INTERTEXTUALITY,
ALLUSION,
AND QUOTATION

Recent Titles in
Bibliographies and Indexes in World Literature

The Independent Monologue in Latin American Theater: A Primary
Bibliography with Selective Secondary Sources
Duane Rhoades, compiler

J.R.R. Tolkien: Six Decades of Criticism
Judith A. Johnson

Bibliographic Guide to Gabriel García Márquez, 1979-1985
Margaret Eustella Fau and Nelly Sfeir de Gonzalez, compilers

Eastern Europe in Children's Literature: An Annotated Bibliography
of English-language Books
Frances F. Povsic

The Literary Universe of Jorge Luis Borges: An Index to References and
Allusions to Persons, Titles, and Places in His Writings
Daniel Balderston, compiler

Film as Literature, Literature as Film: An Introduction to and Bibliography
of Film's Relationship to Literature
Harris Ross

A Guide to Folktales in the English Language: Based on the Aarne-Thompson
Classification System
D. L. Ashliman

Literature for Children about Asians and Asian Americans: Analysis and
Annotated Bibliography, with Additional Readings for Adults
Esther C. Jenkins and Mary C. Austin

A Bibliographical Guide to Spanish American Literature: Twentieth-Century
Sources
Walter Rela, compiler

Themes and Settings in Fiction: A Bibliography of Bibliographies
Donald K. Hartman and Jerome Drost, compilers

The Pinocchio Catalogue: Being a Descriptive Bibliography and Printing
History of English Language Translations and Other Renditions Appearing
in the United States, 1892-1987
Richard Wunderlich, compiler

Robert Burton and *The Anatomy of Melancholy:* An Annotated Bibliography
of Primary and Secondary Sources
Joey Conn, compiler

INTERTEXTUALITY, ALLUSION, AND QUOTATION

An International Bibliography of Critical Studies

Compiled by Udo J. Hebel

Bibliographies and Indexes in World Literature, Number 18

G P

Greenwood Press
New York • Westport, Connecticut • London

Library of Congress Cataloging-in-Publication Data

Hebel, Udo J.
   Intertextuality, allusion, and quotation: an international
bibliography of critical studies / compiled by Udo J. Hebel.
      p.   cm. — (Bibliographies and indexes in world literature,
   ISSN 0742-6801 ; no. 18)
      Bibliography: p.
      Includes indexes.
      ISBN 0-313-26517-8 (lib. bdg. : alk. paper)
      1. Intertextuality—Bibliography.   2. Allusions—Bibliography.
   3. Quotations—Bibliography.   I. Title.   II. Series.
   Z6514.C97H4   1989
   [PN98.I58]
   016.809—dc19   88-38862

British Library Cataloguing in Publication Data is available.

Library of Congress Catalog Card Number: 88-38862
ISBN: 0-313-26517-8
ISSN: 0742-6801

First published in 1989

Greenwood Press, Inc.
88 Post Road West, Westport, Connecticut 06881

Printed in the United States of America

The paper used in this book complies with the
Permanent Paper Standard issued by the National
Information Standards Organization (Z39.48-1984).

10 9 8 7 6 5 4 3 2 1

For Christine

Contents

Preface

Twenty odd years after the first French publication of Julia
Kristeva's pace-setting articles, it has almost become a
commonplace of intertextual studies to call for a stocktak-
ing in this astoundingly productive and extremely diversi-
fied field of scholarship. The present bibliography endorses
such claims and offers a compilation of more than 2000 critical studies that deal not only with the relatively young
concept of intertextuality and its predominantly poststructuralist implications, but also with the time-honored concepts of allusion and quotation, which have seen a remark-
able renaissance in the wake of the intertextual enthusiasm.
     Earliest beginnings of this bibliographical project date
back to the academic year of 1982-1983 when I was able to do
a substantial part of my doctoral research on F. Scott Fitzgerald's use of intertextual techniques at The University of
Michigan in Ann Arbor, Michigan. I discovered that there was
no comprehensive reference work at hand that would direct
newcomers through the labyrinth of intertextual criticism
and that would supply more advanced scholars with further
inspiration. At that time, Carmela Perri's "Allusion Studies: An International Annotated Bibliography, 1921-1977"
(1979) and Don Bruce's "Bibliographie annotée: Ecrits sur
l'intertextualité" (1983) were the only two compilations
available--and they have remained so until today. Perri's
valuable, though sometimes unreliable, collection is limited
to books and articles that employ traditional concepts of
allusion and quotation--and thus too narrow in scope in regard to recent intertextual approaches. Bruce's equally important contribution is rather vague in its inclusion of
general studies on poststructuralism--and thus too broad in
scope in regard to interpretive applications of intertextual, allusional, and quotational theories.
     The present volume is, to the best of my knowledge, the
first comprehensive compilation of its sort and goes beyond
earlier bibliographies, both in scope and quantity. It documents scholarly achievements in the field of intertextual
research and may serve as a guide to previously unexplored
topics. In its scope--intertextuality, allusion, and quota-
tion--it follows scholars such as Gérard Genette, Julia
Kristeva, and Wolf Schmid, who consider allusion and quotation prominent manifestations of intertextuality to be per-

ceived by the reader on the surface of the text. As soon as
intertextuality is defined as the "présence effective d'un
texte dans un autre" (Genette), relations established by
these two concepts move into the limelight of critical attention. From this perspective, the results of long-standing
research on allusion and quotation can be integrated into
the more radical and far-reaching theory of intertextuality,
although possible problems of such a stratification as well
as the yet unsolved question of where to draw a distinct
line between allusion and quotation still deserve further
analysis. Studies on other forms of intertextual relations
such as montage, collage, parody, and pastiche have only
been included if the three central concepts of intertextuality, allusion, and quotation are substantially referred
to. Each of these additional categories might very well lend
itself to another, specialized bibliography that would have
to account for the category's specific requirements. Fur-
thermore, it should be noted that the present bibliography
only contains books and articles preeminently concerned with
at least one of the three critical concepts. The mere mention of an allusion or a quotation in a thematically unre-
lated study forbade the consideration of those titles. With
the exception of Eliot's and Emerson's essays, writers'
views on intertextual phenomena were also excluded; owing to
the different quality of their engagement of intertextuality, allusion, or quotation, comments by John Barth, Jorge
Luis Borges, Samuel Johnson, Stéphane Mallarmé, Osip Mandelstam, Thomas Mann, Robert Musil, and many others should be
brought together under separate cover.

Items presented in the following compilation have been
collected in a number of ways. Besides the two thematic bibliographies mentioned before, the usual annual reference
works available to any scholar in the humanities were naturally the most accessible sources. Computerized searches of
the MLA Bibliography Database and the Comprehensive Dis-
sertation Index Database added a large number of titles. At
the same time, however, this procedure proved to be quite
unsatisfactory because subject indexes to most annual bibliographies are of fairly recent origin and--as any index--
are necessarily incomplete and rather personal. As quite a
few computerized searches were based on a title word index
rather than on a subject index in the sense proper, this
form of technological research clearly evidenced its limita-
tions--especially for items dating back to the times when
scholars had not yet begun to devise the titles of their
studies according to computer requirements. Once these
shortcomings had become obvious, I resorted more thoroughly
to conventional, but indispensable, methods, which is to
say, I systematically scrutinized all articles and books
previously found. In the final analysis, this procedure
yielded more than one-third of all items and led to the discovery of quite a few important older publications.

As a consequence of this procedure, all articles and
books located were actually retrieved, checked in regard to
the bibliographic accuracy of the entry, and assessed as to
their thematic relevance. This method necessitated a less
recent closing date than might be expected from a bibliography that attempts to survey a topic of scholarship so vivid-
ly and controversially debated in academic circles. In the

present case, the closing date is 1986. It seemed more re-
warding to accept this closing date in order to submit a
comprehensive and reliable compilation of items published
through 1986, than to include items brought out in 1987, or
even 1988, without adequately exhausting the scholarly activities of this time span and without being able to base
bibliographical information on personal inspection. It might
also not be too daring to contend that scholarly interest in
intertextuality has slightly waned during the last two years
although any final judgment on that issue is premature.

   Intertextuality, Allusion, and Quotation is organized in
three parts: the introduction, the bibliography, and the
indexes. The introduction surveys the heterogeneous field of
intertextual studies, provides a first insight into the history and development of the critical concepts under examination, and points to important theoretical sources and exemplary analyses of individual writers or specific aspects.

   The largest portion of the book is taken up by the bibliography proper, which comprises a total of 2033 items, ar-
ranged alphabetically and numbered consecutively. This organization was given preference over a broad subject-oriented
division in order to keep work done on the three closely related and often simultaneously applied concepts in one corpus. It avoids an otherwise inevitable system of cross-references and tries to ensure easy usage. Entries are written
according to the MLA format. English translations of foreign
language studies, as in the case of Bakhtin's, Barthes's,
Derrida's, Foucault's, and Kristeva's works, are given in
square brackets immediately after the original titles. For
the sake of ready accessibility, no abbreviations were used
in writing the bibliographical references; this format appeared to be particularly suitable for journals with chang-
ing names.

   The bibliography is followed by two indexes that refer
to the entry numbers. The "Index to Writers and Anonymous
Texts" lists those writers and anonymous texts that are sub-
jects of the studies collected. Notwithstanding its title,
this first index also records the names of composers and
painters whose works have been analyzed in regard to intertextuality, allusion, and quotation; unfortunately, their
number has so far remained small. All entries pertaining to
the works of one writer, or artist in any other field, are
subsumed under his or her name. This method of indexing
proved to be the most fitting one, because hardly any study
on intertextual relations is restricted to the one or two
texts under close examination. Most critics include at least
passing remarks on the writer's general intertextual techniques or his or her preferred intertextual points of reference in other texts. Extended cross-references, double
listings, and an almost endless sequence of texts, which are
mentioned in any of the interpretations, would have been
detrimental to the easy usage of the volume.

   The "Subject Index" first of all allows for the retriev-
al of theoretical studies on intertextuality, allusion, and
quotation as well as of entries dealing with specific aspects of intertextual theory such as autotextuality. Fur-
thermore, it directs the user to categories of literary
scholarship such as irony or satire, and to particular
(literary) forms such as letters or hymns that have been

discussed in regard to the three central concepts, either on
a theoretical basis or in the context of a specific application. In addition, subject words such as "function"
lead the user to analyses of the artistic usage of intertextuality, allusion, and quotation, while broader headings
such as "classical allusion, quotation, and intertextuality"
or "biblical allusion, quotation, and intertextuality" col-
lect work done on larger areas of research. Anyone interested in these recurrent questions of scholarship will find
quite a few inspiring books and articles in the respective
columns. Subject words such as "exegesis," "usage of quotation in research," and "philosophy" will be of interest to
a more limited circle of users. Although items subsumed
under such headings lead away from a strictly literary understanding of intertextuality, allusion, and quotation,
they nicely illustrate the diversity and fecundity of intertextual scholarship.

None of the three parts of the present volume would have
been possible without the generous help of institutions and
friends. I am especially grateful to the interlibrary loan
offices of The University of Michigan, Ann Arbor, Michigan,
and of Johannes Gutenberg-Universitaet, Mainz, West Germany,
which supplied me with items whose very existence I had
often begun to doubt seriously. After my departure from Ann
Arbor, it was above all Martina Kohl, Lioba Ruedell, and
Petra Wacker who kept the transatlantic route open for me
and who retrieved a number of items that I was unable to
locate on this side of the ocean. I am much indebted to Pro-
fessor Dr. Winfried Herget, American Studies Division, Johannes Gutenberg-Universitaet, Mainz, who always took the
time to discuss the project with me when I, a newcomer to
bibliographical research, was about to surrender to its
stumbling blocks. Petra Wacker and Gerald Pike were most
helpful with proofreading the manuscript. Marilyn Brown-
stein, Humanities Editor with Greenwood Press, was a congenial editor who accompanied the project most kindly in its
final stages. Finally, and most of all, I am deeply grateful
to my wife who not only did most of the typing and helped
with the indexes, but also had the patience to bear with me
through all 2033 items.

Mainz, August 1988

INTERTEXTUALITY, ALLUSION, AND QUOTATION

Introduction

Newcomers to the field of intertextual studies will be con-
fronted with the striking paradox that the rise of intertextuality to one of the most celebrated concepts of poststructuralism seems to have focused critical attention on a
feature of texts that actually had always received wide-
spread scholarly interest. The relationships between two
texts or the intricate network of connections among various
texts, as well as the rhetorical or artistic usages of references to other texts, other writers, or any other person
or event outside the text itself, had been the subject of a
myriad of studies even before such relationships began to be
considered manifestations of intertextuality. Nevertheless,
Julia Kristeva's thought-provoking work (#969-#978)[1] and her
contagious neologism truly deserve the credit for resusci-
tating an area of literary scholarship that had been para-
lyzed by basically well-intentioned, but ultimately inconse-
quential, searches for yet another biblical or classical allusion or quotation in yet another text. Kristeva opened up
new perspectives for scholars who had been looking for a
theoretical framework into which the various kinds of atom-
istic "intertextual" observations could be incorporated.
Kristeva and her theory of intertextuality provided for the
umbrella category under which a multiplicity of approaches
and concepts could be subsumed rewardingly. In the wake of
the discussion on intertextuality the analysis of relationships between texts has been liberated from the negative
reputation that futile analogy hunts or stale exercises in
proving a writer's unoriginality had attributed to it.
Kristeva's concept of intertextuality has encouraged scholars to further plow the fruitful field of intertextual research and to further exhaust the interpretive implications
of intertextual relations for a deeper understanding of the
text(s) involved.

Well before Kristeva and her disciples discovered the
potential of intertextuality, and well before poststructuralist notions of text and author destabilized conventional categories of interpretation, it had mainly been quotation and allusion that had served scholars as analytical
tools to come to terms with the traces leading from one text
to another. Especially the concept of quotation had had a

rich tradition of research, which seems to have left a more
lasting imprint on French and German scholars than on
English and American students of literature. Interestingly
enough, none of the prominent English or American handbooks
to literature contains a relevant entry; on the contrary,
corresponding German reference works include substantial
articles on quotation and its features and functions as a
literary device.[2] It may well be speculated whether René
Wellek's and Austin Warren's condescending attitude toward
quotations has affected the editors of English and American
handbooks.[3]

In comparison to the number of German and French studies, the number of English and American studies of quotation
from a theoretical point of view has also remained consider-
ably smaller. Aside from Emerson's essay "Quotation and
Originality" (#514), Kellett's book *Literary Quotation and
Allusion* (#922) deserves mention, even though neither of
these two older works developed a comprehensive theory of
quotation or a usable approach to the analysis of quotations
in literary texts. Credit for such a theory must be given to
the Dutch Germanist Herman Meyer whose book *The Poetics of
Quotation in the European Novel* (#1185) should still be the
point of departure for serious efforts to come to terms with
quotation and its role in literary scholarship. Older German
essays by Bernay (#152), Krause (#968), or Switalski (#1778)
continue to be interesting as stepping-stones in the historical development of the concept; Neumann (#1271) and
Voigts (#1891 and #1892) present more recent views. Simon's
contribution (#1677) must be pointed out as the most encompassing survey article available. It starts with explaining
the use of quotations as rhetorical elements in the speeches
of ancient, medieval, and Renaissance orators and ends with
illustrating the significance of quotations for modernist
montages and collages.

Among studies by scholars of Romance languages, it is
first of all Compagnon's *La seconde main* (#361) that
enhances our understanding of the phenomenon. Gelas (#622)
and Kapp (#912) already establish a connection with intertextual theories. Among newer studies written in English,
Morawski's and Weisgerber's articles (#1226 and #1928) approach the subject from a more theoretical perspective while
Le Comte (#1037), McKinley (#1127), and Perlina (#1353) focus on the writers they chose to analyze.

As far as specific interpretations are concerned, those
by Baerend (#74), Becker-Frank (#125), Brandes (#221), Durzak (#489), Kaiser (#910), Klotz (#950), Metschies (#1182),
Motiramani (#1237), Schneider (#1623), and Voss (#1898)
document the richness of German research and may serve
scholars who are looking for exemplary studies in the field
of German, French, or Russian literature. It appears that
the original German edition of Meyer's book has exercised a
durable influence while its American edition has remained
far less effective. Moreover, older dissertations by Apfel
(#46), Armleder (#50), and Hinman (#799) can be taken as
representative American examples of the lasting vogue of ex-
amining the texts of classical authors in regard to their
usage of quotations that has flourished on both sides of the
Atlantic. In America as well as in Europe (Roettger, #1516),
the starting point for most of those studies was a rhetor-

ical approach rather than an interest in the strictly aes-
thetic functions of quotations.
Titles mentioned up to this point will introduce the
user of the present volume to important perspectives on quotation and will familiarize him or her with exemplary studies. For research on more specialized topics or on interdisciplinary views (e.g., quotations in music or painting),
whose assessment would clearly go beyond the scope of this
introductory essay, the reader is referred to the subject
index. Among publications issued after the closing date of
this bibliography, Plett's article "The Poetics of Quotation"⁴ has to be noted as it tries to give new impetus to a
theory of quotation and marks its author's promising embark-
ment on a larger project on the problem. Diepeveen's disser-
tation "The Modernist Quoting Poem"⁵ continues the analysis
of modernist literature in regard to its quoting habits.
The critical discussion on the concept of quotation and
its major results can best be illustrated by a short passage
from Morawski's valuable article:

> Quotation is the literal reproduction of a verbal text
> of a certain length or of a set of images, notes,
> sounds, movements, or a combination of all or some of
> these elements or some of them with a verbal text,
> wherein what is reproduced forms an integral part of
> some work and can easily be detached from the new whole
> in which it is incorporated....The crucial features of
> the quotation are its LITERALNESS and its DISCRETENESS
> in relation to the structure in which it has been in-
> serted. To the former is related the question of ac-
> curacy or fidelity, the latter is responsible for its
> appearance in inverted commas. (#1226, p. 691)

Morawski's description stresses some of the issues at stake
in many studies of quotation: whether only literal quotations should be considered true quotations or whether more
or less faithful reproductions might not also be acceptable
(Becker-Frank, #125; Metschies, #1182; Meyer, #1185;
Schneider, #1623; Simon, #1677); whether only those elements
reproduced from other texts should be analyzed as quotations
that are marked as such by quotation marks, by italiciza-
tion, or by any other way of indicating their secondary
quality or whether so-called cryptic quotations (Meyer,
#1185) might not also be regarded as quotations (Adel, #4;
Becker-Frank, #125; Neumann, #1271; Wheeler, #1943); whether
only textual elements "of a certain length" should be
treated as quotations (Simon, #1677) or whether names of
characters from other literary texts or titles of other
texts might not also be subsumed under the category in question and be dealt with as title quotations, name quotations,
or simply microquotations (Jensch, #879; Kaiser, #910;
Karrer, #916; Krause, #968; Motiramani, #1237; Neumann,
#1271; Schneider, #1623).
On the whole, most scholars currently tend to de-empha-
size the criterion of literalness, to underscore the aspect
of discreteness, and to include titles and names in a discussion of quotational elements. The consequence is an understanding of quotation that stresses its relational and
genealogical qualities (Helbig, #770; Kosny, #965; Meyer,

#1185; Neumann, #1271; Voss, #1898). It is no longer the
mere extension of the quotational element within the new
context and its fidelity to its original wording that dis-
tinguish it as a quotation proper, but its very ability to
refer the reader to other texts, to make him or her aware of
the text's relations to points of reference outside itself.
Meyer's well-known description of the effect of a quotation
as a tension between assimilation and dissimilation proves
the lasting significance of Meyer's work once more, because
it is this very tension the reader has to cope with when his
or her reading reaches the point where the intratextual continuum is extended into an extratextual frame of reference.
Thus, quotations open up a deeper dimension (Giustiniani,
#645; Wirtz, #1969). They not only refer to their original
contexts, but also represent them in the quoting text (Hoehler, #805; Klotz, #950; Voigts, #1892; Kosny, #965). This
quasi-metonymical presence of the quoted text in the quoting
text is, however, not restricted to the words of the quotation, but goes beyond the limits of the quotation and at-
tains suggestive power (Kaiser, #910; McKinley, #1127). The
quotational element evokes the quoted text as a whole and,
possibly, its author, the latter's *oeuvre*, or the literary
period in which it was written. Any quotation may trigger a
theoretically endless sequence of associations, or--to use
more fashionable terminology--intertextual relations. It is
therefore small wonder that recent studies have begun to
discuss quotation as "another intertextual figure" (Cancogni, #301, p. 147; cf., Stierle, #1749), and that Genette
(#629) and Kristeva (#973) point to this traditional category when describing manifestations of intertextuality on
the surface of the text.

Notions of quotation as a suggestive element whose contribution to the meaning of the quoting text exceeds the
meaning of its very wording accentuate the close, but still
underestimated connection between quotation and current
approaches to allusion. At the same time, a careful assessment of studies on quotation and allusion reveals frequent
terminological insecurities and inconsistencies when it
comes to describing the true nature of this connection. Even
Meyer's characterization of quotation and allusion as "in
some way congenial" (#1185, p. 15) betrays such an insecu-
rity, and two of the most notable contributions to our
understanding of allusion and its role in literary texts,
Schlack's *Continuing Presences: Virginia Woolf's Use of
Allusions* (#1609) and Wheeler's *The Art of Allusion in Victorian Fiction* (#1943), mention allusion in their titles,
but call attention to Meyer's book as one of their central
points of departure. Coinages such as Pollak's term "allusive quotation" (#1387, p. 57) further elucidate scholars'
uncertainties about possible boundaries and affinities between the two concepts.
    The question whether allusion or quotation should be
considered the more encompassing category has been answered
both ways. While Oppenheimer (#1310), Plett (#1378), and
Wheeler (#1943) accept allusion as the generic term under
which quotation should be subsumed, Laub (#1027), Neumann
(#1271), Stierle (#1749), and Tetzeli von Rosador (#1803)
favor quotation as the superior category. Notwithstanding

Genette's attempt to present the two concepts as equally
leveled manifestations of intertextual relationships on the
surface of the text, the following passages will show in
which way quotations can be described as one particular form
of allusion.
   In sharp contrast to quotation, allusion figures promi-
nently in English and American handbooks to literature, and
research on allusion has always had a stronghold in the En-
glish-speaking academe (Brower, #250; Johnson, #889; Kellett, #922; Miner, #1209; Wassermann, #1918). Without unduly
disregarding French, Italian, and Spanish achievements
(Hickey, #783; Morier, #1228; Pasquali, #1340; Sucre,
#1764), recent modifications of the concept of allusion have
to be traced primarily to the theoretical studies of Ben-
Porat (#137, #138, and #139), Coombs (#371), Johnson (#882),
and Perri (#1355 and #1356). Congenial scholars, above all
Rodi (#1509), Schaar (#1596, #1597, and #1598), and Schmid
(#1616) contributed to the redefinition of allusion.
   Among the host of studies on individual writers from
Milton, Swift, Wordsworth, Coleridge, Austen, Thackeray,
Hardy, Ellison, Woolf, and Joyce to Fontane, Borges, and
Gracq, those by Amossy (#30 and #31), Beaumont (#120),
Chandler (#319), Christ (#333), Hollander (#812), Laub
(#1027), Moler (#1219), Nadel (#1255), Newlyn (#1274), Plett
(#1378), Schlack (#1609), Springer (#1721), Stein (#1738),
Thornton (#1817), and Wheeler (#1943) are worth consulting.
As this short list of important titles cannot exhaust the
wide range of studies available on other writers--not to
mention the even higher number of brief notes identifying
concealed allusions--the reader is referred to the "Index to
Writers and Anonymous Texts" at the end of the present volume for further interpretations of writers of his or her own
liking.
   Titles published after the closing date of the bibliography have continued major trends of allusional research.
Thus, Mathews's and Paulien's dissertations[6] illustrate the
enduring interest in topics related to an analysis of the
Bible, while Lass's Dictionary of Classical, Biblical, and
Literary Allusions[7] presents the results of yet another
encyclopedic endeavor. Recent studies on Churchill, Cheever,
Lope de Vega, and Voltaire[8] are examples of further attempts
to closely examine the significance of allusions for one
particular person or one particular text.
   A passage from Harold Bloom's A Map of Misreading may
serve as an introduction to the critical discussion on allusion. It outlines the historical development of the concept by commenting on the various senses provided for the
term by the Oxford English Dictionary:

   The history of "allusion" as an English word goes from
   an initial meaning of "illusion" on to an early Renaissance use as meaning a pun, or word-play in general. But
   by the time of Bacon it meant any symbolic likening,
   whether in allegory, parable or metaphor, as when in The
   Advancement of Learning poetry is divided into "narrative, representative, and allusive." A fourth meaning,
   which is still the correct modern one, follows rapidly
   by the very early seventeenth century, and involves any
   implicit, indirect or hidden reference. The fifth mean-

ing, still incorrect but bound to establish itself, now
equates allusion with direct, overt reference. (#190, p.
126)

Bloom's distinction between the fourth--supposedly "correct"--and the fifth--supposedly "incorrect"--meanings calls
attention to one major point of controversy that has divided
scholars of allusion. Miner's definition of allusion as
"tacit reference to another literary work, to another art,
to history, to contemporary figures, or the like" (#1209, p.
18) still reflects Bloom's fourth meaning, which has been
perpetuated well into the 1980s by some of the reference
works mentioned above. This very understanding of allusion
has induced the myriad of articles that try to trace as many
tacit, unmarked allusions as possible--unfortunately quite
often without paying much attention to the interpretive
potential of the allusive connections retrieved. Even a superficial perusal of the bibliography part of this book will
yield any number of "notes on unknown details" or "notes on
biblical, classical or historical allusions" in just about
any text by any writer from Chaucer to Joyce.

In the 1970s and 1980s, Ben-Porat, Coombs, Johnson,
Perri, and Schaar provided for a new perspective on allusion
--Bloom's "fifth meaning"--which has not only established
itself rightfully by now, but has also enlarged our understanding of the allusive process. Ben-Porat writes as follows:

> The literary allusion is a device for the simultaneous
> activation of two texts. The activation is achieved
> through the manipulation of a special sign: a sign
> (simple or complex) in a given text characterized by an
> additional larger "referent." This referent is always an
> independent text. The simultaneous activation of the two
> texts thus connected results in the formation of inter-
> textual patterns whose nature cannot be predetermined.
> ...The built-in directional signal is often called the
> allusion; but in order not to confuse it with the device
> it triggers, I propose to use the term "marker" for the
> latter. The marker is always identifiable as an element
> or pattern belonging to another independent text. This
> is true even when the pattern is a comprehensive one,
> such as the title of a work or the name of a protag-
> onist. (#139, pp. 107-108)

Ben-Porat's differentiation between allusion as a textual
element within the linear sequence of the alluding text
("signal"/"marker") and allusion as a process of activating
at least one other text ("device") allows for a more precise
description of the signal and supports a more dynamic conception of the allusive process.

Perri favors similar notions when she approaches allusion on the basis of speech act theory and rejects traditional definitions of the concept. More obviously than Ben-
Porat, Perri emphasizes the possibility of including overt
forms of the marker in a discussion of allusion, even if
they "occur as the extreme case of overtness, proper names"
(#1356, p. 298). Additionally, quite a few scholars, fore-
most among them Chandler (#319) and Schaar (#1596, #1597,

and #1598) and to a lesser degree Bergsten (#151), Laub
(#1027), Springer (#1721), and Wassermann (#1918) have concerned themselves with the question of artistic intention.
From their points of view, allusions are no longer regarded
as casual references without any major impact on the meaning
of the text, but rather as particularly intentional elements
within the text's artistic structure.

Similar to studies on quotation mentioned above, newer
analyses of allusion are prone to consider proper names of
persons from outside the textual universe or titles of other
texts as specific forms of the allusion marker (Christ,
#333; Gottschalk, #674; Johnson, #882; Kurth-Voigt, #992;
Nadel, #1255; Pollak, #1387; Schlack, #1609; Wheeler,
#1943). Again, one major consequence of this shifting per-
spective has been a heavier stress on the relational quality
of allusions. Definitions of allusion as "a device for linking texts" (Ben-Porat, #138, p. 588), as "a link between
texts" (Perri, #1356, p. 289), and as "a trope of related-
ness" (Perri, #1355, p. 128) and their disregard for the
controversy over overtness and covertness illustrate these
views nicely. Advancing implicit suggestions made by some
theorists of allusion (Ben-Porat, #139), it then becomes
possible--and only consequential--to accept quotation as yet
another form of the allusional marker that links the quoting
text with the quoted text or, to use the terminology of allusional theory, the alluding text with the allusively
activated text. Quotations are just further forms of intertextual "stumbling blocks" (Riffaterre, #1481, p. 6) that
draw the reader's attention to other levels of meaning. The
question whether allusion or quotation is the superior concept becomes insignificant as soon as any textual element
relating one text with another outside itself is granted the
status and quality of an allusional marker.

Next to the redefinition of the allusion marker, the
description of the allusional process and the concern with
the evocative potential of allusions are noteworthy achievements of recent theories of allusion. Although quite a few
earlier scholars had touched on the ability of allusions to
elicit far-reaching associations (Nelson, #1267; Pasco,
#1339; Yarrison, #1996), it was once again Ben-Porat and to
a lesser degree Coombs, Perri, and Schmid who presented for-
malized models of the process of actualizing an allusion and
its evocative potential. This complex process is outlined by
Ben-Porat as "a movement starting with the recognition of
the marker and ending with intertextual patterning" (#139,
p. 109) and subdivided into four stages: recognition of an
element in a given text as a signal pointing to another independent unity, identification of the evoked text, modifi-
cation of the initial local interpretation of the passage by
forming at least one intertextual pattern, and activation of
the evoked text as a whole and of a theoretically limitless
range of associations in an attempt to form a maximum of intertextual patterns. While Ben-Porat is still hesitant to
extend this model to allusions to nonliterary points of
reference, Perri is less conventional in this respect:

   Allusion-markers act like proper names in that they denote unique individuals (source texts), they also tacit-
   ly specify the property(ies) belonging to the source

> text's connotation relevant to the allusion's meaning.
> ...It must be noted that topical or historical allusions
> to persons or events may fall under any of the marker
> categories discussed thus far. Echoes of past or con-
> temporary real-world texts are not of a different order
> than literary allusions, for they, like all allusions,
> evoke attributes of their referents. (#1356, pp. 291/305)

Thus, the crucial feature of an allusion, no matter whether
a literary allusion in the conventional sense or any other
allusion to a person or event, is its effect to denote a
specific relation between a text and an identifiable point
of reference and its potential to connote additional associations. Johnson's dichotomy of the "denotative nucleus" of
an allusion and its "connotative cytoplasm" (#882, p. 580)
expresses this conception figuratively.

It will be readily understood at this point that such an
approach to the interpretation of allusions emphasizes the
active role of the reader in the process of actualizing a
text and its allusions (Perri, #1356; Schaar, #1596). Allusion markers only direct the reader to certain points of
reference outside the text under examination; in the final
analysis, however, it will be the reader's allusional competence (Rodi, #1509; Schmid, #1616) or his or her prepared-
ness to go through the trouble of collecting further information about the text or person evoked on which a deeper ap-
preciation of the allusion and the alluding text depends.

The above sketch of major developments in the field of
allusion studies hinted at the increasingly intricate connection between this well-known category of literary scholarship and fashionable theories of intertextuality. Even if
one does not go as far as Schmid (#1616) who considers allusion as *the* manifestation of intertextuality, it should be
obvious by now that allusion, the "text-linking device," establishes relations that transgress the boundaries of the
individual text and situate it within its surroundings.
Thus, the allusive system of one text comprises a large portion of what has become known as the intertextuality of the
text, i.e., its always and necessarily being linked with extratextual systems of signification. While theories of allusion account for the working of individual intertextual relationships whose points of departure can be clearly recognized in the alluding text, theories of intertextuality concern themselves more generally with the intertextual quality
of any text.

Any attempt to come to terms with the concept of intertextuality and its implications for literary scholarship
must first of all delineate its roots in poststructuralist
theories as they were developed by the French critics
Barthes (#102-#107), Derrida (#445-#449), Foucault (#565-
#569), Kristeva (#969-#978), and--though of little signif-
icance for the topic under examination--Lacan. The work of
these critics and their followers began to shake academic
circles in France during a time of political, social, and
intellectual upheaval toward the end of the 1960s, and the
enthusiasm for their ideas spilled over to America almost
immediately. Well into the 1980s, translations of Barthes's
books *S/Z* (#106) and *Le plaisir du texte* (#105) appeared to

be musts in the private library of any American graduate
student, and translations of his famous articles "De l'oeuvre au texte" (#103), "La mort de l'auteur" (#104), and
"Texte (Théorie du)" (#107) made Heath's *Image, Music, Text*,
Harari's *Textual Strategies*, and Young's *Untying the Text*
best-sellers in campus bookstores. By the early 1980s, Derrida's *oeuvre* was available in American editions; Foucault's
L'archéologie du savoir (#565) and his *Les mots et les
choses* (#567) had already been published in English as early
as 1971 and 1972. Translations of Foucault's essays "Un fantastique de bibliothèque" (#566) and, above all, "Qu'est-ce
qu'un auteur" (#568) supported the success of Bouchard's
Language, Counter-Memory, Practice as well as the usage of
Harari's *Textual Strategies* as textbook in many graduate
seminars on critical theory. Surprisingly enough, trans-
lators of Kristeva's work were less prolific, and it was not
before 1980 that English versions of her ground-breaking essays "Bakhtine, le mot, le dialogue et le roman" (#969) and
"Le texte clos" (#977) were published in Roudiez's *Desire in
Language*. Nineteen eighty-four finally saw the translation
of *La révolution du langage poétique* (#975).

This brief sketch of the reception of French critical
theory since the late 1960s is to elucidate the extent to
which academic circles in America embraced poststructuralist
ideas in the 1970s and 1980s--a critical craze most likely
without precedent. Among the immense number of secondary
literature on poststructuralism and its effect on scholarship in the humanities, which has only been included in the
present bibliography if intertextuality, allusion, or quotation are substantially treated, survey articles by Arrivé
(#57), Jameson (#865), Said (#1582), and Sprinker (#1723)
and two book-length studies by Culler (#395 and #397) deserve special mention.[9]

"What is a text, for current opinion?" reads the opening
question of Barthes's pivotal essay "Texte (Théorie du)"
(#107, p. 32) which has remained the best introduction
available on poststructuralist theories of the text. This
question hints at Barthes's famous distinction between
traditional and poststructuralist understandings of the
text, which he establishes most succinctly in his essay "De
l'oeuvre au texte" (#103). For Barthes, the conventional
concept of the work relies on the authority of the latter's
stable meaning that is to be accepted as the author's intentional meaning. The act of interpretation is limited to
retrieving this single "true" meaning; interpretation becomes the "re-cognition of the author's meaning"[10]. On the
basis of Kristeva's definition of the text as a "translin-
guistic apparatus that redistributes the order of language
by relating communicative speech, which aims to inform di-
rectly, to different kinds of anterior or synchronic utterances" (#977, p. 36), Barthes stresses five principal features of the text: "signifying practices, productivity,
'signifiance', phenotext and genotext, intertextuality"
(#107, p. 36). Referring the reader of this introduction to
the titles mentioned above for further elaboration on the
wider implications of this definition of the text, it may
suffice to note here that Barthes's efforts to overcome traditional notions of the work has liberated the text from its
author and the requirement to contain any stable meaning.

Barthes pulverizes the text into an intricate network of codes that penetrate and dominate author, text, and reader at the same time. In the wake of Foucault's decentering of the author-subject (#568) he proclaims the "death of the author" (#104). His description of the text as a "galaxy of signifiers" (#106, p. 5), which are no longer restrained by any final signified, clearly shows the influence of Derrida. Finally, Barthes makes the reader emerge as the "place where this multiplicity is focused" (#104, p. 148); the reader's joyful participation in the text's productivity yields any number of readings, none, however, more or less justified than any other (Barthes, #103 and #105). The text is now taken to be an open, dynamic, and polysemous space, an endless process of signification. At the same time, the text is always part of the larger, all-encompassing processes and systems of signification into which man's social and historical practices have been dissolved by poststructuralists. Derrida's view of the "already-thereness of the language or of the culture" (#445, p. 161) and his provocative declaration that "*there is nothing outside of the text*" (#445, p. 158), which gave support to propositions about the general textuality of the world, revolutionized textual theory and left their mark on Barthes's definition of the text as "an entrance into a network with a thousand entrances" (#106, p. 12). To quote Foucault in this context:

> Mais de plus les marges d'un livre ne sont jamais nettes ni rigoureusement tranchées: aucun livre ne peut exister par lui-même; il est toujours dans un rapport d'appui et de dépendance à l'égard des autres; il est un point dans un reseau; il comporte un système d'indications qui renvoient—explicitement ou non—à d'autres livres, ou d'autres textes, ou d'autres phrases. (#569, p. 14)

This short, and necessarily superficial excursion into critical theory outlines the position of Kristeva's concept of intertextuality within poststructuralist notions of text and textuality. Next to her views on the productivity of the text and her dichotonmy of *phéno-texte* and *géno-texte*, her theory of intertextuality has qualified scholars' interpretive practices. Although the term itself appears to be of too recent origin to be widely recognized by handbooks to literature, it has already entered the 1987 edition of Fowler's *A Dictionary of Modern Critical Terms*[11]—a notable proof of the concept's effectiveness even if the entry remains insufficient. Novices to the field of intertextual studies are therefore best advised to consult survey articles offered in English, French, German, or Spanish by Angenot (#41), Ette (#522), Firmat (#548), Lachmann (#997), Morgan (#1227), Pfister (#1365), Ruprecht (#1569), and Zurowski (#2015). Special issues of periodicals or collections of essays devoted to intertextuality (#453, #837-#840, #842-#847, #1377, #1804) document the wealth and diversity of intertextual research performed during the last two decades and may serve as first guides to central issues and methods. A quick glance at some of these titles also shows that the concern with intertextuality has long ceased to be a domain of Romance or Slavic studies, which had naturally taken the lead in the early years of the intertextual enthusiasm.

Instead of more or less arbitrarily singling out individual articles or books at this point, I would rather
like to emphasize four of the collections touched on before,
because these already have to be considered landmarks of
intertextual research on both sides of the Atlantic. First,
Dialog der Texte: Hamburger Kolloquium zur Intertextualitaet
(#453) is a collection of essays on Slavic literature as
well as on theoretical topics (cf., esp. Schmid, #1616;
Stempel, #1740). Second, *Intertextualitaet: Formen, Funktionen, anglistische Fallstudien* (#837) is a collection of
essays on English and American literature that also includes
valuable theoretical articles by Broich (#241 and #244),
Karrer (#916), Pfister (#1365 and #1366), and Plett (#1379).
Third, *Poétique*'s quite early special issue "Intertextualités" (#842) not only tries for the first time to assess
intertextual research and its results until the mid-1970s,
but also contains Jenny's pivotal article, which saw its English translation in 1982 (#878), and Daellenbach's essay
"Intertexte et autotexte" (#402), which concerns itself at
least partly with the question of autotextuality, i.e., the
intertextuality among texts by the same author. Fourth, and
finally, *Intertextuality in Faulkner* (#847) represents the
meritorious endeavor to focus a group of scholars--and thus
a multiplicity of different perspectives--on an author whose
oeuvre just calls for an analysis of intertextuality and
autotextuality. The mere number of special issues and collections, together with the large amount of studies compiled
in the following bibliography, bears further witness to the
productivity of intertextual research whose central category
was created single-handedly by Kristeva only some twenty
years ago.[12]
    Within the broader context of the critical discussion
outlined above and in the wake of a rising interest in Ferdinand de Saussure's anagrams (Arrivé, #55; Starobinski,
#1733), Kristeva revitalized the work of the Russian critic
Mikhail Bakhtin and his concept of the polyphonic novel.[13]
Kristeva now defined the text as "a permutation of texts, an
intertextuality: in the space of a given text, several utterances, taken from other texts, intersect and neutralize
one another" (#977, p. 36). With reference to Bakhtin, she
contended that "any text is constructed as a mosaic of quotations; any text is the absorption and transformation of
another" (#969, p. 66). In "Problèmes de la structuration du
texte" she extended the scope of the concept and defined
intertextuality as a text's relation to the whole of its extratextual surroundings:

La méthode transformationelle nous mène donc à situer la
structure littéraire dans l'ensemble social considéré
comme un ensemble textuel. Nous appellerons *intertextualité* cette interaction textuelle qui se produit à
l'intérieur d'un seul texte. Pour le sujet connaissant,
l'intertextualité est une notion qui sera l'indice de la
façon dont un texte lit l'histoire et s'insère en elle.
(#973, p. 311)

Notwithstanding further attempts of terminological modifi-
cation in *La révolution du langage poétique* (#975), which
remained rather ineffective, these passages comprise the es-

sence of Kristeva's theory of intertextuality as an inherent quality of any text and its process of signification. At the same time, intertextuality situates the single text within a network of relations stretched out between the text and its intertextual surroundings.

According to their respective emphases, intertextualists have stressed either of these two aspects. Barthes (#107), Culler (#396), Lachmann (esp. #998), and, with special regard to the readers' response, Riffaterre (esp. #1464, #1466, #1481, and #1485) have discussed intertextuality as inherent quality of a text and of textuality in general. A second group of scholars has focused on the relations set up by intertextuality, trying to come to terms with their specific nature. Important representatives of this group include, among others, Net (#1270), Schmid (#1616), Stewart (#1747), and, with special regard to psychoanalytical aspects of intertextuality, Bloom (#189 and #190). It must, however, be kept in mind that boundaries between the two camps are only vaguely drawn and that many scholars have favored both views concurrently. Such practices do not reveal scholarly inconsistencies, but are rather the logical consequences of the intricate connections between both facets of intertextuality.

Approaches to intertextuality as inherent quality of any text or of any signifying practice whatsoever, have often underscored the ideological implications of critical theory. Intertextuality became one of the most effective tools to decenter the author- and reader-subject and to destabilize the unity and authority of the text and its meaning—critical positions that were readily embraced and widely acclaimed when traditional categories came under attack in the late 1960s (Pfister, #1365). Early studies of intertextuality were quite frequently limited to assertions that the text under examination showed traces of intertextuality that disrupted its unity and undermined its superficial meaning. The mere proclamation of a text's intertextual polysemy replaced the serious attempt to use these intertextual relations and polysemies for an interpretation of the text. In a slightly different manner, Barthes's studies of Balzac and Poe (#102 and #106) bear witness to this practice of appreciative observation of a text's polysemy that openly rejects any methodological interpretation.

Approaches to intertextuality as a device to establish relations with other texts or other points of reference soon began to emphasize the significance of these relations for the meaning of the individual text. It is almost needless to add that studies along these lines drew heavy fire from diehard poststructuralists for whom any interest in meaning or any revitalization of the interpretive impetus amounted to no less than a betrayal of the pure faith. Laurent Jenny's essay "La stratégie de la forme" must be considered an important turning point in the movement away from the observation of intertextually destabilized texts toward an understanding of intertextuality that accepts "a focal text which keeps control over the meaning" (# 878, p. 40). In the late 1970s and early 1980s, German scholars, most of all Lachmann (#997-#1002), Pfister (#1364-#1366), Schmid (#1614-#1618), Stempel (#1740), and Stierle (#1749) called for the development of analytical methods to further exhaust the semantic potential of intertextually organized texts. *Intertextuali-taet: Formen, Funktionen, anglistische Fallstudien*, a col-lection of essays mentioned earlier, is explicitly committed to a post-poststructuralist model of intertextuality that tries to account for the additional meaning brought into the single text by its intertextual relations. Intertextuality no longer destabilizes the text or disseminates its meaning infinitely, but rather enhances the constitution of meaning. The so-called semantic explosion, triggered by intertextual relations, is utilized to apprehend the semantic potential of the text as far as possible, without unduly disregarding the never-closing gap between the text's polysemy and the individual reader's interpretive—and intertextual—compe-tence. Schmid's concept of "intersemanticity"(#1616, p. 144) expresses this notion quite nicely. It will have become evi-dent at this point that the integration of allusion with its emphasis on the evocative process of actualization into the theory of intertextuality finds its justification in these developments.

Despite the lasting opposition of many poststructuralist critics to any interpretive, and therefore eventually aca-demic, usages of their ideological panacea, it appears safe to contend from today's point of view that an interpretive approach to intertextuality will prove to be the more fruit-ful perspective for scholars of literature, even though the original dimension of this critical concept must not be for-gotten. The reduction of intertextuality to a literary de-vice among all others (e.g., Ugarte, #1846, p. 42) neglects its far-reaching implications and the truly revolutionary influence it has exercised during the last two decades. In-tertextuality should always be dealt with as feature of the text, not as device of the work.

Noteworthy ventures to restructure the field of inter-textual studies, most of all Genette's embedding of inter-textuality into the larger concept of transtextuality, de-fined as "transcendance textuelle du texte" (#629, p. 7), open up further perspectives and support the integration of allusion, quotation, and other categories of traditional literary scholarship into the larger framework of recent critical theory. In the final analysis, however, it will re-main Kristeva's approach and her neologism that will carry the day.

In which way the infinity of possible intertextual re-lations can be utilized in the act of interpretation depends on the individual critic's definition of the intertext. Ba-sically, three definitions have been offered and applied in a number of specific analyses. A first, rather small group of scholars, among them Jenny (#878) and Zamora (#2000), call the single text under examination the intertext: "We use this term in the sense of 'a text absorbing a multi-plicity of texts while remaining oriented by a meaning.'" (Jenny, #878, p. 45)

Two other larger groups locate the intertext outside the single text; what distinguishes them, however, is their view of what exactly lies outside the individual text. Pfister described the two positions with the help of the dichotomy "specific intertextuality" versus "universal intertextual-ity" (#1365, p. 11). Studies primarily concerned with the

interpretive usage of intertextuality for a deeper understanding of a particular text have often favored the idea of
"specific intertextuality," which defines the intertext of a
text as a limited number of points of reference with which
the text enters into semantically productive relationships.
Some scholars have further restricted the range of possible
points of reference to other literary texts proper so that
the intertext often came to be taken as the corpus of all
other literary texts evoked by the text under examination.
Aside from the contributors to *Intertextualitaet: Formen,
Funktionen, anglistische Fallstudien* (#837), Riffaterre
(esp. #1473, #1481, and #1485) and Ugarte (#1846) may be
mentioned as prominent representatives of this position.
    The third group dissolves all boundaries outside the
single text and considers the *texte général* the intertext of
any text. After the aforesaid, it will be obvious that such
ideas have prospered in the wake of Derrida's "notion of
pan-textuality"[14] and Barthes's joyous affirmation of "the
impossibility of living outside the infinite text" (#105, p.
36). Among adherents of such creeds, Culler deserves special
mention (#394, #395, and #397). A somewhat vague, but possibly fruitful compromise to reconcile the various stances
is offered by Arrivé who defines the intertext as "l'ensemble des textes entre lesquels fonctionnent les relations
d'intertextualité" (#57, p. 61). This approach offers a
pragmatic solution that should enable scholars to (re)direct
their energy to the analysis of this network of relations
instead of wasting it in defining artificial and eventually
ineffective limits.
    No matter which of the three--or four--definitions is
actually employed in a practical application, intertextuality emerges as the text's truly dialogic dimension. Kristeva
elaborates on this aspect when she defines the ideologeme:

> The ideologeme is that intertextual function read as
> "materialized" at the different structural levels of
> each text, and which stretches along the entire length
> of its trajectory, giving it its historical and social
> coordinates....The concept of text as ideologeme deter-
> mines the very procedure of a semiotics that, by study-
> ing the text as intertextuality, considers it as such
> within (the text of) society and history. (#977, pp. 36-
> 37)

The theory of intertextuality thus (re)contextualizes the
text and (re)directs scholarly interest to more comprehensive topics of literary history, social history, or literary
reception. It is at this very point, too, where the theory
of intertextuality once again reveals its origins in
Bakhtin's concept of the polyphonic novel as a microcosm of
the social, historical, and literary voices.

    The functional aspect draws our attention to one more
central question of intertextual research that must be
briefly surveyed toward the end of this introduction. In a
narrower, less semiotically oriented sense than employed by
Kristeva and her followers, function has reappeared as a
critical category after Jenny's essay (#878). By and by,
scholars of intertextuality have again become interested in

the various intratextual functions performed within the focal text by the intertextual relations (cf., Schulte-Middelich, #1638). Despite their greater theoretical clarity, recent classifications of functions (Karrer, #916) have generally brought little progress in comparison with traditional classifications developed by studies on allusion and
quotation. Morawski (#1226) distinguishes the appeal to
authorities, the erudite function, the stimulative-ampli-
ficatory function, and the aesthetic-ornamental function and
has therewith presented a catalog that is still very usable.
Within the range of artistic usages, a threefold division
has been repeatedly established: characterization, illus-
tration of themes, and support of composition, with the
latter including a variety of aspects such as foreshadowing
(cf., recently Plett, #1378). Most applications evidence,
however, that a strict separation of these functions is neither possible nor advisable. Owing to the associative nature
of intertextually allusive relations, their majority enhances the meaning of the text in more than one of the given
categories. Nevertheless, the characterizing function must
be considered the front-runner as far as the quantitative
aspect of its usage is concerned. For these very reasons,
the subject index to the following bibliography does without
any further subdivisions of the entry on function. Out of
the large number of titles listed under this heading, the
studies by the following scholars may serve as a fair selection and will provide the user with further details: Brewer
(#227), Brower (#250), Christ (#333), Cowart (#384), Feld
(#540), Forslund (#563), Gruebel (#710), Hines (#797), Kosny
(#965), Little (#1080), Mays (#1177), Metschies (#1182),
Meyer (#1185), Motiramani (#1237), Perlina (#1352), Regalado
(#1431), Sankey (#1588), Schakel (#1602), Schlack (#1609),
Schneider (#1623), Van Nuffel (#1864), Vessels (#1882),
Weisgerber (#1928), Wheeler (#1943), and Wyatt (#1992).
     One special aspect that deserves distinct treatment con-
cerns the stock character of the so-called reading protagonist, which will be a well-known figure to readers of novels
by Austen, Cervantes, Flaubert, Goethe, Plenzdorf, and
Wilde. In most cases, the reading of such characters as Werther or Emma Bovary, not to mention Don Quixote again,
decisively shapes their views of the world and guides their
actions--a phenomenon that has gained new significance in
the context of theories about the textuality of any world
view. Among studies concerned with the reading protagonist,
those by Gerhardt (#634), Herrero (#776), Kleinert (#943 and
#944), Llorens (#1084), Pabst (#1322 and #1323), Stueckrath
(#1760), and Wuthenow (#1988) are worth consulting. Wolpers's collection *Gelebte Literatur in der Literatur: Studien zu Erscheinungsformen und Geschichte eines literarischen Motivs* (#624) bears witness to the unbroken popularity
of this topic in Germany.
     In addition to intratextual functions that concern the
semantic enrichment of the text under examination, scholars
of intertextual relations have also made use of what has
lately become known as metatextuality. The term has to be
traced back to Genette's *Palimpsestes* (#629) and pertains to
the commentating effect of any intertextual relation. In the
very act of establishing a relation to an extratextual point
of reference, the text always comments on the latter. The

extent and implication of this metatextual evaluation
depends on the context in which the extratextual point of
reference is embedded in the alluding text. Although quite a
few scholars have by now recognized the far-reaching possibilities of this perspective, especially for an intertextual history of reception (Beugnot, #159; Beyer, #160;
Fox, #571; Kaiser, #910; Nadel, #1255 and #1256; Newlyn,
#1274; Sondrup, #1708), metatextuality has yet remained a
field of intertextual studies largely unplowed. Scholars
ought to pay more attention to this aspect without, however,
falling victim to the critical pitfalls involved. The principal purpose of any metatextual analysis has to be the
delineation of a text's position within the intertextual
network, not the attempt to prove one writer's reading
habits or his or her literary preferences.

The above introduction to the three closely related concepts that have served as organizing principles for the following bibliography has intentionally focused on literary
scholarship. It is impossible within the limits of an introductory essay of this sort to fully explain the implications
and problems of an extended theory of intertextuality, allusion, and quotation in regard to other areas of artistic
or nonartistic activities. The task of a more comprehensive
account must be left to the more courageous writer of the
long-awaited monograph on the subject. For more specific
questions of literary scholarship as well as for particular
aspects of nonliterary disciplines, the user is referred to
the subject index at the end of this volume, which tries to
do both—to take stock of topics long tackled by critics and
to draw attention to further possibilities of research.
Thus, anybody interested in questions of biblical or
classical intertextuality will find a broad selection of
valuable studies under the respective headings. Students of
theology might also be attracted to titles dealing with
questions of exegesis. Theorists of literature may want to
examine the connections between intertextuality, allusion,
and quotation, on the one hand, and critical concepts such
as satire, irony, or parody, on the other. A very challeng-
ing topic is dealt with in studies on problems of translating intertextually organized texts. Students of literature
may also want to consult work done on specific forms (autobiography, detective fiction, letters) or on particular
parts of a text (title, epigraph). Scholars interested in
interdisciplinary approaches will find further inspiration
in books and articles dealing with intertextuality, allusion, and quotation in music, the fine arts, film, or tele-
vision; he or she might also consult studies available on
allusions to art and music in literary texts. Finally, the
subject index offers the possibility to approach research
performed by linguists and philosophers who have repeatedly
concerned themselves with the ontological status of quotational elements. Last, but not least, teachers of literature
may find useful information on their students' intertextual
competence in any of the items collected under the respective subject word.

However incomplete this brief introductory survey has to
remain, it should nevertheless be able to document the productivity and heterogeneity of intertextual research. The

compiler of the present bibliography can only hope that it
will help its user to find his or her way through the labyrinth of concepts, terms, and approaches related to intertextuality, allusion, and quotation. The present volume will
prove worthy of all efforts if it is able to induce further
interpretive applications aiming at a deeper understanding
of intertextually organized texts.

NOTES

1. Titles included in the following bibliography are referred to by author and entry number. Where available, foreign language studies are quoted in their published English
translations.
2. cf., Karl Beckson and Arthur Ganz, *Literary Terms: A
Dictionary* (New York: Farrar & Giroux, 1975); J. A. Cuddon,
A Dictionary of Literary Terms (Garden City, N.Y.: Double-
day, 1977); Roger Fowler, *A Dictionary of Modern Critical
Terms* (London: Routledge & Kegan Paul, 1973); Northrop Frye,
Sheridan Baker, and George Perkins, *The Harper Handbook to
Literature* (New York: Harper, 1985);   Hugh Holman, *A Hand-
book to Literature*, 4th ed. (Indianapolis, Ind.: Bobbs-Mer-
rill, 1980); Alex Preminger, ed., *Princeton Encyclopedia of
Poetry and Poetics*, enlarged ed. (Princeton, N.J.: Princeton
University Press, 1974); Joseph T. Shipley, *Dictionary of
World Literary Terms* (London: Allen & Unwin, 1955); Guenther
and Irmgard Schweikle, eds., *Metzler Literatur Lexikon*
(Stuttgart, W. Germany: Metzler, 1984); Gero von Wilpert,
Sachwoerterbuch der Literatur, 6th ed. (Stuttgart, W. Germany: Kroener, 1979).
3. cf., René Wellek and Austin Warren, *Theory of Literature*, 3rd ed. (Harmondsworth, UK: Penguin, 1970) 258.
4. Heinrich F. Plett, "The Poetics of Quotation," *Von
der verbalen Konstitution zur symbolischen Bedeutung--From
Verbal Constitution to Symbolic Meaning*, eds. J. S. Petoefi
and T. Olivi (Hamburg, W. Germany: Buske, 1988) 313-334.
5. Leonard Peter Diepeveen, "The Modernist Quoting
Poem," diss., University of Illinois at Urbana-Champaign,
1987. Hilda Brown, "Between Plagiarism and Parody: The Function of the Rimbaud Quotations in Brecht's *Im Dickicht der
Staedte*," *Modern Language Review* 82 (1987): 662-674, deserves mention as it deals with the relationships among the
concepts indicated in its title. The following two articles
represent scholars' activities in the field: Harald Breier,
"Brando Malvolio, ein Mann von (fuenfund)fuenfzig Jahren:
Form und Funktion des Zitats in Martin Walsers Roman *Bran-
dung*," *Literatur in Wissenschaft und Unterricht* 21 (1988):
191-201; Eric Rasmussen, "A Source for Keats's Misquotation
of *Lear*," *Keats-Shelley-Journal* 36 (1987): 20.
6. Susan F. Mathews, "A Critical Evaluation of the Allusions to the Old Testament in Apocalypse 1:1-8:5," diss.,
Catholic University of America, Washington, D.C., 1987; John
Paulien, "Allusions, Exegetical Method, and the Interpretation of Revelation 8:7-12," diss., Andrews University,

Berrien Springs., Mich., 1987. Ben-Dov's essay continues the long-standing tradition of analyzing biblical allusions; cf., Nitza Ben-Dov, "Biblical Allusion in Agnon's *Dance of Death*: A Study of Intertextual Dissonance," *Modern Judaism* 7 (1987): 271-286.

   7. Abraham H. Lass et al., eds., *The Facts on File: Dictionary of Classical, Biblical, and Literary Allusions* (New York: Facts on File, 1987). Encyclopedic endeavors of a different kind are Rathjen's and Weisenburger's companions to Schmidt and Pynchon: Friedhelm Rathjen, *"... schlechte Augen": James Joyce bei Arno Schmidt vor Zettels Traum. Ein annotierender Kommentar* (Muenchen, W. Germany: Edition Text und Kritik, 1988); Steven Weisenburger, *A Gravity's Rainbow Companion: Sources and Contexts for Pynchon's Novel* (Athens, Ga.: University of Georgia Press, 1988).

   8. Darrell Holley, *Churchill's Literary Allusions: An Index to the Education of a Soldier, Statesman, and Litterateur* (Jefferson, N.C.: McFarland, 1987); Horst Kruse, "Parsing a Complex Structure: Literary Allusion and Mythic Evocation in John Cheever's 'The Swimmer,'" *Literatur in Wissenschaft und Unterricht* 20 (1987): 217-231; Debra C. Ames, "The Function of Classical Allusions in the Theater of Lope de Vega," diss., University of Virginia, 1987; Morris Wachs, "The Elusiveness of Topical Allusions: Chapter XII of *Candide* and a Poem by Diderot," *Romance Quarterly* 34 (1987): 233-236.

   9. In addition to the titles mentioned, the reader is advised to consult the following studies: Irmela Arnsperger, "Die Texttheorie der Tel Quel-Gruppe," diss., Berlin, 1975; Richard Bruetting, *"écriture" und "texte": Die franzoesische Literaturtheorie "nach dem Strukturalismus"* (Bonn, W. Germany: Bouvier, 1976); Josué V. Harari, "Critical Factions/ Critical Fictions," *Textual Strategies: Perspectives in Poststructuralist Criticism*, ed. J. V. Harari (Ithaca, N.Y.: Cornell University Press, 1979) 17-72; Klaus W. Hempfer, *Poststrukturale Texttheorie und narrative Praxis* (Muenchen, W. Germany: Fink, 1976); Vincent B. Leitch, *Deconstructive Criticism: An Advanced Introduction* (New York: Columbia University Press, 1983); Frank Lentricchia, *After the New Criticism* (Chicago, Ill.: University of Chicago Press, 1980); Richard Macksey and Eugenio Donato, eds., *The Structuralist Controversy: The Languages of Criticism and the Sciences of Man* (Baltimore, Md.: Johns Hopkins University Press, 1970); Christopher Norris, *Deconstruction: Theory and Practice* (London: Methuen, 1982); Edward Said, *The World, the Text, the Critic* (Cambridge, Mass.: Harvard University Press, 1983).

   10. E. D. Hirsch, *Validity in Interpretation* (New Haven, Conn.: Yale University Press, 1967) 26. The discussion on artistic intention is most accessible in David de Molina, ed., *On Literary Intention* (Edinburgh, UK: University Press, 1976).

   11. cf., Roger Fowler, *A Dictionary of Modern Critical Terms*, rev. and enlarged ed. (New York: Routledge & Kegan Paul, 1987).

   12. Items published after the closing date of the present bibliography have not brought any new developments. The following titles represent the ongoing discussion: Donald M. Bruce, "De l'intertextualité à l'interdiscursivité: Evolu-

tion d'un concept théorique," diss., University of Toronto, Canada, 1987; Paul Francis Bryce-Almendral, "The Crossroads of the Underworld and Intertextual Practices: Carnival, Discursive Formations, and the Archeology of Domination in Nineteenth-Century Literature," diss., University of Michigan, 1987; Miranda Haddad, "The Writer as Reader: A Study of Intertextual Influence in the Works of Dante, Ariosto and Spenser," diss., Yale University, New Haven, Conn., 1987; Ingeborg Hoesterey, "The Intertextual Loop: Kafka, Robbe-Grillet, Kafka," *Kafka and the Contemporary Performance: Centenary Readings*, ed. Alan Udoff (Bloomington, Ind.: Indiana University Press, 1987) 58-75; Wanda Rulewicz, "Intertextuality, Competence, Reader," *Kwartalnik Neofilologiczny* 34 (1987): 229-241; Françoise Sammarcelli, "Mise en scène d'une manipulation: *Letters* de John Barth ou les pièges de l'intertexte," *Revue Française d'Études Américaines* 32 (1987): 171-182.

13. Owing to the history of his reception, Bakhtin poses serious problems for any bibliographer. As the present volume singles out the English editions of his most important works, the reader is referred to the following titles that offer further bibliographies of Bakhtin's works, their translations, and secondary literature on Bakhtin and his disciples: Michail M. Bachtin, *Die Aesthetik des Wortes*, ed. Rainer Gruebel (Frankfurt, W. Germany: Suhrkamp, 1979) 79-88; Bakhtin (#82) pp. xxxii-xxxiv; Todorov (#1823) pp. 173-176; Bruce (#258) pp. 220-223. In addition to entries #208, #454, #648, #841, #852, #969, #977, and #1571, the following titles deserve special mention: Katerina Clark and Michael Holquist, *Mikhail Bakhtin* (Cambridge, Mass: Belknap Press, 1984); "Mikhail Bakhtin," *Critical Inquiry*, special issue 10.2 (1983); "Mikhail Bakhtin," *Studies in Twentieth Century Literature*, special issue 9.1 (1984); I. R. Titunik, "M. M. Baxtin (The Baxtin School) and Soviet Semiotics," *Dispositio* 1 (1976): 327-338.

14. Robert Alter, "Deconstruction in America," *The New Republic* (April 25, 1983): 30.

Bibliography

0001. Abraham, Lyndy. "Literary Allusion in Nabokov's *Pale Fire.*" *Dutch Quarterly Review of Anglo-American Letters* 13 (1983): 241-266.

0002. Ackerley, C. J. "*Under the Volcano.* A Check-List of Unknown Details." *Malcolm Lowry Review* 17-18 (1985-86): 121-133.

0003. Ackermann, Carl. *The Bible in Shakespeare.* 1936; Folcroft Library Editions, 1971.

0004. Adel, Kurt. "Das Zitat in der Lyrik." *Literatur und Kritik* 61 (1972): 235-245.

0005. Aden, John M. "'The Change of Sceptors, and Impending Woe': Political Allusion in Pope's 'Statius.'" *Philological Quarterly* 52 (1973): 728-738.

0006. Adorno, Theodor W. "Versuch, das *Endspiel* zu verstehen." Theodor W. Adorno. *Noten zur Literatur II.* Frankfurt, W. Germany: Suhrkamp, 1961. 188-235.

0007. Ahrendt, Peter. "Vom Nutzen der Zettelkaesten: Selbstzitate bei Arno Schmidt." *Bargfelder Bote* 69-70 (1983): 26-30.

0008. Alazraki, Jaime. "Aproximación a la prosa narrativa de Jorge Luis Borges." *Symposium* 24 (1970): 5-16.

0009. -----. "El texto como palimpsesto: Lectura intertextual de Borges." *Hispanic Review* 52 (1984): 281-302.

0010. Albrecht, Wolfgang. "Bemerkungen zu Funktion und Leistung der Goethe-Zitate in Plenzdorfs *Die neuen Leiden des jungen W.*: Eine linguistische Untersuchung auf literaturwissenschaftlicher Interessengrundlage." *Die Funktion der Sprachgestaltung im literarischen Text.* Ed. Willi Steinberg. Halle, E. Germany: Martin Luther Universitaet, 1981. 251-267.

0011. Alderman, Taylor. "*The Great Gatsby* and *Hopalong Cassidy.*" *Fitzgerald/Hemingway Annual* (1975): 83-87.

0012. Alderson, William L. "A Checklist of Supplements to Spurgeon's Chaucer Allusions." *Philological Quarterly* 32 (1953): 418-427.

0013. -----. "A Collection of Chaucer Allusions." William L. Alderson and Arnold C. Henderson. *Chaucer and Augustan Scholarship.* University of California English Studies 35. Berkeley and Los Angeles: University of California Press, 1970. 189-241.

0014. -----. "On Two Chaucer Allusions." *Modern Language Notes* 71 (1956): 166-167.

0015. Alexiou, Margaret. "C. P. Cavafy's 'Dangerous' Drugs: Poetry, Eros and the Dissemination of Images." Eds. Margaret Alexiou and Vassilis Lambropoulos. *The Text and Its Margins: Post-Structuralist Approaches to Twentieth-Century Greek Literature.* New York: Pella, 1985. 157-196.

0016. Alford, John A. "More Unidentified Quotations in *Piers Plowman.*" *Modern Philology* 81 (1983-84): 278-285.

0017. -----. "The Role of the Quotations in *Piers Plowman.*" *Speculum* 52 (1977): 80-99.

0018. ----. "Some Unidentified Quotations in *Piers Plowman.*" *Modern Philology* 72 (1974-75): 390-399.

0019. Allard, Jacques. "L'idéologie du pays dans le roman québécois contemporain: *Il n'y a pas de pays sans grand-père* et l'intertexte national." *Voix et Images* 5 (1979): 117-132.

0020. Allen Gay W. "Biblical Analogies for Walt Whitman's Prosody." *Revue Anglo-Américaine* 10 (1933): 490-507.

0021. -----. "Biblical Echoes in Whitman's Works." *American Literature* 6 (1934): 302-315.

0022. Allen, Judson. "Utopian Literature: The Problem of Literary Reference." *Cithara: Essays in the Judaeo-Christian Tradition* 11.2 (1972): 40-55.

0023. Allen, William Rodney. "All the Names of Death: Allusion and the Theme of Suicide in the Novels of Walker Percy." Diss. Duke University, Durham, N. C., 1982.

0024. Almeida, Ivan. "Paysage intertextuel." *Sémiotique & Bible* 15 (1979): 1-3.

0025. -----. "Trois cas de rapports intratextuels: La citation, la parabolisation, le commentaire." *Sémiotique & Bible* 15 (1979): 23-42.

0026. Alonso-Hernandez, José Luis. "Multiplicidad significativa en Quevedo (Analisa de un soneto)." *Bulletin Hispanique* 87 (1985): 245-276.

0027. Altman, Charles F. "Intratextual Rewriting: Textuality as Language Formation." *The Sign in Music and Literature*. Ed. Wendy Steiner. Austin, Texas: University of Texas Press, 1981. 39-51.

0028. Alvarez-Borland, Isabel. "Victor Hugo, Gabriela Mistral, y *l'intertextualité*." *Revista de Estudios Hispanicos* 18 (1984): 371-380.

0029. Amoroso, Guiseppe. "Il surrealismo archeologico di Savinio." *Letteratura* 25 (1961): 59-68.

0030. Amossy, Ruth. *Les jeux de l'allusion littéraire dans Un beau ténébreux de Julien Gracq*. Neuchâtel, Switzerland: Baconnièrre, 1980.

0031. -----. "Un procédé du récit réfléchi: Les allusions à Rimbaud dans *Un beau ténébreux*." *Revue des Sciences Humaines* 151 (1973): 469-484.

0032. Andersen, Harry. "Nogle allusioner i Sophus Claussens Digtning." *Danske Studier* 57 (1962): 118-125.

0033. Anderson, Charles. "Hemingway's Other Style." *Modern Language Notes* 76 (1961): 434-442.

0034. Anderson, David G. "Internal Structure and Intertextuality in the *Odas* of Pablo Neruda." Diss. Vanderbilt University, Nashville, Tenn., 1985.

0035. Andersson, Hans. "Quotations and Allusions: An Aspect of the Use of English." *Moderna Sprak* 79 (1985): 201-207, 289-297.

0036. Andreu, Alicia. "*El folletin*: De Galdós a Manuel Puig." *Revista Iberoamericana* 49 (1983): 541-546.

0037. Andrew, Malcolm. "Chaucer's 'General Prologue' to the *Canterbury Tales*." *Explicator* 43.1 (1984) 5-6.

0038. Andrieu, J. "Procédés de citation et de raccord." *Revue des Etudes Latines* 26 (1948): 268-293.

0039. Angenot, Marc. "Intertextualité, interdiscursivité, discours social." *Texte* 2 (1983): 101-112.

0040. -----. "Lecture intertextuelle d'un texte de Freud." *Poétique* 56 (1983): 387-396.

0041. -----. "L'intertextualité?: Enquête sur l'émergence et la diffusion d'un champ notionnel." *Revue des Sciences Humaines* 189 (1983): 121-135.

0042. Anschuetz, Carol. "Bely's *Petersburg* and the End of the Russian Novel." *The Russian Novel from Pushkin to Pasternak*. Ed. John Garrard. New Haven, Conn.: Yale

University Press, 1983. 125-153.

0043. Anthony, J. Philip. "Donne's 'The Relique.'" *Explicator* 44.2 (1986): 13-15.

0044. Anthony, Mary. "Emily Dickinson's Scriptural Echoes." *Massachusetts Review* 2 (1961): 557-561.

0045. Anzalone, John. "Golden Cylinders: Inscription and Intertext in *L'Eve future.*" *L'Esprit Créateur* 26 (1986): 38-47.

0046. Apfel, Henrietta Veit. "Literary Quotation and Allusion in Demetrius and Longinus." Diss. Columbia University, New York, 1935.

0047. Applegate, James E. "Classical Allusions in Prose Work in Robert Greene." Diss. Johns Hopkins University, Baltimore, Md., 1954.

0048 Araújo, Helena. "Valenzuela's *Other Weapons.*" *Review of Contemporary Fiction* 6.3 (1986): 78-81.

0049. Armisén, Antonio. "Intensidad y altura: Lope de Vega, César Vallejo y los problemas de la escritura poética." *Bulletin Hispanique* 87 (1985): 277-303.

0050. Armleder, Paul John. "Quotation in Cicero's Letters." Diss. University of Cincinnati, Ohio, 1957.

0051. Armstrong, David T. "Literary Allusions." *English Journal* 34 (1945): 218-219.

0052. Aron, Thomas. "La Fontaine ou la 'Mise en scene' de la parole." *Europe: Revue Littéraire Mensuelle* 59 (1981): 202-204.

0053. Arpad, Joseph J. "The Fight Story: Quotation and Originality in Native American Humor." *Journal of the Folklore Institute* 10 (1973): 141-172.

0054. Arrathoon, Leigh A. "'For craft is al, whoso that do it kan': The Genre of *The Merchant's Tale.*" *Chaucer and the Craft of Fiction.* Ed. Leigh A. Arrathoon. Rochester, Mich.: Solaris, 1986. 241-328.

0055. Arrivé, Michel. "Intertexte et intertextualité chez Ferdinand de Saussure." *Le plaisir de l'intertexte: Formes et fonctions de l'intertextualité (roman populaire, surréalisme, André Gide, nouveau roman).* Eds. Raimund Theis and Hans T. Siepe. Bern, Switzerland: Lang, 1986. 11-31.

0056. -----. *Les langages de Jarry: Essai de sémiotique littéraire.* Paris: Klincksieck, 1972.

0057. -----. "Pour une théorie des textes poly-isotopiques." *Langages* 31 (1973): 54-63.

0058. Asensio, Jaime. "¿Es Tirso 'el otro' de el *Viaje del Parnaso* de Cervantes?" *Revista Canadiense de Estudios Hispánicos* 10 (1986): 155-172.

0059. Ashton, J. W. "Three Sixteenth-Century Allusions to Chaucer." *Philological Quarterly* 13 (1934): 82-83.

0060. Astro, Richard. "*Vandover and the Brute* and *The Beautiful and Damned*: A Search for Thematic and Stylistic Reinterpretations." *Modern Fiction Studies* 14 (1968): 397-413.

0061. Atherton, James A. *The Books at the Wake: A Study of Literary Allusions in James Joyce's Finnegans Wake.* Carbondale, Edwardsville, Ill.: Southern Illinois University Press, 1959.

0062. Atkinson, Dorothy F. "Chaucer Allusions." *Notes and Queries* 169 (1935): 116, 205.

0063. -----. "Some Further Chaucer Allusions." *Modern Language Notes* 55 (1940): 361-362.

0064. -----. "Some Further Chaucer Allusions." *Modern Language Notes* 59 (1944): 568-570.

0065. Attrey, Roshan. "The Function of Oriental Allusions in James Joyce's *Ulysses.*" Diss. University of Tennessee, 1986.

0066. Audhuy, Letha. "*The Waste Land*: Myth and Symbolism in *The Great Gatsby.*" *Etudes Anglaises* 33 (1980): 41-54.

0067. Authier-Revuz, Jacqueline. "Hétérogènéité(s) énonciative(s)." *Langages* 73 (1984): 98-111.

0068. Awkward, Michael. "A Circle of Sisters: An Intertextual Analysis of Afro-American Women's Novels." Diss. University of Pennsylvania, 1986.

0069. Ayers, Robert W. "*Robinson Crusoe*: 'Allusive Allegorick History.'" *Publications of the Modern Language Association* 82 (1967): 399-407.

0070. Backscheider, Paula R. "Personality and Biblical Allusions in Defoe's Letters." *South Atlantic Bulletin* 47 (1982): 1-20.

0071. Bader, Bernd. *Die klassisch-altertumswissenschaftliche Zeitschriftenliteratur: Eine Zitateanalyse.* Giessen, W. Germany: Universitaetsbibliothek, 1981.

0072. Baenzinger, Hans. "'Ab posse ad esse valet': Zu einem Zitat im Spiel 'Biografie.'" *Frisch: Kritik-Thesen-Analysen: Beitraege zum 65. Geburtstag.* Ed. Manfred Jurgensen. Bern, Switzerland: Francke, 1977. 11-25.

0073. -----. "Leben im Zitat: Zu *Montauk*: Ein Formulierungsproblem und dessen Vorgeschichte." *Max Frisch:*

Aspekte des Prosawerkes. Ed. Gerhard Knapp. Bern, Switzerland: Lang, 1978. 267-284.

0074. Baerend, Irmhild. "Das Bibelzitat als Strukturelement im Werk Wilhelm Raabes." Diss. Freie Universitaet Berlin, W. Germany, 1969.

0075. -----. "Das Bibelzitat als Strukturelement im Werk Wilhelm Raabes." *Jahrbuch der Raabe-Gesellschaft* (1969): 33-52.

0076. Bailey, John A. "*Jumpers* by Tom Stoppard: The Ironist as Theistic Apologist." *Michigan Academician* 11 (1979): 237-250.

0077. Baker, Christopher P. "Milton's Nativity Ode and *In Memoriam.*" *Victorian Poetry* 18 (1980): 202-203.

0078. -----. "Spenser and 'The City in the Sea.'" *Poe Studies* 5 (1972): 55.

0079. Baker, Deborah L. *Narcissus and the Lover: Mythic Recovery and Reinvention in Scève's Délie.* Saratoga, Cal.: Anma Libri, 1986.

0080. Baker, Harry T. "Shakespeare Misquoted." *Modern Language Notes* 42 (1927): 87-94.

0081. Baker, Sheridan. "Political Allusion in Fielding's *Author's Farce, Mock Doctor,* and *Tumble Down Dick.*" *Publications of the Modern Language Association* 77 (1962): 221-231.

0082. Bakhtin, Mikhail. *The Dialogic Imagination: Four Essays.* Ed. Michael Holquist; transl. Caryl Emerson and Michael Holquist. Austin, Texas: University of Texas Press, 1981.

0083. -----. *Problems of Dostoevsky's Poetics.* Transl. R. W. Rotsel. Ann Arbor: Ardis, 1973. [cf. also: Mikhail Bakhtin. *Problems of Dostoevsky's Poetics.* Transl. Caryl Emerson. Minneapolis, Minn.: University of Minnesota Press, 1984.]

0084. -----. *Rabelais and His World.* Transl. H. Iswolsky. Cambridge, Mass.: MIT Press, 1968.

0085. Bakker, Jan. "Parallel Water Journeys into the American Eden in John Davis' *The First Settlers of Virginia* and F. Scott Fitzgerald's *The Great Gatsby.*" *Early American Literature* 16 (1981): 50-53.

0086. Balderston, Daniel. *The Literary Universe of Jorge Luis Borges: An Index to References and Allusions to Persons, Titles, and Places in His Writings.* Bibliographies and Indexes in World Literature 9. Westport, Conn.: Greenwood, 1986.

0087. Baldridge, Wilson. "The Time-Crisis in Mallarmé and

Proust." *French Review* 59 (1986): 564-570.

0088. Baldwin, Anna. "Reference in *Piers Plowman* to the Westminster Sanctuary." *Notes and Queries* 29 (1982): 106-108.

0089. Ball, Robert. "Góngora's Parodies of Literary Conventions." Diss. Yale University, New Haven, Conn., 1976.

0090. -----. "Poetic Imitation in Góngora's *Romance de Angélica y Medoro.*" *Bulletin of Hispanic Studies* 57 (1980): 33-54.

0091. Balmas, Enea. "Rhétorique et originalité chez les poètes de la Pléiade." *Textes et intertextes: Etudes sur le XVIe siècle pour Alfred Glauser.* Eds. Floyd Gray and Marcel Tetel. Paris: Nizet, 1979. 11-28.

0092. Balmas, Nerina Clerici. "Un ami de Marc Papillon: Le médicien Pierre Pena." *Mélanges sur la littérature de la Renaissance à la mémoire de V. L. Saulnier.* Ed. P. G. Castex. Geneva, Switzerland: Droz, 1984. 681-689.

0093. Bandera, Cesareo. "Oú nous entraîne l'intertextualité?" *Violence et vérité autour de René Girard.* Ed. Paul Dumouchel. Paris: Grasset, 1985. 468-482.

0094. Barclay, Dean Arne. "Enormous Tradition: Literary Allusion in Thackeray and Dickens." Diss. Harvard University, Cambridge, Mass., 1986.

0095. Bargad, Warren. "The Poetics of Allusion and the Hebrew Literary Tradition." *Judaism* 26 (1977): 481-488.

0096. Barker, Francis, and Peter Hulme. "Nymphs and Reapers Heavily Vanish: The Discursive Con-Texts of *The Tempest.*" *Alternative Shakespeares.* Ed. John Drakakis. London: Methuen, 1985. 191-205.

0097. Barnes, A. D. "'Kent's Holy Cords': A Biblical Allusion in *King Lear* II, ii 74-76." *English Language Notes* 22.2 (1984): 20-22.

0098. Barnouw, Dagmar. "Literat und Literatur: Robert Musils Beziehung zu Franz Blei." *Modern Austrian Literature* 9 (1976): 168-199.

0099. Barr, Helen. "The Use of Latin Quotations in *Piers Plowman* with Special Reference to Passus XVIII of the 'B' Text." *Notes and Queries* 33 (1986): 440-448.

0100. Barrenechea, Ann Maria. *Borges: The Labyrinth Maker.* New York: New York University Press, 1965.

0101. Barry, Peter. "Finnegans Waste Land." *A Wake Newslitter* 17.2 (1980): 21-23.

0102. Barthes, Roland. "Analyse textuelle d'un conte d'Edgar Poe." *Sémiotique narrative et textuelle.* Ed. Claude

Chabrol. Paris: Larousse, 1973. 29-54. [Engl. trans. by G. Bennington: "Textual Analysis of Poe's 'Valdemar.'" *Untying the Text: A Poststructuralist Reader.* Ed. Robert Young. Boston, Mass.,: Routledge & Co., 1981. 133-161.]

0103. -----. "De l'oeuvre au texte." *Revue d'Esthétique* 24 (1971): 225-232. [Engl. trans. by Stephen Heath: "From Work to Text." *Image, Music, Text.* Ed. Stephen Heath. New York: Hill & Wang, 1977. 155-164. For another English translation cf., "From Work to Text." *Textual Strategies: Perspectives in Post-Structuralist Criticism.* Ed. Josué V. Harari. Ithaca, N.Y.: Cornell University Press, 1979. 73-81.]

0104. -----. "La mort de l'auteur." *Manteia* 5 (1968): 12-17. [Engl. trans. by Stephen Heath: "The Death of the Author." *Image, Music, Text.* Ed. Stephen Heath. New York: Hill & Wang, 1977. 142-148.]

0105. -----. *Le plaisir du texte.* Paris: Seuil, 1973. [Engl. trans. by Richard Miller: *The Pleasure of the Text.* New York: Hill & Wang, 1975.]

0106. -----. *S/Z.* Paris: Seuil, 1970. [Engl. trans. by Richard Miller: *S/Z.* New York: Hill & Wang, 1974.]

0107. -----. "Texte (Théorie du)." *Encyclopædia Universalis.* Paris: Encyclopædia Universalis, 1973. 15: 1013-1017. [Engl. trans. by Ian McLeod: "Theory of the Text." *Untying the Text: A Poststructuralist Reader.* Ed. Robert Young. Boston, Mass.: Routledge & Co., 1981. 31-47.]

0108. Bartlett, Phyllis. "Other Countries, Other Wenches." *Modern Fiction Studies* 3 (1957-58): 345-349.

0109. Bartschi, Helen. *The Doing and Undoing of Fiction: A Study of Joseph Andrews.* Bern, Switzerl.: Lang, 1983.

0110. Bastian, Katherine. *Joyce Carol Oates's Short Stories Between Tradition and Innovation.* Frankfurt, W. Germany: Lang, 1983.

0111. Batchelor, R. E. "L'art de l'allusion dans *Moïra.*" *Nottingham French Studies* 5 (1966): 40-49.

0112. Bate, A. Jonathan. "Hazlitt's Shakespearean Quotations." *Prose Studies* 7 (1984): 26-37.

0113. Batt, Kurt. "Leben im Zitat: Notizen zu Peter Handke." *Sinn und Form* 26 (1974): 603-623.

0114. Bauer, George H. "Uòmo di lettere - Lhomme letre - B's XYZ Game." *Intertextuality: New Perspectives in Criticism.* Eds. Jeanine P. Plottel and Hanna Charney. New York Literary Forum 2. New York: Literary Forum, 1978. 139-156.

0115. Bauerle, Ruth. "Two Unnoted Musical Allusions." *James*

Joyce Quarterly 9 (1971): 140-142.

0116. Baumgartner, Emmanuèle. "Les citations lyriques dans le *Roman de la rose* de Jean Renart." *Romance Philology* 35 (1981): 260-266.

0117. Bawcutt, Priscilla. "Dunbar's *Tretis of the Tua Mariit Wemen and the Wedo* 185-187 and Chaucer's *Parson's Tale.*" *Notes and Queries* 209 (1964): 332-333.

0118. Baxter, Charles. "De-Faced America: *The Great Gatsby* and *The Crying of Lot 49.*" *Pynchon Notes* 7 (1981): 22-37.

0119. Beaujour, Michel. "Is Less More?" *Intertextuality: New Perspectives in Criticism.* Eds. Jeanine P. Plottel and Hanna Charney. New York Literary Forum 2. New York: Literary Forum, 1978. 237-243.

0120. Beaumont, Charles Allen. *Swift's Use of the Bible: A Documentation and a Study in Allusion.* University of Georgia Monographs 14. Athens, Ga.: University of Georgia Press, 1965.

0121. Bebermeyer, Renate. "'Gefluegelte Zitate' - gestern und heute." *Sprachspiegel* 40 (1984): 66-70.

0122. Beck, Adolf. "Unbekannte franzoesische Quellen fuer *Dantons Tod* von Georg Buechner." *Jahrbuch des Freien Deutschen Hochstifts* (1963): 489-538.

0123. Beck, G. "Gaensefuesse als Pferdefuesse: Ueber Formen und Normen direkter und indirekter Zitierung." *Sprache und Literatur in Wissenschaft und Unterricht* 17.2 (1986): 85-98.

0124. Beck, Michael. "Die Koranzitate bei Sibawaih." Diss. Muenchen, W. Germany, 1959.

0125. Becker-Frank, Sigrid W. *Das Spaetwerk Thomas Manns: Eine Untersuchung zur Integration des Zitats, besonders im Doktor Faustus.* Quickborn/Hamburg, W. Germany: Schnelle, 1963. [Diss. Tuebingen, W. Germany, 1963.]

0126. Begnal, Michael H. "*Bend Sinister*: Joyce, Shakespeare, Nabokov." *Modern Language Studies* 15.4 (1985): 22-27.

0127. Behar, Henri. "La réécriture comme poétique - ou le même et l'autre." *Romanic Review* 72 (1981): 51-65.

0128. Beichner, Paul E. "Absolon's Hair." *Mediaeval Studies* 12 (1951): 222-233.

0129. Bell, Robert F. "Metamorphoses and Missing Halves: Allusions in Paul Theroux's *Picture Palace.*" *Critique* 22.3 (1981): 17-30.

0130. Bellamy, Joe David. "The Dark Lady of American Letters: An Interview with Joyce Carol Oates." *Atlan-*

tic Monthly 229 (February 1972): 63-67.

0131. Bellmann, Samuel. "Henry James's 'The Tree of Know-
      ledge': A Biblical Parallel." *Studies in Short Fiction*
      1 (1964): 226-228.

0132. Bellmann, Werner. "'Bedlam' und 'Kasperle' auf dem li-
      terarischen Schuetzenplatz in Jena: Anmerkungen zu
      Brentanos satirischem Fruehwerk." *Aurora* 42 (1982):
      166-177.

0133. -----. "'Cacatum non est pictum' - Ein Zitat in Heines
      'Wintermaerchen.'" *Wirkendes Wort* 33 (1983): 213-215.

0134. Benjamin, Walter. "Das Kunstwerk im Zeitalter seiner
      technischen Reproduzierbarkeit." W. Benjamin. *Illumi-
      nationen*. Frankfurt, W. G.: Suhrkamp, 1961. 148-184.

0135. Bennani, Ben. "Translating Arabic Poetry: An Inter-
      pretative, Intertextual Approach." *Translation Spec-
      trum: Essays in Theory and Practice*. Ed. Marilyn G.
      Rose. Albany, N. Y.: State University of New York,
      1981. 135-139.

0136. Bennett, John Zebulun. "Detail, Allusion, and Theme in
      the 'Telemachus' Episode of James Joyce's *Ulysses*."
      Diss. University of North Carolina, Chapel Hill, N.C.,
      1967.

0137. Ben-Porat, Ziva. "The Poetics of Allusion." Diss. Uni-
      versity of California, Berkeley, Cal., 1973.

0138. -----. "The Poetics of Allusion: A Text-Linking Device
      In Different Media of Communication." *A Semiotic
      Landscape: Proceedings of the First Congress of the
      International Association For Semiotic Studies*. Ed. S.
      Chatman. The Hague, Holland: Mouton, 1979. 588-593.

0139. -----. "The Poetics of Literary Allusion." *PTL: A
      Journal for Descriptive Poetics and Theory of Litera-
      ture* 1 (1976): 105-128.

0140. Benrekassa, Georges. "Swiat Kultury w 'Pawle i
      Wirginii': Tekst a Intertekst." *Pamietnik Literacki* 72
      (1981): 201-226.

0141. Benson, C. David. "A Chaucerian Allusion and the Date
      of the Alliterative *Destruction of Troy*." *Notes and
      Queries* 219 (1974): 206-207.

0142. Benson, Douglas K. "Convenciones de lenguaje y alu-
      siones literarias en la poesía de Francisco Brines:
      Insistencias en Luzbel." *Hispania* 69 (1986): 1-11.

0143. Benson, Jackson J. "Literary Allusion and the Private
      Irony of Hemingway." *Pacific Coast Philology* 4 (1969):
      24-29.

0144. Benstock, Bernard. "Reflections on *Ruby*." *James Joyce*

Quarterly 19 (1982): 339-341.

0145. Bentley, Greg. "Donne's 'Witchcraft by a Picture.'" *Explicator* 42.3 (1984): 15-17.

0146. Berger, Dieter A. "'Damn the Mottoe': Scott and the Epigraph." *Anglia* 100 (1982): 373-396.

0147. Berger, Harry. "The Discarding of Malbecco: Conspicuous Allusion and Cultural Exhaustion in *The Faerie Queene* III, IX-X." *Studies in Philology* 66 (1969): 135-154.

0148. Bergman, Herbert. "Whitman and Tennyson." *Studies in Philology* 51 (1954): 492-504.

0149. Bergner, Heinz. "Text und kollektives Wissen: Zu Begriff und System der Praesupposition." *Text-Leser-Bedeutung.* Ed. Herbert Grabes. Grossen-Linden, W. Germany: Hoffmann, 1977. 1-18.

0150. Bergquist, Bruce Allen. "Walt Whitman and the Bible: Language Echoes, Images, Allusions, and Ideas." Diss. University of Nebraska, Lincoln, Nebr., 1979.

0151. Bergsten, Staffan. "Illusive Allusion: Some Reflections on the Critical Approach to the Poetry of T. S. Eliot." *Orbis Litterarum: International Review of Literary Studies* 14 (1959): 9-18.

0152. Bernay, Michael. "Zur Lehre von den Citaten und Noten." Michael Bernay. *Schriften zur Kritik und Litteraturgeschichte.* Berlin: Behr, 1899. 4: 253-347.

0153. Bernucci, Leopoldo M. "'La guerra del fin del mundo' de Mario Vargas Llosa: Un estudio transtextual." Diss. University of Michigan, Ann Arbor, Mich., 1986.

0154. Bernstein, Michael André. "'Bringing It All Back Home': Derivations and Quotations in Robert Duncan and the Poundian Tradition." *Sagetrieb* 1 (1982): 176-189.

0155. Berta, Michel. "Le non-dit religieux dans *Germinal*." *Cahiers Naturalists* 59 (1985): 93-99.

0156. Berthiaume, André. "Pratique de la citation dans les *Essais* de Montaigne." *Renaissance and Reformation* 8 (1984): 91-105.

0157. Betz, Friedrich. "'Wo Sich Herz Zum Herzen Find't': The Question of Authorship and Source of the Song and Subtitle in Fontane's *Frau Jenny Treibel*." *German Quarterly* 49 (1976): 312-317.

0158. Beugnot, Bernard. "Dialogue, entretien et citation à l'époque classique." *Canadian Review of Comparative Literature* 3 (1976): 39-50.

0159. -----. "Un aspect textuel de la réception critique: La citation." *Oeuvres & Critiques* 1.2 (1976): 5-19.

0160. Beyer, Renate. "Untersuchungen zum Zitatgebrauch in der deutschen Lyrik nach 1945." Diss. Goettingen, W. Germany, 1975.

0161. Bidney, Martin. "Faulkner's Variations on Romantic Themes: Blake, Wordsworth, Byron, and Shelley in *Light in August.*" *Mississippi Quarterly* 38 (1985): 277-286.

0162. -----. "Victorian Vision in Mississippi: Tennysonian Resonances in Faulkner's *Dark House / Light in August.*" *Victorian Poetry* 23 (1985): 43-57.

0163. Bier, Jean Paul. "Heinrich Mann und die Naivitaet." *Littérature et culture allemandes: Hommages à Henri Plard.* Ed. Michel Vanhelleputte. Bruxelles, Belgium: Editions de l'Université de Bruxelles, 1985. 237-270.

0164. -----. "James Joyce et Karl Bleibtreu: Sens et fonction d'une allusion littéraire dans *Ulysses.*" *Revue de Littérature Comparée* 44 (1970): 215-223.

0165. Bigelow, John C. "Contexts and Quotation [I]." *Linguistische Berichte* 38 (1975): 1-21.

0166. -----. "Contexts and Quotation [II]." *Linguistische Berichte* 39 (1975): 1-21.

0167. Bilous, Daniel. "Intertexte/pastiche: L'intermimotexte." *Texte* 2 (1983): 135-160.

0168. -----. "Réécrire l'intertexte: La Bruyère pasticheur de Montaigne." *Cahiers de Littérature du XVIIIème Siècle* 4 (1982): 101-117.

0169. Binns, Ron. "Lowry and *Dead of Night.*" *Malcolm Lowry Review* 16 (1985): 85-87.

0170. Birck, Friedrich Paul. *Literarische Anspielungen in den Werken Ben Jonsons.* Strassburg: DuMont Schauberg, 1908. [Diss. Strassburg, 1908.]

0171. Bismut, Roger. "L'appareil littéraire dans *Madame Bovary.*" *Les Lettres Romanes* 39 (1985): 27-43.

0172. Bjornson, Richard. "Translation and Literary Theory." *Translation Review* 6 (1980): 13-16.

0173. Black, Jeremy. "Political Allusions in Fielding's *Coffee-House-Politician.*" *Theoria* 62 (1984): 45-56.

0174. Black, Robert. "Chaucer's Allusion to the 'Sermon on the Mount' in the 'Miller's Tale.'" *Revue de l'Université d'Ottawa* 55 (1985): 23-32.

0175. Blackall, Jean F. "Literary Allusion as Imaginative Event in *The Akward Age.*" *Modern Fiction Studies* 26 (1980): 179-197.

0176. Blackwelder, James Ray. "Literary Allusions in *Look Homeward, Angel*: The Characters' Expressions." *Thomas Wolfe Review* 9.2 (1985): 36-46.

0177. -----. "Literary Allusions in *Look Homeward, Angel*: The Narrator's Perspective." *Thomas Wolfe Review* 8.2 (1984): 14-25.

0178. Blaensdorf, Juergen. "Senecas *Apocolocyntosis* und die Intertextualitaetstheorie." *Poetica* 18 (1986): 1-26.

0179. Blake, Nancy. "Creation and Procreation: The Voice and the Name, or Biblical Intertextuality in *Absalom, Absalom!*" *Intertextuality in Faulkner*. Eds. Michel Gresset and Noel Polk. Jackson, Miss.: University Press of Mississippi, 1985. 128-143.

0180. -----. "'An Exact Precession': Leonardo, Gertrude, and Guy Davenport's *DaVinci's Bicycle*." *Critical Angles: European Views of Contemporary American Literature*. Ed. Marc Chénetier. Carbondale, Ill.: Southern Illinois University Press, 1986. 145-152.

0181. Blakemore, Steven. "DeQuincey's Transubstantiation of Opium in the *Confessions*." *Massachusetts Studies in English* 9.3 (1984): 32-41.

0182. -----. "Language and Ideology in Orwell's *1984*." *Social Theory and Practice* 10 (1984): 349-356.

0183. Blaydes, Sophia. "Literary Allusion as Satire in Simon Gray's *Butley*." *Midwest Quarterly* 18 (1977): 374-391.

0184. Bledsoe, Robert T. "*Vanity Fair* and Singing." *Studies in the Novel* 13 (1981): 51-63.

0185. Bleicher, Thomas. *Homer in der deutschen Literatur. (1450-1740)*. Stuttgart, W. Germany: Metzler, 1972.

0186. Bleikasten, André. "'Cet affreux goût d'encore': Emma Bovary's Ghost in *Sanctuary*." *Intertextuality in Faulkner*. Eds. Michel Gresset and Noel Polk. Jackson, Miss.: University Press of Mississippi, 1985. 36-56.

0187. Bliss, Lee. "Defending Fletcher's Shepherds." *Studies in English Literature 1500-1900* 23 (1983): 295-310.

0188. Blodgett, E. D. "Intertextual Designs in Hugh Mac-Lennan's *The Watch that Ends the Night*." *Canadian Review of Comparative Literature* 5 (1978): 280-288.

0189. Bloom, Harold. *The Anxiety of Influence: A Theory of Poetry*. New York: Oxford University Press, 1973.

0190. -----. *A Map of Misreading*. New York: Oxford University Press, 1975.

0191. Bloomfield, Morton W. "Quoting and Alluding: Shakespeare in the English Language." *Harvard English*

Studies 7 (1976): 1-20.

0192. Blumenfeld-Kosinski, Renate. "The Poetics of Continuation in the Old French *Paon*-Cycle." *Modern Philology* 39 (1986): 437-447.

0193. Blythe, Hal and Charlie Sweet. "Classical Allusions in John Cheever's 'The Swimmer.'" *Notes on Modern American Literature* 8.1 (1984): Item 1.

0194. Boehm, Rudolf. *Das Motto in der englischen Literatur des 19. Jahrhunderts.* Muenchen, W. Germany: Fink, 1975.

0195. Boekhoff, Hermann. "Wilhelm Raabes Weltverhaeltnis in der Entwicklung seiner literarhistorischen und geistesgeschichtlichen Beziehungen." Diss. Kiel, W. Germany, 1948.

0196. Bohn, Willard. "Semiosis and Intertextuality in Breton's 'Femme et oiseau.'" *Romanic Review* 76 (1985): 415-428.

0197. Bolduc, Stevie Anne. "A Study of Intertextuality: Thomas Mann's *Tristan* and Richard Wagner's *Tristan und Isolde.*" *Rocky Mountain Review of Language and Literature* 37 (1983): 82-90.

0198. Boller, Paul F. *Quotemanship: The Use and Abuse of Quotations for Polemical and Other Purposes.* Dallas, Texas: Southern Methodist University Press, 1967.

0199. Bollnow, Otto F. "Ueber den Gebrauch von Zitaten." O. F. Bollnow. *Mass und Vermessenheit des Menschen.* Goettingen, W. Germany: Vandenhoeck, 1962. 198-213.

0200. Bond, Richmond P. "A Collection of Chaucer Allusions." *Studies in Philology* 28 (1931): 481-512.

0201. -----, Millican, C. B., Bowjer, J., and G. H. Smith. "Some Eighteenth Century Chaucer Allusions." *Studies in Philology* 25 (1928): 316-339.

0202. Bonnet, Pierre. "La source d'une citation latine de Montaigne." *Bulletin de la Société des Amis de Montaigne* 19 (1969): 43-49.

0203. Bornstein, George. "The Arrangement of Browning's *Dramatic Lyrics* (1842)." *Poems in Their Place: The Intertextuality and Order of Poetic Collections.* Ed. Neil Fraistat. Chapel Hill, N. C.: University of North Carolina Press, 1986. 273-288.

0204. Boswell, Jackson C. "Chaucer Allusions: Addenda to Spurgeon." *Notes and Queries* 222 (1977): 493-495.

0205. -----. "Chaucer and Spenser Allusions Not in Spurgeon and Wells." *Analytical and Enumerative Bibliography* 1 (1977): 30-32.

0206. -----, and H. R. Woudhuysen. "Some Unfamiliar Sidney Allusions." *Sir Philip Sidney: 1586 and the Creation of a Legend.* Eds. Jan van Dorsten, Dominic Baker-Smith, and Arthur F. Kinney. Leiden, Holland: Brill, 1986. 221-237.

0207. Bouché, Claude. *Lautréamont, du lieu commun à la parodie.* Paris: Larousse, 1974.

0208. Bové, Mastrangelo Carol. "The Text as Dialogue in Bakhtin and Kristeva." *University of Ottawa Quarterly* 53 (1983): 117-124.

0209. Bovie, S. P. "Classical Allusions." *Classical World* 52 (1958): 1-6.

0210. Bowen, Zack. "Allusion to Musical Works in *Point Counter Point.*" *Studies in the Novel* 9 (1977): 488-508.

0211. -----. *Musical Allusions in the Works of James Joyce: Early Poetry Through Ulysses.* Dublin, Ireland: Gill & Macmillan, 1975.

0212. Bowers, Alice Tremain. "Allusions to the Private Life of Louis XIV in the Dramatic Literature of the Seventeenth Century." Diss. University of Missouri, 1968.

0213. Bowers, R. H. "Impingham's Borrowings from Chaucer." *Modern Language Notes* 73 (1958): 327-329.

0214. -----. "Thomas Randolph Alludes to Chaucer." *Philological Quarterly* 12 (1933): 314.

0215. Bowman, Frank Paul. "Flaubert dans l'intertexte des discours sur le mythe." *La Revue de Lettres Modernes* 777 (1986): 5-57.

0216. Box, Mark. "A Quotation in *The Pleasures of Imagination* Identified." *Notes and Queries* 31 (1984): 9-10.

0217. Boys, Richard C. "Some Chaucer Allusions 1705-1799." *Philological Quarterly* 17 (1938): 263-270.

0218. Braden, Gordon. "Herrick's Classical Quotations." *"Trust To Good Verses": Herrick Tercentenary Essays.* Pittsburgh, Pa.: University of Pittsburgh Press, 1978. 127-147.

0219. Bradley, Jesse Franklin, and Joseph Q. Adams. *The Jonson Allusion-Book: A Collection of Allusions to Ben Jonson from 1597 to 1700.* New Haven, Conn.: Yale University Press, 1922. [Diss. Cornell University, Ithaca, N. Y., 1919.]

0220. Brandell, Gunnar. "Konsten att citera." *Gunnar Brandell. Konsten att citera och andra aterblickar.* Stockholm, Sweden: Bonnier, 1966. 7-18.

0221. Brandes, Ute. *Zitat und Montage in der neueren DDR-Prosa*. Frankfurt, W. Germany: Lang, 1984.

0222. Brandt, Per Aage. "La pensée du texte (de la littéralité de la littérarité)." *Essais de la théorie du texte*. Ed. Charles Bonazis. Paris: Galilée, 1973. 183-215.

0223. Brater, Enoch. "The *Company* Beckett Keeps: The Shape of Memory and One Fablist's Decay of Lying." *Samuel Beckett: Humanistic Perspectives*. Ed. Morris Beja. Columbus, Ohio: Ohio State University, 1983. 157-171.

0224. Braun, Peter. "Sprichwoerter-Redensarten-Zitate-Titel: Oder die Tendenz zur Abwandlung von Formeln." Peter Braun. *Tendenzen in der deutschen Gegenwartssprache*. Stuttgart, W. Germany: Kohlhammer, 1979. 159-164.

0225. Brée, Germaine. "The Archaeology of Discourse in Malraux's *Anti-memoirs*." *Intertextuality: New Perspectives in Criticism*. Eds. Jeanine P. Plottel and Hanna Charney. New York Literary Forum 2. New York: Literary Forum, 1978. 3-13.

0226. Breitkreuz, Hartmut. "Literarische Zitatanalyse und Exemplaforschung." *Fabula: Zeitschrift fuer Erzaehlforschung* 12 (1971): 1-7.

0227. Bremer, Thomas. "Historia social de la literatura e intertextualidad: Funciones de la lectura en las novelas latino-americanas del siglo XIX (el caso del 'libro en el libro')." *Revista de Crítica Literaria Latinoamericana* 24 (1986): 31-49.

0228. Brennan, Anthony S. "Winnie's Golden Treasure: The Use of Quotation in *Happy Days*." *Arizona Quarterly* 35 (1979): 205-227.

0229. Brennan, Matthew C. "Plotting Against Chekhov: Joyce Carol Oates and 'The Lady With the Dog.'" *Notes on Modern American Literature* 9.3 (1985): Item 13.

0230. Bresnahan, Mary Isabelle. "Finding Our Feet: Problems in Interpreting a Foreign Text." Diss. University of Michigan, Ann Arbor, Mich., 1985.

0231. Breunig, LeRoy C. "From *Rem* to *Rien* and Back." *Intertextuality: New Perspectives in Criticism*. Eds. Jeanine P. Plottel and Hanna Charney. New York Literary Forum 2. New York: Literary Forum, 1978. 209-217.

0232. Brewer, Maria Minich. "An Energetics of Reading: Intertextual in Claude Simon." *Romanic Review* 73 (1982): 489-504.

0233. Bright, Michael. "John the Baptist in Browning's 'Fra Lippo Lippi.'" *Victorian Poetry* 15 (1977): 75-77.

0234. Brinker-Gabler, Gisela. "'Ich weiss nicht, ob mich ei-

ner versteht, Leute': Funktions- und Wirkungspotential
von Teenagersprache und Werther-Zitat in Ulrich Plenzdorfs *Die neuen Leiden des jungen W.*" *Literatur in
Wissenschaft und Unterricht* 11 (1978): 80-92.

0235. Brinkmann, Hennig. "Wiederholung als Gestaltung in
Sprache und als Wiederverwendung von Sprache." *Wirkendes Wort* 33 (1983): 71-93.

0236. Brisset, Annie. "Intertextualité et traduction: Un
poème de W. H. Auden." *Journal Canadien de Recherche
Sémiotique* 8 (1980/81): 201-214.

0237. Brisson, Marie. "L'admirateur admiré: Le masque au
service de la flatterie: Etude d'une lettre de
Boileau." *Revue Frontenac* 3 (1985): 59-70.

0238. Brode, Hanspeter. "Studien zu Gottfried Benn: II. Anspielung und Zitat als sinngebende Elemente moderner
Lyrik. Benns Gedicht 'Widmung.'" *Deutsche Vierteljahrsschrift fuer Literaturwissenschaft und Geistesgeschichte* 47 (1973): 286-309.

0239. Brody, Jules. "'Let There Be Night': Intertextuality
in a Poem of Victor Hugo." *Romanic Review* 75 (1984):
216-229.

0240. Brogunier, Joseph. "An Incident in *The Great Gatsby*
and *Huckleberry Finn.*" *Mark Twain Journal* 16 (1972):
1-3.

0241. Broich, Ulrich. "Formen der Markierung von Intertextualitaet." *Intertextualitaet: Formen, Funktionen,
anglistische Fallstudien.* Eds. U. Broich and M.
Pfister. Tuebingen, W. Germany: Niemeyer, 1985. 31-47.

0242. ------. "Intertextualitaet in Fieldings *Joseph
Andrews.*" *Intertextualitaet: Formen, Funktionen, ang-
listische Fallstudien.* Eds. U. Broich and M. Pfister.
Tuebingen, W. Germany: Niemeyer, 1985. 262-278.

0243. ------. "Zu den Versetzungsformen der Intertextualitaet." *Intertextualitaet: Formen, Funktionen, anglistische Fallstudien.* Eds. U. Broich and M. Pfister.
Tuebingen, W. Germany: Niemeyer, 1985. 135-137.

0244. ------. "Zur Einzeltextreferenz." *Intertextualitaet:
Formen, Funktionen, anglistische Fallstudien.* Eds. U.
Broich and M. Pfister. Tuebingen, W. Germany: Nie-
meyer, 1985. 48-52.

0245. Bromwich, David. "Parody, Pastiche, and Allusion."
Lyric Poetry: Beyond New Criticism. Eds. Chavia Hosek
and Patricia Parker. Ithaca, N. Y.: Cornell University
Press, 1985. 328-344.

0246. Bronkhorst, Johannes. "On Some Vedic Quotations in
Bhartrhari's Works." *Studien zur Indologie und
Iranistik* 7 (1981): 173-175.

0247. Brooks, Douglas. "Richardson's *Pamela* and Fielding's *Joseph Andrews.*" *Essays in Criticism* 17 (1967): 158-168.

0248. Brooks, Harold F. "The 'Imitation' in English Poetry. Especially in Formal Satire, Before the Age of Pope." *Review of English Studies* 25 (1949): 124-140.

0249. Brousseau-Beuermann, Christine Marie. "La *Copie* de Montaigne: Etude sur les citations dans les *Essais.*" Diss. Harvard University, Cambridge, Mass., 1986.

0250. Brower, Reuben Arthur. *Alexander Pope: The Poetry of Allusion.* Oxford, UK: Clarendon Press, 1959.

0251. -----. "An Allusion to Europe: Dryden and Tradition." *Journal of English Literary History* 19 (1952): 38-48.

0252. Brown, Emerson. "Allusion in Chaucer's 'Merchant's Tale.'" Diss. Cornell University, Ithaca, N. Y., 1967.

0253. -----. "Chaucer and a Proper Name: January in 'The Merchant's Tale.'" *Names* 31 (1983): 79-87.

0254. -----. "Of Mice and Women: Thoughts on Chaucerian Allusion." *Chaucer and the Craft of Fiction.* Ed. Leigh A. Arrathoon. Rochester, Mich.: Solaris, 1986. 63-84.

0255. Brown, James Neil. "'Hence with the Nightingale Will I Take Part': A Virgilian Orphic Allusion in Spenser's 'August.'" *Thoth* 13 (1972-1973): 13-18.

0256. Brownlee, Marina S. "The Generic Status of the *Siervo libre de amor*: Rodriguez de Padrón's Reworking of Dante." *Poetics Today* 5 (1984): 629-643.

0257. Brownson, Robert Charles. "Techniques of Reference, Allusion, and Quotation in Thomas Mann's *Doktor Faustus* and William Gaddis' *The Recognitions.*" Diss. University of Colorado, Boulder, Colo., 1976.

0258. Bruce, Don. "Bibliographie annotée: Ecrits sur l'intertextualité." *Texte* 2 (1983): 217-258.

0259. Bruce-Novoa, Juan. "Julieta Campos' *Salina*: In the Labyrinth of Intertextuality." *Third Woman* 2.2 (1984): 43-63.

0260. Bruckner, Matilda T. "En guise de conclusion." *Littérature* 41 (1981): 104-108.

0261. Bruhn, Gert. "Parodistischer Konservatismus: Zur Funktion des Selbstzitats in Thomas Manns *Zauberberg.*" *Neophilologus* 58 (1974): 208-224.

0262. -----. "Das Selbstzitat bei Thomas Mann." Diss. Princeton, N. J., 1967.

0263. Brumm, Ursula. "Das Motiv *Gelebte Literatur* in Tabitha

Tenneys *Female Quixotism.*" *Gelebte Literatur in der Literatur: Studien zu Erscheinungsformen und Geschichte eines literarischen Motivs.* Ed. Theodor Wolpers. Goettingen, W. Germany: Vandenhoeck & Ruprecht, 1986. 163-167.

0264. -----. "Das Motiv 'Gelebte Literatur' in William Faulkners 'Old Man.'" *Gelebte Literatur in der Literatur: Studien zu Erscheinungsformen und Geschichte eines literarischen Motivs.* Ed. Theodor Wolpers. Goettingen, W. Germany: Vandenhoeck & Ruprecht, 1986. 298-310.

0265. Brunet-Weinmann, Monique. "De l'intertexte à l'interartialité: A propos de l'impressionisme verlainien." *Europa* 4 (1981): 91-101.

0266. Brydon, Diana. "Resisting 'the tyranny of what is written': Christina Stead's Fiction." *Ariel: A Review of International English Literature* 17.4 (1986): 3-15.

0267. Brysch, E. "Zitate aus der Literatur in Solzenicyns Roman *Krebsstation.*" *Seminarbeitraege zum Werk Aleksander Solzenicyns.* Ed. Irene Nowikowa. Hamburg, W. Germany: Buske, 1972. 77-82.

0268. Buchbinder, Reinhard. *Bibelzitate, Bibelanspielungen, Bibelparodien, theologische Vergleiche und Analogien bei Marx und Engels.* Philologische Studien und Quellen 84. Berlin, W. Germany: Schmidt, 1976.

0269. Buckridge, Pat. "Katherine Susannah Prichard and the Literary Dynamics of Political Commitment." *Gender, Politics, and Fiction: Twentieth Century Australian Women's Novels.* Ed. Carole Ferrier. St. Lucia, Queensland: University of Queensland, 1985. 85-100.

0270. Budde, Elmar. "Zitat, Collage, Montage." *Die Musik der sechziger Jahre.* Ed. Rudolf Stephan. Veroeffentlichungen des Instituts fuer neue Musik und Musikerziehung Darmstadt 12. Mainz, W. Germany: Schott, 1972. 26-38.

0271. Buder, Guido. *Titel und Text: Information und Wirkung des italienischen Novellentitels (G. Verga, L. Pirandello, A. Moravia) vor und waehrend der Textlektuere.* Rheinfelden, W. Germany: Schaeuble, 1982.

0272. Buergel, J. Ch. "A New Arabic Quotation from Plato's *Phaido* and Its Relation to a Persian Version of the Phaido." *Actas do IV. congreso de estudos arabes e islamicos.* Leiden, Holland: Brill, 1971. 281-290.

0273. Buermann, Theodore B. "Chaucer's 'Book of Genesis' in *The Canterbury Tales*: The Biblical Scheme of the First Fragment." Diss. University of Illinois, 1967.

0274. Bugge, John. "Tell-Tale Context - Two Notes on Biblical Quotation in *The Canterbury Tales.*" *American Notes and Queries* 14 (1976): 82-85.

0275. Bulhof, Francis. "*Le grand meaulnes* and *The Great Gatsby.*" *Dichter und Leser: Studien zur Literatur.* Eds. Ferdinand van Ingen et al. Groningen, Holland: Wolters-Noordhoff, 1972. 276-286.

0276. Bulman, James C. "*Coriolanus* and the Matter of Troy." *Mirror up to Shakespeare: Essays in Honour of G. R. Hibbard.* Ed. John C. Gray. Toronto, Canada: University of Toronto Press, 1984. 242-260.

0277. Bump, Jerome. "Influence and Intertextuality: Hopkins and the School of Dante." *Journal of English and Germanic Philology* 83 (1984): 355-379.

0278. Bunn, Olena S. "A Bibliography of Chaucer in English and American Belles-Lettres Since 1900." *Bulletin of Bibliography* 19 (1949): 205-208.

0279. Burgess, William. *The Bible in Shakespeare: A Study of the Relation of the Works of William Shakespeare to the Bible with Numerous Parallel Passages, Quotations, References, Paraphrases, and Allusions.* 1903; New York: Haskell, 1968.

0280. Burling, William J. "'The Feast of Belshazzar' and *Sister Carrie.*" *American Literary Realism* 17 (1984): 40-43.

0281. -----. "Virginia Woolf's *Lighthouse*: An Allusion to Shelley's *Queen Mab.*" *English Language Notes* 22.2 (1984): 62-65.

0282. Burnet, R. A. L. "Shakespeare and the First Seven Chapters of the Genevan Job." *Notes and Queries* 29 (1982): 127-128.

0283. Burnley, J. D. "Chaucer's Art of Verbal Allusion: Two Notes." *Neophilologus* 56 (1972): 93-99.

0284. Burns, E. Jane "Feigned Allegory: Intertextuality in the *Queste del Saint Graal.*" *Kentucky Romance Quarterly* 29 (1982): 347-364.

0285. Burns, Gerald. "In Medias [Olson's] K." *Sagetrieb* 4 (1985): 109-113

0286. Burton, Thomas Glen. "Tennyson's Use of Biblical Allusions." Diss. Vanderbilt University, Nashville, Tenn., 1966.

0287. Burwick, Frederick. "Coleridge's 'Limbo' and 'Ne plus ultra': The Multeity of Intertextuality." *Romanticism Past and Present* 9.1 (1985): 35-45.

0288. Busby, Keith. "*Le roman des eles* as Guide to the *Sens* of *Méraugis de Portlesguez.*" *The Spirit of the Court: Selected Proceedings of the 4th Congress of the International Courtly Literature Society.* Eds. G. Burgess and R. Taylor. Dover, N. H.: Brewer, 1985. 79-89.

0289. Busch, Ulrich. "Gogol's 'Mantel' - Eine verkehrte Er-
      zaehlung: Schriftsteller, Autor, Erzaehler in intra-
      und intertextueller Beziehung." *Dialog der Texte: Ham-
      burger Kolloquium zur Intertextualitaet.* Eds. Wolf
      Schmid and Wolf-Dieter Stempel. Wiener Slawistischer
      Almanach Sonderband 11. Wien, 1983. 189-203.

0290. Bush, Douglas. "Ironic and Ambiguous Allusion in
      Paradise Lost." *Journal of English and Germanic Phi-
      lology* 60 (1961): 631-640.

0291. Bush, Sargent. "The End and Means in *Walden*: Thoreau's
      Use of the Catechism." *Journal of the American Re-
      naissance* 31 (1985): 1-10.

0292. Bushoff, Klaus. "Wortzitate/Bildzitate." *Zeitschrift
      fuer Kunstpaedagogik* (1975): 7-16.

0293. Busi, Frederick. "Joycean Echoes in *Waiting for
      Godot.*" *Research Studies* 43 (1975): 71-87.

0294. Buss, Hannelore. "Goethe und Freud: Eine Untersuchung
      anhand der Goethe-Zitate im Werk Sigmund Freuds."
      Diss. University of Southern California, 1975.

0295. Buttram, Sara Mac Weed. "A Content Analysis of Eight
      Major Literary Selections Studied by High School
      Students to Discover the Nature and Frequency of Bib-
      lical Allusions; with Implications for Teaching Lit-
      erature." Diss. Auburn University, Auburn, Ala., 1970.

0296. Calin, Françoise. "D'Alain Robbe-Grillet à Claude
      Ollier: 'Mise en scène' d'un intertexte." *Stanford
      French Review* 5 (1981): 363-379.

0297. Calin, William. "Poetry and Eros: Language, Communi-
      cation, and Intertextuality in *Le roman du castelain
      de Couci.*" *French Forum* 6 (1981): 197-211.

0298. -----. "The Poets' Poet: Intertextuality in Louis
      Aragon." *Symposium* 40 (1986): 3-15.

0299. Campbell, Gertrude H. "Chaucer's Prophecy in 1586."
      Modern Language Notes 29 (1914): 195-196.

0300. Cancogni, Annapaola. *The Mirage in the Mirror:
      Nabokov's Ada and Its French Pre-Texts.* New York:
      Garland, 1985.

0301. -----. "'My Sister, Do You Still Recall?': Chateau-
      briand/Nabokov." *Comparative Literature* 35 (1983):
      140-166.

0302. Cappello, Mary. "'Rappacini's Daughter' as Trans-
      lation." *Philological Quarterly* 65 (1986): 263-277.

0303. Carlos, Alberto J. "*Nacha Regules y Santa*: Problemas
      de intertextualidad." *Symposium* 36 (1982): 301-306.

0304. Carlson, Anni. "Ibsenspuren im Werk Fontanes und Thomas Manns." *Deutsche Vierteljahrsschrift fuer Literaturwissenschaft und Geistesgeschichte* 43 (1969): 289-296.

0305. Carlton, Jill Margo. "The Genesis of *Il barone rampante*." *Italica* 61 (1984): 195-206.

0306. Carrier, David. "On the Depiction of Figurative Representational Pictures Within Pictures." *Leonardo* 12 (1979): 197-200.

0307. Carroll, John. "Richardson at Work: Revisions, Allusions, and Quotations in *Clarissa*." *Studies in the Eighteenth Century: Papers Presented at the Second David Nichol Smith Memorial Seminar, Canberra, 1970.* Ed. R. F. Brissenden. Canberra, Australia: Australian National University Press, 1973. 53-71.

0308. Carter, Ernest. "Classical Allusion as the Clue to Meaning in Conrad's 'Il conde.'" *Conradiana* 3 (1971-1972): 55-62.

0309. Cash, Jean W. "Styron's Use of the Bible in *The Confessions of Nat Turner*." *Resources for American Literary Studies* 12 (1982): 134-142.

0310. Cass, Colin S. "The Look of Hemingway's 'In Another Country.'" *Studies in Short Fiction* 18 (1981): 309-313.

0311. Cauthen, I. B. "Another Chaucer Allusion in Harsnet (1603)." *Notes and Queries* 203 (1958): 248-249.

0312. Cawley, Robert R. "A Chaucerian Echo in Spenser." *Modern Language Notes* 41 (1926): 313-314.

0313. Caws, Mary Ann. "Baroque Lighting in René Char." *Intertextuality: New Perspectives in Criticism.* Eds. Jeanine P. Plottel and Hanna Charney. New York Literary Forum 2. New York: Literary Forum, 1978. 197-205.

0314. ------. "Whatever is Fitting in a Text." *Intertextuality: New Perspectives in Criticism.* Eds. Jeanine P. Plottel and Hanna Charney. New York Literary Forum 2. New York: Literary Forum, 1978. 275-280.

0315. Cederborg, Else. "Mytologien som forlsningsmodel: Karen Blixens *Karyatiderne*." *Edda* 84 (1984): 1-8.

0316. Chalendar, Pierette, and Gérard Chalendar. "A fabricaçao do sentito em *O rio triste* de Fernando Namora." *Colóquio* 86 (1985): 24-32.

0317. Chalk, E. S. "Chaucer Allusion." *Notes and Queries* 169 (1935): 241.

0318. Champagne, Roland A. "The Writer Within the Intertext." *Intertextuality: New Perspectives in Criticism.*
Eds. Jeanine P. Plottel and Hanna Charney. New York
Literary Forum 2. New York: Literary Forum, 1978. 129-
137.

0319. Chandler, J. K. "Romantic Allusiveness." *Critical Inquiry* 8 (1981): 461-487.

0320. Chapman, Robert William. "The Art of Quotation." *The
Portrait of a Scholar and Other Essays Written in
Macedonia 1916-1918.* London: Milford, 1920. 80-89.

0321. Charney, Hanna. "Variations by James on a Theme of
Balzac." *Intertextuality: New Perspectives in Criticism.* Eds. Jeanine P. Plottel and Hanna Charney. New
York Literary Forum 2. New York: Literary Forum, 1978.
69-75.

0322. Charney, Maurice. "The Complex Unbuttoning of *Tristram
Shandy.*" *Intertextuality: New Perspectives in Criticism.* Eds. Jeanine P. Plottel and Hanna Charney. New
York Literary Forum 2. New York: Literary Forum, 1978.
257-261.

0323. -----. "Shakespeare's *Ha*: Paralinguistic Hermeneutics." *Intertextuality: New Perspectives in Criticism.*
Eds. Jeanine P. Plottel and Hanna Charney. New York
Literary Forum 2. New York: Literary Forum, 1978. 35-
42.

0324. Chase, Cynthia. "'Viewless Wings': Intertextual Inter-
pretation of Keats' 'Ode to a Nightingale.'" *Lyric
Poetry: Beyond New Criticism.* Eds. Chavia Hosek and
Patricia Parker. Ithaca, N. Y.: Cornell University
Press, 1985. 208-225.

0325. *Chaucer and the Scriptural Tradition.* Ed. David Lyle.
Ottawa, Canada: University of Ottawa Press, 1984.

0326. Chaves-Abad, Maria-José. "Ficción e historia en *El
acoso*: Un estudio de la intertextualidad." *Revista de
Estudios Hispanicos* 10 (1983): 91-104.

0327. Cheney, Patrick. "Hemingway and Christian Epic: The
Bible in *For Whom the Bell Tolls.*" *Papers on Language
and Literature* 21 (1985): 170-191.

0328. -----. "Poe's Use of *The Tempest* and the Bible in 'The
Masque of the Red Death.'" *English Language Notes*
20.3-4 (1983): 31-39.

0329. Cheng, Vincent J. "Shakespearean Reversals in *Finnegans Wake.*" *English Language Notes* 22.3 (1985): 58-61.

0330. Chisolm, Marsha Katz. "Portraits of the Artists: The
Rhetoric of Self-Allusion in the Poetry of Pope and
Swift." Diss. Vanderbilt University, Nashville, Tenn.,
1977.

0331. Chou, Shan. "Allusion and Periphrasis as Modes of
      Poetry in Tu Fu's *Eight Laments.*" *Harvard Journal of
      Asiatic Studies* 45 (1985): 77-128.

0332. -----. "Tu Fu's *Eight Laments*: Allusion and Imagery as
      Modes of Poetry." Diss. Harvard University, Cambridge,
      Mass., 1984.

0333. Christ, Ronald J. *The Narrow Act: Borges' Art of Al-
      lusion.* New York: New York University Press, 1969.

0334. Christensen, Bente. "L'intertextualité: Système clos
      de reproduction ou ouverture relative?" *Etudes fran-
      çaises en Europe non francophone.* Ed. Josef Heistein.
      Warsaw, Poland, 1981. 167.

0335. -----. "Problèmes méthodologiques d'une lecture inter-
      textuelle: Prise de la prose." *Revue Romane* 17.2
      (1982): 55-63.

0336. Ciplijauskaité, Biruté. "El verso ajeno en el poema."
      Hispania 69 (1986): 784-787.

0337. Clark, Eva Lee. *Hidden Allusions in Shakespeare's
      Plays: A Study of the Early Court Revels and Personal-
      ities of the Times.* New York: Payson, 1931.

0338. Clark, M. L. "A Quotation in Gibbon's Autobiography."
      Notes and Queries 32 (1985): 246.

0339. Classen, C.J. "The References to Classical Authors in
      Buchanan's *Rerum scoticarum historia.*" *Acta Conventus
      Neo-Latini Sanctandreani: Proceedings of the Fifth
      International Congress of Neo-Latin Studies.* Ed. I. D.
      McFarlane. Binghamtom, N. Y.: Medieval & Renaissance
      Texts & Studies, 1986. 3-29.

0340. Clayton, J. Douglas. "Night and Wind: Images and Allu-
      sions as the Source of the Poetic in Turgenev's
      Rudin." *Canadian Slavonic Papers* 26 (1984): 10-14.

0341. Clouser, Robin A. "The Pilgrim of Consciousness:
      Hauptmann's Syncretistic Fairy Tale." *Hauptmann-For-
      schung: Neue Beitraege/Hauptmann Research: New Direc-
      tions.* Eds. Peter Sprengel und Philip Mellen. Frank-
      furt, W. Germany: Lang, 1986. 303-322.

0342. Coates, John. "Byzantine References in *The Twyborn
      Affair.*" *Australian Literary Studies* 11 (1984): 508-
      513.

0343. Coatu, Nicoleta. "Intertextualitate la nivelul textu-
      lui oral-folcloric." *Studii si Cercetari Lingvistice*
      36 (1985): 64-72.

0344. Coffee, Jessie McGuire. *Faulkner's Un-Christlike
      Christians: Biblical Allusions in the Novels.* Ann
      Arbor, Mich.: UMI Research Press, 1983. [Diss. Uni-
      versity of Nevada, Reno, Nev., 1971.]

0345. Coffler, Gail H. *Melville's Classical Allusions: A Comprehensive Index and Glossary.* Westport, Conn.: Greenwood, 1985.

0346. Cohen, Alain. "Proust and the President Schreber: A Theory of Primal Quotation or *For a Psychoanalytics of (-desire-in) Philosophy.*" *Yale French Studies* 52 (1975): 189-205.

0347. Cohen, Hennig. "An Early American Chaucer Allusion." *Notes and Queries* 203 (1958): 245.

0348. Cohen, Martin S. "Allusive Conversation in *A Handful of Dust* and *Brideshead Revisited.*" *Evelyn Waugh Newsletter* 5.2 (1971): 1-6.

0349. Cohen, Philip. "'Ahenobarbus' Vestal': Belle Mitchell and Nero." *Notes on Contemporary Literature* 14.2 (1984): 8-9.

0350. Cohen, Ralph. "Literary History and the Ballad of George Barnwel." *Augustan Studies: Essays in Honor of Irvin Ehrenpreis.* Eds. Douglas Lane Patey and Timothy Keegan. Newark, Del.: University of Delaware Press, 1985. 13-31.

0351. Cohen, Richard. *Literary References and Their Effect Upon Characterization in the Novels of Samuel Richardson.* Bangor, Me.: Husson College Press, 1970.

0352. Cohn, Ruby. *Modern Shakespeare Offshoots.* Princeton, N. J.: Princeton University Press, 1976.

0353. Colby, Elbridge. *The Echo-Device in Literature.* New York: New York Public Library, 1920.

0354. Coldwell, Patricia Carothers. "Allusion in Byron's *Don Juan.*" Diss. Yale University, New Haven, Conn., 1983.

0355. Colie, Rosalie L. "The Energies of Endurance: Biblical Echo in *King Lear.*" *Some Facets of King Lear: Essays in Prismatic Criticism.* Eds. Rosalie L. Colie and F. T. Flahiff. Toronto, Canada: University of Toronto Press, 1974. 117-144.

0356. Colker, Marvin L. "Walter of Chatillon, Rigord of Saint-Denis, and an Alleged Quotation from Juvenal." *Classical Folia: Studies in the Christian Perpetuation of the Classics* 24 (1970): 89-95.

0357. Collett, Jonathan H. "Milton's Use of Classical Mythology in *Paradise Lost.*" *Publications of the Modern Language Association* 85 (1970): 88-96.

0358. Collier, Peter. "Nerval in Apollinaire's 'La chanson du mal-aimé.'" *French Studies Bulletin* 6 (1983): 9-13.

0359. Collinson, W. E. "Some English Book-Titles." *Moderna Sprak* 43 (1949): 168-186.

0360. Compagnon, Antoine. "Montaigne: De la traduction des autres a la traduction de soi." *Littérature* 55 (1984): 37-44.

0361. -----. *La seconde main: Ou le travail de la citation.* Paris: Seuil, 1979.

0362. Conley, Tom. "Catching Z's." *Intertextuality: New Perspectives in Criticism.* Eds. Jeanine P. Plottel and Hanna Charney. New York Literary Forum 2. New York: Literary Forum, 1978. 113-128.

0363. Connaughton, Michael E. "Richardson's Familiar Quotations: *Clarissa* and Bysshe's *Art of English Poetry.*" *Philological Quarterly* 60 (1981): 183-195.

0364. Conner, Edwin Lee. "'The Squire's Tale' and Its Teller: Medieval Tradition and Chaucer's Artistry of Allusion." Diss. Vanderbilt University, Nashville, Tenn., 1985.

0365. Connolly, Julian W. "The Function of Literary Allusion in Nabokov's *Despair.*" *Slavic and East European Journal* 26 (1982): 302-313.

0366. Conte, Gian Biagio. *Memoria dei poeti e sistema letterario. Catullo, Virgilio, Ovidio, Lucano.* Turin, Italy: Einaudi, 1974. [Engl. trans. by Charles Segal: *The Rhetoric of Imitation: Genre and Poetic Memory in Virgil and Other Latin Poets.* Ithaca, N. Y.: Cornell University Press, 1986.]

0367. Contini, Gianfranco. "Dante et la mémoire poétique." *Poétique* 27 (1976): 297-316.

0368. Cook, Dayton G. "'Es soll nicht sein' - *Doktor Faustus* and *Die Raeuber.*" *Modern Language Notes* 96 (1981): 629-631.

0369. Cook, Eleanor. "The Senses of Eliot's Salvages." *Essays in Criticism* 34 (1984): 309-318.

0370. Cooke, John William. "The Optical Allusion: Perception and Form in Stoppard's *Travesties.*" Diss. American University, Washington, D. C., 1978.

0371. Coombs, James H. "Allusion Defined and Explained." *Poetics* 13 (1984): 475-488.

0372. Cooper, Linda F. "The Literary Reflectiveness of Jean Renart's *Lai de l'ombre.*" *Romance Philology* 35 (1981): 250-260.

0373. Coppinger, Rebecca. "Analoguus Journeys: William Golding and T. S. Eliot." *Modern Language Studies* 11 (1981): 83-87.

0374. Cornelia, Marie. "Images and Allusion in Hopkins' 'Carrion Comfort.'" *Renascence* 27 (1974): 51-55.

0375. Cornilliat, François. "L'autre géant: Les *chroniques gargantuines* et leur intertexte." *Littérature* 55 (1984): 85-97.

0376. -----. "Intertexte phénix." *Littérature* 55 (1984): 5-9.

0377. Corral, Wilfredo H. "¿Qué es releer la historia por la alusión, leer el texto cultural y consumir lo leído en la ficcionalización?" *Escritura* 8 (1983): 191-206.

0378. Correale, Robert M. "Nicholas of Clairvaux and the Quotation from Seint Bernard in 'The Parson's Tale.'" *American Notes and Queries* 20 (1981): 130-132.

0379. -----. "The Source of the Quotation from 'Crisostom' in 'The Parson's Tale.'" *Notes and Queries* 27 (1980): 101-102.

0380. Cosgrove, Mark Francis. "Biblical, Liturgical, and Classical Allusions in *The Merchant of Venice.*" Diss. University of Florida, Gainesville, Fla., 1970.

0381. Coste, Didier. "Nabokov, la référence et ses doubles." *Fabula* 2 (1983): 29-47.

0382. Coursen, Herbert R. "The Mirror of Allusion: *The Ambassadors.*" *New England Quarterly* 34 (1961): 382-384.

0383. Cowan, James C. "The Function of Allusions and Symbols in D. H. Lawrence's *The Man Who Died.*" *American Imago* 18 (1960): 241-253.

0384. Cowart, David. *Thomas Pynchon: The Art of Allusion.* Carbondale, Ill.: Southern Illinois University Press, 1980. [Diss. Rutgers University, N. J., 1977.]

0385. Craig, Randall. "Good Places and Promised Lands in *The Comedians.*" *Renascence* 39 (1986): 312-324.

0386. Craik, T. W. "Congreve as a Shakespearean." *Poetry and Drama 1570-1700: Essays in Honour of Harold F. Brooks.* Ed. Anthony Coleman. London, New York: Methuen, 1981. 186-199.

0387. Crawford, Gary W. "Stephen King's American Gothic." *Discovering Stephen King.* Ed. Darrell Schweitzer. Starmont Studies in Literary Criticism 8. Mercer Island, Wash.: Starmont, 1985. 41-45.

0388. Creese, Richard Alan. "Graham Greene and Modern Narrative Practice." Diss. University of California, Los Angeles, 1984.

0389. Cresswell, M. J. "Quotational Theories of Propositional Attitudes." *Journal of Philosophical Logic* 9 (1980): 17-40.

0390. Crider, J.R. "Jupiter Pluvius in *Guest of the Nation.*"

Studies in Short Fiction 23 (1986): 407-411.

0391. Crockett, H. Kelley. "The Bible and *The Grapes of Wrath.*" *College English* 24 (1962): 193-196.

0392. Cuddy, Lois A. "Sounding the Secular Depths of *Ash-Wednesday*: A Study of Eliot's Allusional Design and Purpose." *Studia Neophilologica* 55 (1983): 167-179.

0393. Culler, Jonathan. "Changes in the Study of the Lyric." *Lyric Poetry: Beyond New Criticism.* Eds. Chavia Hosek and Patricia Parker. Ithaca, N. Y.: Cornell University Press, 1985. 38-54.

0394. -----. "In Pursuit of Signs." *Daedalus: Journal of the American Academy of Arts and Sciences* 106.4 (1977): 95-111.

0395. -----. *On Deconstruction: Theory and Criticism After Structuralism.* Ithaca: Cornell University Press, 1982.

0396. -----. "Presupposition and Intertextuality." *Modern Language Notes* 91 (1976): 1380-1396.

0397. -----. *The Pursuit of Signs: Semiotics, Literature, Deconstruction.* Ithaca, N. Y.: Cornell University Press, 1981.

0398. -----. "Semiotics and Deconstruction." *Poetics Today* 1 (1979): 137-141.

0399. -----. *Structuralist Poetics.* Ithaca, N. Y.: Cornell University Press, 1975.

0400. Cuny, Pascale. "La *Première sepmaine* de Du Bartas: Spiritualité d'une forme." *Mélanges sur la littérature de la Renaissance à la mémoire de V. L. Saulnier.* Ed. P. G. Castex. Geneva, Switzerl.: Droz, 1984. 255-260.

0401. Daalder, Joost. "Some Renaissance Elements in Malcolm Lowry's *Under the Volcano.*" *American Notes and Queries* 21 (1983): 115-116.

0402. Daellenbach, Lucien. "Intertexte et autotexte." *Poétique* 27 (1976): 282-296.

0403. -----. *Le livre et ses mirroirs dans l'oeuvre romanesque de Michel Butor.* Archives des Lettres Modernes 8. Paris: Minard, 1972.

0404. Dale, James. "Biblical Allusion in Vaughan's 'The World.'" *English Studies* 51 (1970): 336-339.

0405. Daly, Robert. "Fideism and the Allusive Mode in 'Rappaccini's Daughter.'" *Nineteenth-Century Fiction* 28 (1973): 25-37.

0406. Dane, Joseph. "The Ovids of Ben Jonson in *Poetaster* and in *Epicoene.*" *Drama in the Renaissance: Com-*

parative and Critical Essays. Eds. Clifford Davidson,
C. J. Gianakaris, and John H. Stroupe. New York: AMS
Press, 1986. 103-115.

0407. Daniele, Antonio. "Intorno al sonetto del Petrarca 'Il
mal mi preme et me mi spaventa il peggio.'" *Giornale
Storico della Letteratura Italiana* 103 (1986): 44-62.

0408. Da Silveira, Jorge Fernandes. "Poetas leitores de
Pessoa." *Actas do II. congreso internacional de estu-
dos pessoanos*. Oporto, Portugal: Centre de Estudos
Pessoanos, 1985. 569-578.

0409. Dassonville, Michel. "Sortilèges de Rabelais." *Textes
et intertextes: Etudes sur le XVIe siècle pour Alfred
Glauser*. Eds. Floyd Gray and Marcel Tetel. Paris:
Nizet, 1979. 69-78.

0410. D'Avanzo, Mario L. "Gatsby and Holden Caulfield."
Fitzgerald Newsletter. Ed. Matthew J. Bruccoli. Washington: Microcard Editions, 1969. 270-271.

0411. -----. "Hightower and Tennyson in *Light in August*."
South Carolina Review 14 (1981): 66-71.

0412. Davidson, Arnold. "Silencing the Word in Howard
O'Hagan's *Tay John*." *Canadian Literature* 110 (1986):
30-44.

0413. Davidson, Peter. "An Early Echo of Poems by Marvell."
Notes and Queries 33 (1986): 41.

0414. Davies, Howard. "*Les mots* as *Essai sur le don*.
Contribution to an Origin of Myth." *Yale French
Studies* 68 (1985): 57-72.

0415. Davis, Betty J. "The Phrygian Code in Du Bellay's
'Telle que dans son char le Berecynthienne.'" *Literary
Onomastics Studies* 13 (1986): 25-40.

0416. Davis, J. Madison. "Walker Percy's *Lancelot*." *Shakespeare and Southern Writers: A Study in Influence*. Ed.
Philip Kolin. Jackson, Miss.: University Press of Mississippi, 1985. 159-172.

0417. Davis, William. "Large and Startling Figures: The
Place of 'Parker's Back' in Flannery O'Connor's
Canon." *Antigonish Review* 28 (1977): 71-87.

0418. -----. "Quentin's Death Ritual: Further Christian Allusions in *The Sound and the Fury*." *Notes on Mississippi Writers* 6 (1973): 27-32.

0419. Davison, Dennis. "Marvell's Quotation from Rochester."
Notes and Queries 20 (1973): 394-395.

0420. Davison, Ned J. "'The Raven' and 'Out of the Cradle
Endlessly Rocking.'" *Poe Newsletter* 1 (April 1968): 5-
6.

0421. Davison, Richard Allan. "*The Great Gatsby* and *Hopalong Cassidy*: Fitzgerald's Anachronism." *Fitzgerald/Hemingway Annual* (1979): 155-157.

0422. Daw, C. P. "Swift's Favorite Books of the Bible." *Huntington Library Quarterly* 43 (1980): 201-212.

0423. Dawson, Anthony B. "Much Ado About Signifying." *Studies in English Literature* 22 (1982): 211-221.

0424. Deats, Sara Munson. "Ironic Biblical Allusion in Marlowe's *Doctor Faustus*." *Medievalia et Humanistica* 10 (1981): 203-216.

0425. Debicki, Andrew P. "Intertextuality and Reader Response in the Poetry of José Angel Valente, 1967-1970." *Hispanic Review* 51 (1983): 251-267.

0426. Debusscher, Gilbert. "*Educating Rita* Or, An Open University *Pygmalion*." *Communiquer et traduire: Hommages à Jean Dierickx*. Eds. G. Debusscher and J. P. Van Noppen. Bruxelles, Belgium: Editions de l'Université de Bruxelles, 1985. 303-317.

0427. -----. "'Minting Their Separate Wills': Tennessee Williams and Hart Crane." *Modern Drama* 26 (1983): 455-476.

0428. Dees, Jerome S. "The Ship Conceit in *The Faerie Queene*: 'Conspicuous Allusion' and Poetic Structure." *Studies in Philology* 72 (1975): 208-225.

0429. DeFalco, Joseph M. "Whitman's Changes in 'Out of the Cradle' and Poe's 'Raven.'" *Walt Whitman Review* 16 (March 1970): 22-27.

0430. Defaux, Gérard. "Sur des vers de Virgile: Alissa et le mythe gidien du bonheur." *Revue des Lettres Modernes* 331-335 (1972): 97-121.

0431. De Graaf, Daniel A. "Une allusion à la mort de Gérard de Nerval dans l'oeuvre de Hugo." *Neophilologus* 41 (1957): 222-225.

0432. Dekker, George, and Joseph Harris. "Supernaturalism and the Vernacular Style in *A Farewell To Arms*." *Publications of the Modern Language Association* 94 (1979): 311-318.

0433. De Lajarte, Phillipe. "Modes du discours et formes d'alterité dans les 'Nouvelles' de Marguerite de Navarre." *Littérature* 55 (1984): 64-73.

0434. Delas, Daniel. "Propositions pour une théorie de la production textuelle et intertextuelle en poésie: 'Airs' de Philippe Jaccottet." *Romanic Review* 66 (1975): 123-139.

0435. De Ley, Margo, and James O. Crosby. "Originality, Imi-

tation, and Parody in Quevedo's Ballad of the Cid and
the Lion ('Medio día era por filo')." *Studies in Philology* 66 (1969): 155-167.

0436. De Libera, Alain. "De la lectura à la paraphrase:
Remarques sur la citation au Moyen Ages." *Langages* 73
(March 1984): 17-29.

0437. Delorme, J. "Le discours de l'intertextualité dans le
discours exegetique." *Sémiotique & Bible* 15 (1979):
56-62.

0438. De Luca, V. A. "A Wall of Words: The Sublime as Text."
Unnam'd Forms: Blake and Textuality. Eds. Thomas A.
Vogler and Nelson Hilton. Berkeley, Cal.: University
of California Press, 1986. 218-241.

0439. De Man, Paul. "Hypogram and Inscription: Michael Riffaterre's Poetics of Reading." *Diacritics* 11 (Winter
1981): 17-35.

0440. Dembrowski, Peter. "Intertextualité et critique des
textes." *Littérature* 41 (1981): 17-29.

0441. Deming, Robert H. "Theorizing Televison: Text, Textuality, Intertextuality." *Journal of Communication
Inquiry* 10.3 (1986): 32-44.

0442. De Negri, Enrico. "The Legendary Style of the *Decamerone*." *Romanic Review* 43 (1952): 166-189.

0443. Der, Don W. "Jonson's 'On My First Sonne.'" *Explicator*
44.2 (1986): 16-18.

0444. De Roeck, Galina. "The Art Symbol as Root Metaphor: An
Intertextual Analysis." Diss. City University of New
York, 1985.

0445. Derrida, Jacques. *De la grammatologie*. Paris: Minuit,
1967. [Engl. trans. by Gayatri C. Spivak: *Of Gram-
matology*. Baltimore, Md.: Johns Hopkins University
Press, 1976.]

0446. -----. *La dissemination*. Paris: Seuil, 1972. [Engl.
trans. by Barbara Johnson: *Dissemination*. Chicago,
Ill.: University of Chicago Press, 1981.]

0447. -----. *L'écriture et la différence*. Paris: Seuil,
1967. [Engl. trans. by Alan Bass: *Writing and
Difference*. Chicago, Ill.: University of Chicago
Press, 1978.]

0448. -----. *Positions*. Paris: Minuit, 1972. [Engl. trans.
by Alan Bass: *Positions*. Chicago, Ill.: University of
Chicago Press, 1981.]

0449. -----. *La voix et le phénomène*. Paris: Presses
Universitaires de France, 1967. [Engl. trans. by David
B. Allison: *Speech and Phenomenon and Other Essays on*

Husserl's Theory of Signs. Evanston, Ill.: Northwestern University Press, 1973.]

0450. De Sà Rego, Enylton. "Machado de Assis e a sátira menipéia: Um diálogo com os textos de Luciano." *Letterature d'America* 4.18 (1983): 15-38.

0451. Des Places, Edouard. "Citations et paraphrases de poètes chez Démosthène et Platon." *Mélanges offerts à M. Octave Navarre par ses élèves et ses amis*. Toulouse, France: E. Privat, 1935. 129-137.

0452. De Tamargo, Paloma López. "La intertextualidad de 'La picara Justina.'" Diss. Johns Hopkins University, Baltimore, Md., 1979.

0453. *Dialog der Texte: Hamburger Kolloquium zur Intertextualitaet*. Eds. Wolf Schmid and Wolf-Dieter Stempel. Wiener Slawistischer Almanach Sonderband 11. Wien, 1983.

0454. *Dialogizitaet*. Ed. Renate Lachmann. Muenchen, W. Germany: Fink, 1982.

0455. Diaz, Janet W. "Origins, Aesthetics and the 'Nueva novela española.'" *Hispania* 59 (1976): 109-117.

0456. Dibos, William G. "Concerning a Quotation Commonly Attributed to Abraham Lincoln." *Romance Notes* 11 (1970): 579-580.

0457. Di Cesare, Mario A. "Image and Allusion in Herbert's 'Prayer (I).'" *English Literary Renaissance* 11 (1981): 304-328.

0458. Didier, Beatrice. "L'opera fou des bijoux." *Europe* 661 (1984): 142-150.

0459. Dietrich, Manfred. "A Goethe Quotation in a Letter of Matthew Arnold." *Notes and Queries* 23 (1976): 395-396.

0460. Dietze, Walter. "Purpurmantel und dunkle Kutten: Ueber ein unerkanntes Lenau-Zitat bei Marx." *Impulse* 9 (1986): 316-328.

0461. Di Iorio, Francesca. "Sur une citation latine de Stendhal." *Stendhal-Club* 3.11 (1961): 107-110.

0462. Dillon, Bert. *A Chaucer Dictionary: Proper Names and Allusions, Excluding Place Names*. Boston, Mass.: Hall, 1974. [Diss. Duke University, Durham, N. C., 1972.]

0463. Dillon, John B. "Marius and Carbo: A Ciceronian Allusion in Mantuan's *Aegloga secunda*." *The Early Renaissance: Virgil and the Classical Tradition*. Ed. Anthony L. Pellegrini. Binghamtom, N. Y.: Center for Medieval & Early Renaissance Studies, 1984. 57-78.

0464. Dilworth, Thomas. "Cowper's 'Lines Written During a

Period of Insanity.'" *Explicator* 42.2 (1984): 8-9.

0465. -----. "The Technique of Allusion in the Major Poems of David Jones." Diss. University of Toronto, 1977.

0466. Dingley, R. J. "Rochester as Slave: An Allusion in *Jane Eyre.*" *Notes and Queries* 31 (1984): 66.

0467. Ditmas, E. M. R. "A Reappraisal of Geoffrey of Monmouth's Allusions to Cornwall." *Speculum* 48 (1973): 510-524.

0468. Ditsky, John F. "F. Scott Fitzgerald and the Jacob's Ladder." *Journal of Narrative Technique* 7 (1977): 226-228.

0469. "Diversification des lectures bibliques et problèmes de l'intertextualité." *Sémiotique & Bible* 15 (1979): 43-55.

0470. Dobbins, Austin C. "Chaucer Allusions: 1619-1732." *Modern Language Quarterly* 18 (1957): 309-312.

0471. -----. "More Seventeenth-Century Chaucer Allusions." *Modern Language Notes* 68 (1953): 33-34.

0472. Dodds, M. H. "A Chaucer Allusion of 1610." *Notes and Queries* 159 (1930): 258.

0473. Doherty, William E. "*Tender Is the Night* and 'Ode to a Nightingale.'" *Explorations of Literature.* Ed. Rima D. Reck. Baton Rouge, La.: Louisiana State University Press, 1966. 100-114.

0474. Dollerup, Cay. "Spenser's Concord and the Danish Princess Anna." *Notes and Queries* 32 (1985): 23-25.

0475. Donaldson, Scott. "'No, I'm Not Prince Charming': Fairy Tales in *Tender Is the Night.*" *Fitzgerald/Hemingway Annual* (1973): 105-112.

0476. Donker, Marjorie. "*The Waste Land* and the *Aneid.*" *Publications of the Modern Language Association* 89 (1974): 164-173.

0477. Donoghue, Denis. "On 'Gerontion.'" *Southern Review* 21 (1985): 934-946.

0478. Draskau, Jennifer. "Stanza XXVIII of Villon's Testament: A Literary Quotation in Translation." *Essays Presented to Knud Schibsbye on His 75th Birthday.* Eds. Michael Chesnutt et al. Copenhagen, Denmark: Akademisk, 1979. 82-87.

0479. Drijkoningen, Fernand F. J. "Comment lire un poème-objet." *Le plaisir de l'intertexte: Formes et fonctions de l'intertextualité (roman populaire, surréalisme, André Gide, nouveau roman).* Eds. Raimund Theis and H. T. Siepe. Bern, Switzerl.: Lang, 1986. 91-110.

0480. Driscoll, Irene Joan. "Visual Allusion in the Work of Théophile Gautier." *French Studies* 27 (1973): 418-428.

0481. Driskell, Daniel. "Lucretius and 'The City in the Sea.'" *Poe Studies* 5 (1972): 54-55.

0482. Dryden, Edgar A. "From the Piazza to the Enchanted Isles: Melville's Textual Rovings." *After Strange Texts: The Role of Theory in the Study of Literature.* Eds. Gregory S. Jay and David L. Miller. University, Ala.: University of Alabama, 1985. 46-68.

0483. Dudek, Louis. "Exotic References in the Cantos of Ezra Pound." *Antigonish Review* 11 (1972): 55-66.

0484. Duffy, Jean H. "*Les géorgiques* by Claude Simon: A Work of Synthesis and Renewal." *Australian Journal of French Studies* 21 (1984): 161-179.

0485. Duncan, Alastair B. "Claude Simon's *Les géorgiques*: An Intertextual Adventure." *Romance Studies* 2 (1983): 90-107.

0486. Duncan-Jones, E. E. "Marvell's Quotation from Rochester." *Notes and Queries* 19 (1972): 176-177.

0487. Dupras, Joseph A. "The Tempest of Intertext in 'Caliban Upon Setebos.'" *Concerning Poetry* 19 (1986): 75-82.

0488. Durham, Philip. "Jay Gatsby and Hopalong Cassidy." *Themes and Directions in American Literature.* Eds. Ray B. Browne and Donald Pizer. Lafayette, Ind.: Purdue University, 1969. 163-170.

0489. Durzak, Manfred. "Zitat und Montage im deutschen Roman der Gegenwart." *Die deutsche Literatur der Gegenwart.* Ed. M. Durzak. Stuttgart, W. Germany: Reclam, 1971. 211-229.

0490. Dvoretzky, Edward. "Goethe's *Werther* and Lessing's *Emilia Galotti.*" *German Life and Letters* 16 (1962): 23-26.

0491. Ebel, Uwe. *Rezeption und Interpretation skandinavischer Literatur in Thomas Manns Buddenbrooks.* Neumuenster, W. Germany: Wacholtz, 1974.

0492. Eberwein, Jane D. "Dickinson's 'I had some things that I called mine.'" *Explicator* 42.3 (1984): 31-33.

0493. Echeverría, Lidia N. "Lo verosímil y la intertextualidad en *El otoño del patriarca.*" *Hispamerica* 12 (1983): 87-99.

0494. Ecker, Gisela. "'A Map for Rereading': Intertextualitaet aus der Perspektive einer feministischen Literaturwissenschaft." *Intertextualitaet: Formen, Funktionen, anglistische Fallstudien.* Eds. U. Broich and M.

Pfister. Tuebingen, W. Germ.: Niemeyer, 1985. 297-311.

0495. Eco, Umberto, "*Casablanca*: Cult Movies and Intertextual Collage (1984)." Umberto Eco. *Travels in
Hyperreality: Essays*. New York: Harcourt, Brace, Jovanovich, 1986. 197-211.

0496. Edwards, A. S. G. "An Early Allusion to Wyatt." *Notes
and Queries* 29 (1982): 402.

0497. Edwards, Anthony Thomas. "Odysseus Against Achilles:
The Role of Allusion in the Homeric Epic." Diss.
Cornell University, Ithaca, N. Y., 1981.

0498. Edwards, Bateman. "An Aesopic Allusion in the *Roman
d'Alexandre*." *Studies in Honor of Frederick W.
Shipley*. Washington University Studies, New Series:
Language and Literature 14. St. Louis, Mo.: Washington
University Press, 1942. 95-99.

0499. Egan, Mary J. "Allusions to Keats in Wallace Stevens'
'Autumn Refrain.'" *Wallace Stevens Journal* 2 (1985):
98-100.

0500. Egan, Michael. "A Notable Sermon: The Subtext of Hao-
Ran's Fiction." *Popular Chinese Literature and
Performing Arts in the People's Republic of China
1949-1979*. Ed. Bonnie S. McDougall. Berkeley, Cal.:
University of California Press, 1984. 224-243.

0501. Eggenschwiler, David. "Nabokov's *The Vane Sisters*:
Exuberant Pedantry and a Biter Bit." *Studies in Short
Fiction* 18 (1981): 33-39.

0502. Ehrenpreis, Irvin. *Acts of Implication: Suggestion and
Covert Meaning in the Works of Dryden, Swift, Pope,
and Austen*. Berkeley, Cal.: University of California
Press, 1980.

0503. Eigeldinger, Marc. "L'inscription du théâtre dans
l'oeuvre narrative du Gautier." *Romantisme* 12 (1982):
141-150.

0504. Eisenzweig, Uri. "Un concept plein d'intérêts." *Texte*
2 (1983): 161-170.

0505. Ekelund, Erik. "Diktens aura." E. Ekelund. *Synvinklar*.
Lund, Sweden: Gleerups Foerlag, 1956. 226-254.

0506. Elbaz, Françoise. "Le profit du change: L'intertextualité dans l'essai de Montaigne 'De ne contre-
faire le malade.'" *Littérature* 55 (1984): 74-84.

0507. Elias, Eduardo F. "Carlos Fuentes and Movie Stars (Intertextuality in a Mexican Drama)." *Latin American
Theatre Review* 19 (1986): 67-77.

0508. Eliot, T. S. "Tradition and the Individual Talent." T.
S. Eliot. *Selected Essays*. London: Faber, 1932. 13-22.

0509. -----. "*Ulysses*, Order, and Myth." *Dial* 75 (1923): 480-483.

0510. Ellis, Frank H. "Notes on *A Tale of a Tub.*" *Swift Studies* 1 (1986): 9-14.

0511. Ellis, James. "The 'Stoddard Lectures' in *The Great Gatsby.*" *American Literature* 44 (1972): 470-471.

0512. -----. "Wallace Stegner's Art of Literary Allusion - 'The Marriage of Heaven and Hell' and 'Faust' in 'Maiden in a Tower.'" *Studies in Short Fiction* 17 (1980): 105-111.

0513. Elm, Theo. "Schreiben im Zitat: Max Frischs Poetik des Vorurteils." *Zeitschrift fuer deutsche Philologie* 103 (1984): 225-243.

0514.. Emerson, Ralph Waldo. "Quotation and Originality." *The Works of Ralph Waldo Emerson.* Standard Library Edition. Boston, Mass.: Houghton Mifflin, [no year]. 8: 167-194.

0515. Endo, Kenichi. "How to Interpret a Literary Allusive Text." *Journal of the English Institute* 12 (1981): 45-88, 122-123.

0516. Ensor, Allison. "Thoreau and the Bible: Preliminary Considerations." *Emerson Society Quarterly* 33 (1963): 65-70.

0517. Eshelman, Raoul. "Mandelstam and Mystification: Notes on His Early Concept of Intertextuality." *Wiener Slawistischer Almanach* 12 (1983): 163-180.

0518. Espey, J. J. *Ezra Pound's Mauberley: A Study in Composition.* 1955; Berkeley, Cal.: University of California Press, 1974.

0519. Espmark, Kjell. "Ekeloef och Eliot: En Studie kring 'Faerjesang.'" *Bonniers Litterara Magasin* (1959): 683-690.

0520. Esrock, Ellen. "Literature and Philosophy as Narrative Writing." *Ideas of Order in Literature and Film.* Eds. Peter Ruppert, Eugene Crook, and Walter Forehand. Tallahassee, Fla.: University Press of Florida, 1980. 18-31.

0521. Estes, David C. "Granny 'Weatherall's Dying Moment: Katherine Anne Porter's Allusions to Emily Dickinson." *Studies in Short Fiction* 22 (1985): 437-442.

0522. Ette, Ottmar. "Intertextualitaet: Ein Forschungsbericht mit literatursoziologischen Anmerkungen." *Romanistische Zeitschrift fuer Literaturgeschichte* 9 (1985): 497-519.

0523. Evans, Elizabeth. "Musical Allusions in *The Age of In-*

nocence." *Notes on Contemporary Literature* 4 (1974):
4-7.

0524. Evans, Lawrence Grove. "A Biblical Allusion in *Troilus
and Criseyde.*" *Modern Language Notes* 74 (1959): 584-
587.

0525. Evans, Michael. "Intertextual Labyrinth: 'El inmortal'
by Borges." *Forum for Modern Language Studies* 20
(1984): 275-281.

0526. -----. "Intertextual Triptych: Reading Across *La
bataille de Pharsale*, *La jalousie*, and *A la recherche
du temps perdu.*" *Modern Language Review* 76 (1981):
839-847.

0527. -----. "Two Uses of Intertextuality: References to Im-
pressionist Painting and *Madame Bovary* in Claude
Simon's *Leçon de choses.*" *Nottingham French Studies* 19
(1980): 33-45.

0528. Fairlie, Alison. "'Entre les lignes': Mallarmé's Art
of Allusion in His Thank-You Letters." *Baudelaire,
Mallarmé, Valery: New Essays in Honour of Lloyd
Austin*. Eds. Malcolm Bowie et al. Cambridge, UK: Cambridge University Press, 1982. 181-201.

0529. Fallon, Stephen M. "Satan's Return to Hell: Milton's
Concealed Dialogue with Homer and Virgil." *Milton
Quarterly* 18.3 (1984): 78-81.

0530. Falzarano, James V. "Adam in Houyhnhnmland: The Presence of *Paradise Lost.*" *Milton Studies* 21 (1985): 179-
197.

0531. Faria, Almeida. "O autor, a intertextualidade e o
leitor." *Coloquio Letras* 75 (1983): 54-57.

0532. Farmer, B. C. D. "Mythological, Biblical, and Literary
Allusions in Donald Barthelme's *The Dead Father.*"
International Fiction Review 6 (1979): 40-48.

0533. Farrell, Joseph A. "Thematic Allusions to Lucretius in
Vergil's *Georgics.*" Diss. University of North
Carolina, 1983.

0534. Feather, John. "A Shakespearean Quotation in 1628."
Notes and Queries 22 (1975): 175-176.

0535. Fechter, Werner. "Die Zitate aus der antiken Dichtung
in den *Ecbasis captivi.*" *Der altsprachliche Unterricht*
12.4 (1969): 5-30.

0536. Fehr, Bernhard. "Das gelbe Buch in Oscar Wildes *Dorian
Gray.*" *Englische Studien* 55 (1921): 237-256.

0537. Fehrman, Carl. "Dante i Sverige: En oeversikt." *Dante
i Sverige: Jubileumsskrift*. Lund, Sweden: Bonnier,
1965. 21-37.

0538. Fehse, Wilhelm. "Die literarischen Symbole in den *Akten des Vogelsangs.*" *Mitteilungen fuer die Gesellschaft der Freunde Wilhelm Raabes* 11 (1921): 8-20.

0539. -----. "Selbstzitate und Motivwandlungen bei Raabe." *Mitteilungen fuer die Gesellschaft der Freunde Wilhelm Raabes* 9 (1919): 33-42.

0540. Feld, Willi. "Funktionale Satire durch Zitieren in Robert Musils Roman *Der Mann ohne Eigenschaften*, mit Exkursen zu Buechner und Frisch." Diss. Muenster, W. Germany, 1981.

0541. Fendrick, John Wendell. "Servius' Knowledge of Juvenal: An Analysis of the Juvenalian Quotations in Servius' Commentary on Vergil." Diss. University of Southern California, 1971.

0542. Fenoaltea, Doranne. "Scève's *Délie* and Marot: A Study of Intertextualities." *Pre-Pléiade Poetry.* Ed. Jerry C. Nash. French Forum Monographs 57. Lexington, Ky.: French Forum, 1985. 136-149.

0543. Ferran, Peter W. "Brecht und Farquhar: The Critical Art of Dramatic Adaptation." Diss. University of Michigan, Ann Arbor, Mich., 1972.

0544. Ferry, Anne Davidson. "Poetic Contexts: Parody, Imitation, Allusion." Anne Davidson Ferry. *Milton and the Miltonic Dryden.* Cambridge, Mass.: Harvard University Press, 1968. 21-40.

0545. Fetty, Audrey Mae Shelley. "Biblical Allusions in the Fiction of Willa Cather." Diss. University of Nebraska, Lincoln, Nebr., 1973.

0546. Field, P. J. C. "Authoritative Echo in Dryden." *Durham University Journal* 31 (1970): 137-151.

0547. Finnell, Susanna. "*Jean Rivard* comme biblio-texte dans *Les enfantômes* de Réjean Ducharme." *Voix et Images* 11 (1985): 96-102.

0548. Firmat, Gustavo Pérez. "Apuntes para un modelo de la intertextualidad en literatura." *Romanic Review* 69 (1978): 1-14.

0549. Fischer-Lamberg, Hanna. "Das Bibelzitat beim jungen Goethe." *Gedenkschrift fuer Ferdinand Josef Schneider (1879-1954).* Ed. Karl Bischoff. Weimar, E. Germany: Boehlau, 1956. 201-221.

0550. Fisher, Craig B. "Several Allusions in Brant's *Narrenschiff.*" *Modern Language Notes* 68 (1953): 395-397.

0551. Fisk, William Craig. "Formal Themes in Medieval Chinese and Modern Western Literary Theory: Mimesis, Intertextuality, Figurativeness, and Foregrounding." Diss. University of Wisconsin, 1976.

0552. Fitch, Brian T. "Des écrivains et des bavards: L'intra-intertextualité camusienne." *Albert Camus: Oeuvre fermée, oeuvre ouverte?.* Eds. Raymond Gay-Crosier and Jacqueline Lévi-Valensi. Paris: Gallimard, 1985. 267-283.

0553. -----. "L'intra-intertextualité interlinguistique de Beckett: La problématique de la traduction de soi." *Texte* 2 (1983): 85-100.

0554. -----. "Just Between Texts: Intra-Intertextuality." Brian Fitch. *The Narcissistic Text: A Reading of Camus' Fiction.* University of Toronto Romance Series 42. Toronto, London: University of Toronto Press, 1982. 89-108.

0555. Fleischauer, Charles. "Voltaire poète: Citations et adaptations." *Colloque 76: Voltaire. Acts of the Eighth Colloquium Organized by the Department of French, University of Western Ontario.* Ed. Robert L. Walters. Ontario, Canada: Department of French, 1983. 117-140.

0556. Fletcher, Alan J. "Line 30 of the Man of Law's Tale and the Medieval Malkyn." *English Language Notes* 24.2 (1986): 15-20.

0557. Fletcher, Harris. "A Chaucer Allusion (Latin), 1619." *Notes and Queries* 211 (1966): 254.

0558. -----. "Milton's Use of Biblical Quotations." *Journal of English and Germanic Philology* 26 (1927): 145-165.

0559. Flora, Joseph M. "Biblical Allusion in The Old Man and the Sea." *Studies in Short Fiction* 10 (1973): 143-147.

0560. Fo, Alessandro. "Note a Merobaude: Influssi claudianei e tecniche allusive; questioni critico-testuali." *Romanobarbarica* 6 (1981-82): 101-128.

0561. Fogel, Daniel Mark. "henryJAMESjoyce: The Succession of the Masters." *Journal of Modern Literature* 11 (1984): 199-229.

0562. Folkenflik, Robert. "'Homo Alludens' in the Eighteenth Century." *Criticism* 24 (1982): 218-232.

0563. Forslund, David Erland. "The Function of Allusions in the Poetry of Wallace Stevens." Diss. University of Arizona, Tucson, Ariz., 1965.

0564. Forster, Jannette. "Use of Dialogue in a Dibabawon Narrative Discourse." *Philippine Journal of Linguistics* 14 (1983): 45-60.

0565. Foucault, Michel. *L'archéologie du savoir.* Paris: Gallimard, 1969. [Engl. trans. by A. M. Sheridan Smith: *The Archaeology of Knowledge.* New York: Pantheon, 1972.]

0566. -----. "Un fantastique de bibliothèque." *Cahiers Renaud-Barrault* 59 (1967): 7-30. [Engl. trans. by Donald F. Bouchard and Sherry Simon: "Fantasia of the Library." Michel Foucault. *Language, Counter-Memory, Practice: Selected Essays and Interviews*. Ed. Donald F. Bouchard. Ithaca, N. Y.: Cornell University Press, 1977. 87-109.]

0567. -----. *Les mots et les choses: Une archéologie des sciences humaines*. Paris: Gallimard, 1966. [Engl. trans.: *The Order of Things: An Archeology of the Human Sciences.*. New York: Pantheon, Random House, 1971.]

0568. -----. "Qu'est-ce qu'un auteur." *Bulletin de la Société Française de Philosophie* 63.3 (1969): 73-104. [Engl. trans. by Donald F. Bouchard and Sherry Simon: "What is an Author?" Michel Foucault. *Language, Counter-Memory, Practice: Selected Essays and Interviews*. Ed. Donald F. Bouchard. Ithaca, N. Y.: Cornell University Press, 1977. 113-138. Another translation with the same title was included by Josué V. Harari in his *Textual Strategies: Perspectives in Post-Structuralist Criticism*. Ithaca, N. Y.: Cornell University Press, 1979. 141-160.]

0569. -----. "Réponse au Cercle d'Epistémologie." *Cahiers pour l'Analyse* 9 (1968): 9-40.

0570. Fowler, Marilyn S. "The Prism of Self: The Fiction of Philip Roth." Diss. University of California, San Diego, Cal., 1984.

0571. Fox, Alice. "Literary Allusion as Feminist Criticism in *A Room of One's Own*." *Philological Quarterly* 63 (1984): 145-161.

0572. Fraley, William. "Intertextuality and the Dictionary: Toward a Deconstructionist Account of Lexicography." *Dictionaries* 7 (1985): 1-20.

0573. Francon, Marcel. "Sur les allusions de Montaigne à des faits historiques." *Bulletin de la Société des Amis du Montaigne* 5.6 (1973): 60-61.

0574. Franklin, Ursula. "Laforgue and His Philosophers: The 'Paratext' in the Intertextual Maze." *Nineteenth-Century French Studies* 14 (1986): 324-340.

0575. Franko, Mark. "An Intertextual Model for the Interaction of Dancer and Spectator in the Renaissance." Diss. Columbia University, New York, 1981.

0576. Franz, Arthur. "Dante zitiert." *Deutsches Dante-Jahrbuch* 28 (1949): 16-64, and 29-30 (1951): 41-105.

0577. Freed, Edwin Dreese. "The Old Testament Quotations in the Gospel of John." Diss. Harvard University, Cambridge, Mass., 1959.

0578. Freedman, William. "The Garden of Eden in *The Rape of the Lock.*" *Renascence* 34 (1981): 34-40.

0579. Freeman, Joanna Mae. "Biblical Allusions as a Rhetorical Device in *The Way of All Flesh.*" Diss. University of Kansas, 1973.

0580. Freeman, Michelle A. "*Cligés.*" *The Romances of Chrétien de Troyes: A Symposium.* Ed. Douglas Kelly. Lexington, Ky.: French Forum, 1985. 89-131.

0581. -----. "Structural Transpositions and Intertextuality: Chrétien's *Cligés.*" *Medievalia et Humanistica* 11 (1982): 149-163.

0582. -----. "Transpositions structurelles et intertextualité: Le *Cligés* de Chrétien." *Littérature* 41 (1981): 50-61.

0583. Freese, Peter. "Zwei unbekannte Verweise in J. D. Salingers *The Catcher in the Rye*: Charles Dickens und Ring Lardner." *Archiv fuer das Studium der neueren Sprachen und Literaturen* 211 (1974): 68-72.

0584. Freiberg, Medeea. "Interferenta stilistica in *Luceafarul.*" *Limba si Literatura* 3 (1985): 319-324.

0585. French, A. L. "Death by Allusion?" *Essays in Criticism* 20 (1970): 269-271.

0586. French, Robert W. "'My Stuffe is Flesh': An Allusion to Job in George Herbert's 'The Pearl.'" *Notes and Queries* 27 (1980): 329-331.

0587. Frenzel, Elisabeth. "Annaeherung an Werther: Literarisches Modell als Mittel der Selbstfindung fuer Ulrich Plenzdorfs Wibeau." *Gelebte Literatur in der Literatur: Studien zu Erscheinungsformen und Geschichte eines literarischen Motivs.* Ed. Theodor Wolpers. Goettingen, W. Germany: Vandenhoeck & Ruprecht, 1986. 321-343.

0588. -----. "Der doppelgesichtige Leverkuehn: Motivverschraenkungen in Thomas Manns *Doktor Faustus.*" *Gelebte Literatur in der Literatur: Studien zu Erscheinungsformen und Geschichte eines literarischen Motivs.* Ed. Theodor Wolpers. Goettingen, W. Germany: Vandenhoeck & Ruprecht, 1986. 311-320.

0589. -----. "Missverstandene Lektuere: Musaeus' *Grandison der Zweite* und Wielands *Die Abenteuer des Don Sylvio von Rosalva* - zwei deutsche Donquichottiaden des 18. Jahrhunderts." *Gelebte Literatur in der Literatur: Studien zu Erscheinungsformen und Geschichte eines literarischen Motivs.* Ed. Theodor Wolpers. Goettingen, W. Germany: Vandenhoeck & Ruprecht, 1986. 110-133.

0590. Freund, Elizabeth. "'Ariachne's Broken Woof': The Rhetoric of Citation in *Troilus and Cressida.*" *Shake-*

speare and the Question of Theory. Ed. Patricia Parker. New York: Methuen, 1985. 19-36.

0591. Fricke, Dietmar. "Mythes et pseudo-mythes chez Robbe-
Grillet: Une approche intertextuelle." *Le plaisir de
l'intertexte: Formes et fonctions de l'intertextualité
(roman populaire, surréalisme, André Gide, nouveau
roman).* Eds. Raimund Theis and Hans T. Siepe. Bern,
Switzerland: Lang, 1986. 297-316.

0592. Fried, Debra. "Valves of Attention: Quotation and Context in the Age of Emerson." Diss. Yale University,
New Haven, Conn., 1983.

0593. Frieden, Kenneth. "Genius and Monologue: Intertextual
Approaches to the Rhetoric of Inspiration and Individ-
uality." Diss. Yale University, New Haven, Conn.,1984.

0594. Frost, Carolyn O. "The Use of Citations in Literary
Research: A Preliminary Classification of Citation
Functions." *Library Quarterly* 49 (1979): 399-414.

0595. Frost, Kate G. "An Unreported *Hamlet*-Allusion." *Notes
and Queries* 31 (1984): 220-221.

0596. Frow, John. "Who Shot Frank Hardy?: Intertextuality
and Textual Politics." *Southern Review* (Adelaide) 15
(1982): 22-39.

0597. Fruehwald, Wolfgang. "Leben im Zitat." *Liebe, Leid und
Lust: Ueber Clemens Brentano.* Ed. Wolfgang Boehme.
Karlsruhe, W. Germany: Tron, 1979. 27-43.

0598. -----. "Leben im Zitat: Anmerkungen zum Werk Clemens
Brentanos." *Zeitwende* 50 (1979): 73-89.

0599. Frye, Northrop. *The Great Code: The Bible in Literature.* New York: Harcourt, Brace, Jovanovich, 1982.

0600. Fulghum, Walter B. *A Dictionary of Biblical Allusions
in English Literature.* New York: Holt, Rinehart,
Winston, 1965.

0601. Fulkerson, Tahita. "Ibsen in 'The Ice Palace.'" *Fitz-
gerald/Hemingway Annual* (1979): 169-171.

0602. Furia, Philip. "Nuances of a Theme by Milton: Wallace
Stevens's 'Sunday Morning.'" *American Literature* 46
(1974): 83-87.

0603. Furst, Lilian R. "Dostoyevsky's *Notes from Underground*
and Salinger's *The Catcher in the Rye.*" *Canadian
Review of Comparative Literature* 5 (1978): 72-85.

0604. Fussell, Edwin. "Hemingway and Mark Twain." *Accent* 14
(1954): 199-206.

0605. Gale, Robert L. "Religion Imagery in Henry James's
Fiction." *Modern Fiction Studies* 3 (1957): 64-72.

0606. Gallinaro, Luprini, and Maria Bianca. "Riferimenti puskiniani in Bulgakov." *Atti del convegno "Michail Bulgakov," Gargnano del Garda, 17 - 22 Settembre 1984.* Eds. Eridano Bazzarelli and Jitka Kresálkova. Milan, Italy: Univ. degli Studi di Milano, 1984. 313-334.

0607. Gallop, Jane. *Intersections: A Reading of Sade with Bataille, Blanchot, and Klossowski.* Lincoln, Nebr.: University of Nebraska Press, 1981.

0608. Gambla, Richard Joseph. "Verse Quotation in the *Epistulae morales* of Seneca." Diss. Northwestern University, Evanston, Ill., 1981.

0609. Garavini, Fausta. "*Le misanthrope travesti*: Hypertexte occitan." *Littérature* 50 (1983): 91-103.

0610. Garcia, José M. "Caeiro traditore." *Colóquio* 88 (1985): 48-56.

0611. Garcia-Antezuma, Jorge. "Intertextualidad mítica en *Alturas de Machu Picchu.*" *Revista de Critica Literaria Latinoamericana* 21-22 (1985): 75-83.

0612. Gardner, C. O. "'No Worst There is None,' and *King Lear*: An Experiment in Criticism." *Theoria* 36 (1971): 11-37.

0613. Gardner, John. "Imagery and Allusion in the Wakefield Noah Play." *Papers on Language and Literature* 4 (1968): 3-12.

0614. Gardner, Traci. "Tennyson's 'Locksley Hall.'" *Explicator* 44.2 (1986): 23-24.

0615. Garrison, James D. "A Quotation from Waller in Dryden's *Love Triumphant.*" *English Language Notes* 15 (1977): 27-29.

0616. Garver, Milton. "Sources of the Allusions to Animals in the Italian Lyric of the Thirteenth Century." Diss. Yale University, New Haven, Conn., 1904.

0617. Gast, Marlene. "Wordsworth and Milton: Varieties of Connection." Diss. Boston College, Mass., 1985.

0618. Gatch, Katherine Haymes. "Shakespeare's Allusions to the Older Drama." *Philological Quarterly* 7 (1928): 27-44.

0619. Gay-Crosier, Raymond. "De l'intertextualité à la métatextualité: *Les géorgiques* de Claude Simon." *Le plaisir de l'intertexte: Formes et fonctions de l'intertextualité (roman populaire, surréalisme, André Gide, nouveau roman).* Eds. Raimund Theis and Hans T. Siepe. Bern, Switzerland: Lang, 1986. 317-344.

0620. Gefin, Laszlo K. "False Exits: The Literary Allusion in Modern Fiction." *Papers on Language and Literature*

20 (1984): 431-452.

0621. Geier, Manfred. *Die Schrift und die Tradition: Studien zur Intertextualitaet.* Muenchen, W. Germ.: Fink, 1985.

0622. Gelas, Bruno. "Elements pour une étude de la citation." *Sémiologiques* 6 (1977): 175.

0623. Gelber, Mark H. "Die literarische Umwelt zu Gustav Freytags *Soll und Haben* und die Realismustheorie der *Grenzboten.*" *Orbis Litterarum* 39 (1984): 38-53.

0624. *Gelebte Literatur in der Literatur: Studien zu Erscheinungsformen und Geschichte eines literarischen Motivs.* Ed. Theodor Wolpers. Goettingen, W. Germany: Vandenhoeck & Ruprecht, 1986.

0625. Gellrich, Jesse M. "The Parody of Medieval Music in the 'Miller's Tale.'" *Journal of English and Germanic Philology* 73 (1974): 176-188.

0626. Geloin, Ghislaine. "La pratique du livre: Intertextualité dans le jeune cinéma." Diss. University of Illinois, Urbana-Champaign, Ill., 1981.

0627. Genette, Gérard. "Demotivation in *Hérodias.*" *Flaubert and Postmodernism.* Eds. Naomi Schor and Henry F. Majewski. Lincoln: University of Nebraska Press, 1984. 192-201.

0628. -----. *Introduction à l'architexte.* Paris: Seuil, 1979.

0629. -----. *Palimpsestes: La littérature au second degré.* Paris: Seuil, 1982.

0630. -----. "Proust palimpseste." Gérard Genette. *Figures I.* Paris: Seuil, 1966. 39-67.

0631. -----. "Transtextualités." *Magazine Littéraire* 192 (1983): 40-41.

0632. Geninasca, Jacques. "Le dialogisme intratextuel chez Stendhal." *Etudes de Lettres* 3.3 (1984): 13-26.

0633. -----. "L'identité intra- et intertextuelle des grandeurs figuratives." *Exigences et perspectives de la sémiotique: Recueil d'hommages pour Algirdas Julien Greimas.* Paris: Benjamins, 1985. 1: 203-214.

0634. Gerhardt, Mia I. "*Don Quijote*: La vie et les livres." *Medelingen der Koninklijke Nederlandse Akademie van Vetenschappen, Afd. Letterkunde.* Nieuwe Reeks, Deel 18.2. Amsterdam, Holland, 1955. 1-41.

0635. Gerigk, Horst J. "Zweimal 'Die Dame mit dem Huendchen': Anton Tschechow und Joyce Carol Oates." *Literary Theory and Criticism: Festschrift Presented to René Wellek in Honor of His Eightieth Birthday.* Ed. J.

P. Strelka. Bern, Switzerl.: Lang, 1984. 1: 871-891.

0636. German, Howard. "The Range of Allusions in the Novels of Iris Murdoch." *Journal of Modern Literature* 2 (1971): 57-85.

0637. Gerstenberger, Donna. "*The Waste Land* in *A Farewell to Arms.*" *Modern Language Notes* 76 (1961): 24-25.

0638. Gervais, Ronald J. "Fitzgerald's 'Euganean Hills' Allusion in *The Crack-Up.*" *American Notes and Queries* 21 (1983): 139-141.

0639. Gibbs, Jack. "Las mocedades de Mainete." *Guillaume d'Orange and the Chanson de geste.* Eds. Wolfgang van Emden and Philip Bennett. Reading, UK: Société Rencesvals, 1984. 33-42.

0640. Gibson, William M. "Metaphor in the Plot of *The Ambassadors.*" *New England Quarterly* 24 (1951): 291-306.

0641. Gier, Albert. "*Cil dormi et cele veilla*: Ein Reflex des literarischen Gespraechs in den *Fabliaux.*" *Zeitschrift fuer romanische Philologie* 102 (1986): 88-93.

0642. Gill, Stephen C. "Allusion in *Bleak House*: A Narrative Device." *Nineteenth Century Fiction* 22 (1967): 145-154.

0643. Gish, Robert Franklin. *Literary Allusion and the Homilectic Style of E. M. Forster: A Study in the Relationship Between the Tales and the Novels.* Albuquerque, N. Mex.: University of New Mexico, 1972.

0644. Giustiniani, Vito R. "Intertestualita, allusioni, reminiscenze letterarie nella poesia pascoliana." *Revista di Studi Italiani* 1.2 (1983): 30-49.

0645. -----. "Zitat und literarische Anspielung in der modernen italienischen Lyrik." *Ideen und Formen: Festschrift fuer Hugo Friedrich.* Ed. Fritz Schalk. Frankfurt, W. Germany: Klostermann, 1965. 105-142.

0646. Glass, Malcolm S. "T. S. Eliot: Christian Poetry Through Liturgical Allusion." *The Twenties: Poetry and Prose: Twenty Critical Essays.* Eds. Richard Langford and William E. Taylor. DeLand, Florida: Everett Edward Press, 1966. 42-45.

0647. Glausser, Wayne. "Spots of Meaning: Literary Allusions in Max Apple's 'Vegetable Love.'" *Studies in Short Fiction* 20 (1983): 255-263.

0648. Glowinski, Michal. "Der Dialog im Roman." *Poetica* 6 (1974): 1-16.

0649. Gobin, Pierre. "Michel Tremblay: An Interweave of Prose and Drama." *Yale French Studies* 65 (1983): 106-123.

0650. Goebel, Gerhard. "Funktionen des 'Buches im Buche' in Werken zweier Repraesentanten des *nouveau roman*." *Interpretationen und Vergleich: Festschrift fuer Walter Pabst.* Eds. Eberhard Leube and Ludwig Schrader. Berlin, W. Germany: Schmidt, 1972. 34-52.

0651. Goetsch, Paul. "Leserfiguren in der Erzaehlkunst." *Germanisch-Romanische Monatsschrift* 33 (1983): 199-215.

0652. Gold, Elise. "Keats Reads Shelley: An Allusion to *The Revolt of Islam* in *Lamia*." *American Notes and Queries* 23 (1985): 74-77.

0653. Goldbeck, Ingeborg. "Gefluegelte Buchtitel." *Muttersprache* 63 (1953): 225-236.

0654. Golden, Samuel A. "Chaucer in Minsheu's *Guide Into the Tongues*." *Chaucer Review* 4 (1970): 49-54.

0655. Goldensohn, Lorrie. "Quotation." *Yale Review* 70 (1981): 415.

0656. Goldhurst, William M. "Poe's Multiple King Pest: A Source Study." *Tennessee Studies in English* 20 (1972): 107-121.

0657. Goldman, Michael. "Shaw and the Marriage in Dionysus." *The Play and Its Critic: Essays for Eric Bentley.* Ed. Michael Bertin. Lanham, Md.: University Press of America, 1986. 97-111.

0658. Goldman, Stephen H. "Immortal Man and Mortal Overlord: The Case for Intertextuality." *Death and the Serpent: Immortality in Science Fiction and Fantasy.* Eds. Carl Yoke and Donald Hassler. Westport, Conn.,: Greenwood, 1985. 193-208.

0659. Goldstein, Sanford, and Bernice Goldstein. "Some Zen References in Salinger." *Literature East & West* 15 (1971): 83-95.

0660. Goldwyn, Merrill. "A Note on Shakespearean Overtones in Henry David Thoreau's 'Lost Journal.'" *Concord Saunterer* 18.2 (1985): 45-47.

0661. Goltschnigg, Dietmar. *Mystische Tradition im Roman Robert Musils: Martin Bubers Ekstatische Konfessionen im Mann ohne Eigenschaften.* Poesie und Wissenschaft 34. Heidelberg, W. Germany: Stiehm, 1974.

0662. Gomez-Moriana, Antonio. "Don Quichotte ou l'évocation comme proédé narratif." *Canadian Review of Comparative Literature* 11 (1984): 521-558.

0663. ------. "Intertextualité, interdiscursivité et parodie: Pour une sémanalyse du roman picaresque." *Journal Canadien de Recherche Sémiotique* 8 (1980-81): 15-32.

0664. -----. "La subversión del discurso ritual: Una lectura intertextual del *Lazarillo de Tormes.*" *Revista Canadiense de Estudios Hispanicos* 4 (1980): 133-154.

0665. Gontard, Marc. "La rhétorique chinoise dans l'univers formel de Victor Segalen: *Stéles.* Une poétique de l'intertextualité." *Revue de Littérature Comparée* 51 (1977): 192-201.

0666. Good, Dorothy Ballweg. "'A Romance and a Reading List': The Literary References in *This Side of Paradise.*" *Fitzgerald/Hemingway Annual* (1976): 35-64.

0667. Goodman, Nelson. "On Some Questions Concerning Quotation." *The Monist: An International Quarterly Journal of General Philosophical Inquiry* 58 (1974): 294-306.

0668. -----. "Routes of Reference." *Critical Inquiry* 8 (1981): 121-132. [German trans.: "Wege der Referenz." *Zeitschrift fuer Semiotik* 3 (1981): 11-22.]

0669. Gordon, Andrew. "Shakespeare's *The Tempest* and Yeats' 'Sailing to Bysantium' in *Seize the Day.*" *Saul Bellow Journal* 4.1 (1985): 45-51.

0670. Gormely, Lane. "The Inflected Hero: A Study of Intratextual Fiction in the Stendhalian Novel." Diss. University of California, Santa Barbara, Cal., 1979.

0671. Gorski, Konrad. "Aluzja literacka: Istota zjawiska i jego typologia." Konrad Gorski. *Z Historii i teorii literatury. Seria Druga.* Warsaw, Poland, 1964. 7-32.

0672. Gosselin, Claudia. "Voices of the Past in Claude Simon's *La bataille de Pharsale.*" *Intertextuality: New Perspectives in Criticism.* Eds. Jeanine P. Plottel and Hanna Charney. New York Literary Forum 2. New York: Literary Forum, 1978. 23-33.

0673. Gottlieb, Sidney. "An Allusion to Lipsius in *The Changeling*, III. iii 175-177." *Notes and Queries* 32 (1985): 63-65.

0674. Gottschalk, Jane. "Sophisticated Jokes: The Use of American Authors in *Invisible Man.*" *Renascence* 30 (1978): 69-77.

0675. Gould, Robert. "*Die gerettete Zunge* und *Dichtung und Wahrheit*: Hypertextuality in Autobiography and Its Implications." *Seminar* 21 (1985): 79-107.

0676. -----. "Literary Quotations and References in the Friederike and Lili-Episodes of *Dichtung und Wahrheit.*" *Carleton Germanic Papers* 9 (1981): 41-71.

0677. Goulet, Alain. "Narcisse au travail dans l'oeuvre d'André Gide." *Le plaisir de l'intertexte: Formes et fonctions de l'intertextualité (roman populaire, surréalisme, André Gide, nouveau roman).* Eds. Raimund

Theis and Hans T. Siepe. Bern, Switzerl.: Lang, 1986.
185-208.

0678. Grabo, Carl. "Astronomical Allusions in Shelley's *Pro-
metheus Unbound.*" *Philological Quarterly* 6 (1927):
362-378.

0679. Grabski, Michael. "Quotations as Indexicals and Demon-
stratives." *Words, Worlds, and Contexts: New Approaches in Word Semantics.* Eds. H. J. Eikmeyer and H.
Rieser. Berlin, New York: Gruyter, 1981. 151-167.

0680. Graham, Audrey. "Froissart's Use of Classical Allusion
in His Poems." *Medium Aevum* 32 (1963): 24-33.

0681. Graham, Don. "The Common Ground of *Goodbye, Columbus*
and *The Great Gatsby.*" *Forum* 13 (1976): 68-71.

0682. -----. "Fitzgerald's Valley of Ashes and Frank Norris'
'Sordid and Grimy Wilderness.'" *Fitzgerald/Hemingway
Annual* (1972): 303-306.

0683. Grave, Rolf. *Biblicismer och liknande inslag i Sara
Lidmans Tjaerdalen.* Lund, Sweden: Studentlitteratur,
1969.

0684. Gravely, William H. "New Sources for Poe's 'Hans
Pfall.'" *Tennessee Studies in Literature* 17 (1972):
139-149.

0685. Graves, Thornton S. "Some Chaucer Allusions (1561-
1700)." *Studies in Philology* 20 (1923): 469-478.

0686. Gray, Floyd. "Pragmatisme et naturalisme dans l'*Apolo-
gie de Raimond Sebond.*" *Textes et intertextes: Etudes
sur le XVIe siècle pour Alfred Glauser.* Eds. Floyd
Gray and Marcel Tetel. Paris: Nizet, 1979. 79-92.

0687. Gray, Nick. "Langland's Quotations from the Peniten-
tial Tradition." *Modern Philology* 84 (1986-87): 53-60.

0688. Gray, Richard. "'All's o'er, and Ye Know Him Not': A
Reading of *Pierre.*" *Herman Melville: Reassessments.*
Ed. Robert A. Lee. London: Vision, 1984. 116-134.

0689. Green, David B. "A Chaucer Allusion in Edward DuBois'
Old Nick." *Notes and Queries* 199 (1954): 417.

0690. Greenberg, Robert A. "Plexuses and Ganglia: Scientific
Allusion in *Middlemarch.*" *Nineteenth Century Fiction*
30 (1975): 33-52.

0691. Greene, Donald. "Reality Into Art: Some Detective
Notes on Waugh." *Evelyn Waugh Newsletter* 20.1 (1986):
1-9.

0692. Greene, Robert W. "Quotation, Repetition, and Ethical
Competence in *Un amour de Swann.*" *Contemporary
Literature* 25 (1984): 136-155.

0693. Greene, Thomas M. *The Light in Troy: Imitation and Discovery in Renaissance Poetry*. New Haven, Conn.: Yale University Press, 1982.

0694. -----. "Rescue from the Abyss: Scève's Dizain 378." *Textual Analysis: Some Readers Reading*. Ed. Mary Ann Caws. New York: Modern Language Association of America, 1986. 14-25.

0695. Greenwood, Sam L. "Geographical Allusion in Attic Tragedy." Diss. University of Chicago, Ill., 1939.

0696. Grene, Nicholas. "Synge's *The Shadow of the Glen*: Repetition and Allusion." *Modern Drama* 17 (1974): 19-25.

0697. Grennen, Joseph E. "Chaucer in a Chapel Perilous: *The Waste Land* 1-18 and 230-242." *English Record* 13.2 (1962): 42-44.

0698. Gresset, Michel. "Introduction: Faulkner Between the Texts." *Intertextuality in Faulkner*. Eds. Michel Gresset and Noel Polk. Jackson, Miss.: University Press of Mississippi, 1985. 3-15.

0699. -----. "Of Sailboats and Kites: The 'Dying Fall' in Faulkner's *Sanctuary* and Beckett's *Murphy*." *Intertextuality in Faulkner*. Eds. Michel Gresset and Noel Polk. Jackson, Miss.: University Press of Mississippi, 1985. 57-72.

0700. Griffith, George V. "Guernica in Hollywood: A Picasso Allusion in *The Day of the Locust*." *Notes on Modern American Literature* 6.3 (1982): Item 22.

0701. -----. "Jarrell According to Garp." *Notes on Modern American Literature* 5.3 (1981): Item 20.

0702. Grimm, Reinhold. "Luther's Language in the Mouth of Brecht: A Parabolic Survey with Some Examples, Detours, and Suggestions." *Michigan Germanic Studies* 10 (1984): 159-204.

0703. -----. "Die Luthersprache im Munde Brechts (Ein essayistischer Vortrag)." *Deutsche Sprache* 14 (1986): 235-242.

0704. Grivel, Charles. "Quant à l'intertexte: Plan d'un livre ou possible ou futur." *Mélanges de linguistique et de littérature offerts à Lein Geschiere*. Amsterdam: Rodopi, 1975. 153-180.

0705. -----. "Serien textueller Perzeption: Eine Skizze." *Dialog der Texte: Hamburger Kolloquium zur Intertextualitaet*. Eds. Wolf Schmid and Wolf-Dieter Stempel. Wiener Slawistischer Almanach Sonderband 11. Wien, 1983. 53-83.

0706. -----. "Thèses préparatoires sur les intertextes." *Dialogizitaet*. Ed. Renate Lachmann. Muenchen, W. Germany: Fink, 1982. 237-248.

0707. -----. "Les universaux de texte." *Littérature* 30 (1978): 25-50.

0708. Grover, Dorothy. "Propositional Quantification and Quotation Contexts." *Truth, Syntax, and Modality*. Ed. Hugues Leblanc. Studies in Logic and the Foundations of Mathematics 68. Amsterdam, Holland: North-Holland, 1973. 101-110.

0709. Grube, John. "*Tender Is the Night*: Keats and Scott Fitzgerald." *Dalhousie Review* 44 (1964-65): 433-441.

0710. Gruebel, Rainer. "Die Geburt des Textes aus dem Tod der Texte: Strukturen und Funktionen der Intertextualitaet in Dostoevskijs Roman *Die Brueder Karamazov* im Lichte seines Mottos." *Dialog der Texte: Hamburger Kolloquium zur Intertextualitaet*. Eds. Wolf Schmid and Wolf-Dieter Stempel. Wiener Slawistischer Almanach Sonderband 11. Wien, 1983. 205-271.

0711. -----. "'Physiker und Lyriker': Zur Kontextualitaet, Intextualitaet und Intertextualitaet des Topos von den 'Zwei Kulturen' in der sovietrussischen Lyrik der 60er Jahre." *Voz'mi na radost: To Honour Jeanne van der Eng-Liedmeier*. Amsterdam, Holland: Slavic Seminar, 1980. 207-229.

0712. Guenther, Vincent J. "Spiegelungen *Hamlets* im Roman und im Drama: Goethe, Innes, Brešan." *Teilnahme und Spiegelungen: Festschrift fuer Horst Ruediger*. Eds. Beda Allemann, Erwin Koppen, and Dieter Gutzen. Berlin, New York: Gruyter, 1975. 165-172.

0713. Guillerm, Luce. "L'auteur, les modèles, et le pouvoir ou la topique de la traduction au XVIe siècle en France." *Revue des Sciences Humaines* 180 (1980): 5-31.

0714. -----. "L'intertextualité démontée: Le discours sur la traduction." *Littérature* 55 (1984): 54-63.

0715. Guimaraés, Denise. "A presença de literatura portuguesa na obra de Salvador José Correia Coelho." *Arquivos* 4.2 (1983): 57-67.

0716. Guise, René. "Intertextualité et roman populaire." *Le plaisir de l'intertexte: Formes et fonctions de l'intertextualité (roman populaire, surréalisme, André Gide, nouveau roman)*. Eds. Raimund Theis and Hans T. Siepe. Bern, Switzerland: Lang, 1986. 37-43.

0717. Gumbrecht, Hans Ulrich. "Intertextualitaet und Herbst/ Herbst und neuzeitliche Rezeption des Mittelalters." *Dialog der Texte: Hamburger Kolloquium zur Intertextualitaet*. Eds. Wolf Schmid and Wolf-Dieter Stempel. Wiener Slawistischer Almanach Sonderband 11. Wien, 1983. 111-139.

0718. Guss, Donald L. "Wyatt's Petrarchism: An Instance of
Creative Imitation in the Renaissance." *Huntington
Library Quarterly* 29 (1965): 1-15.

0719. Guttmann, Allen. "From *Typee* to *Moby Dick*: Melville's
Allusive Art." *Modern Language Quarterly* 24 (1963):
237-244.

0720. Gwynn, Frederick L. "The Functional Allusions in
Conrad Aiken's 'Mr. Arcularis.'" *Twentieth Century
Literature* 2 (1956): 21-25.

0721. Gyurko, Lanin A. "The Artist Manqué in Fuentes' *Cambio
de piel.*" *Symposium* 31 (1977): 126-150.

0722. Habel, Thomas. "Wilhelm Ehrenfried Neugebauers *Der
teutsche Don Quichotte*: Zur Don Quijote-Rezeption und
Fiktionskritik im deutschen Roman des 18. Jahrhun-
derts." *Gelebte Literatur in der Literatur: Studien zu
Erscheinungsformen und Geschichte eines literarischen
Motivs.* Ed. Theodor Wolpers. Goettingen, W. Germany:
Vandenhoeck & Ruprecht, 1986. 72-109.

0723. Hackett, Jeremiah. "The Use of a Text Quotation from
Meister Eckhart by Jordan of Quedlinburg (Saxony),
O.S.A." *Proceedings of the PMR Conference: Annual
Publication of the Patristic, Mediaeval and Renais-
sance Conference* 2 (1977): 97-102.

0724. Haegert, John. "The Author as Reader as Nabokov: Text
and Pretext in *Pale Fire.*" *Texas Studies in Literature
and Language* 26 (1984): 405-424.

0725. Hagan, John. "Une ruse de style: A Pattern of Allusion
in *Madame Bovary.*" *Studies in the Novel* 1 (1969): 6-
16.

0726. Hagendahl, Harald. "Methods of Citation in Postclas-
sical Latin Prose." *Eranos* 45 (1947): 114-128.

0727. Hahn, Ingrid. "Hartmanns Buechlein-Zitat im 'Grego-
rius'." *"Sagen mit Sinne": Festschrift fuer Marie-
Luise Dittrich zum 65. Geburtstag.* Eds. Helmut Ruecker
and Kurt Otto Seidel. Goeppingen, W. Germany: Kuemmerle, 1976. 95-108.

0728. Hahn, Stephen. "Williams's Homage to Keats in *A Voyage
to Pagany.*" *William Carlos Williams Review* 11.1
(1985): 6-12.

0729. Hall, Gaston. "L'allusion chez Molière: L'innocence
d'Agnès et le dénouement de *Tartuffe.*" *Dramaturgies:
Langages dramatiques. Mélanges pour Jacques Scherer.*
Paris: Nizet, 1986. 333-339.

0730. Hall, William F. "Hawthorne, Shakespeare and *Tess*:
Hardy's Use of Allusion and Reference." *English
Studies* 52 (1971): 533-542.

0731. Hallig, Rudolf. "Ueber Form und Eingliederung der woertlichen Rede in den 'Memoiren' des Duc de Saint Simon." *Syntactica und Stilistica: Festschrift fuer Ernst Gramillscheg.* Tuebingen, W. Germany: Niemeyer, 1957. 191-213.

0732. Hambidge, Joan. "Intertekstualiteit versus inter-tekstualiteit." *Standpunte* 39 (1986): 35-43.

0733. Hamilton, Kenneth. "One Way to Use the Bible: The Example of J. D. Salinger." *Christian Scholar* 47 (1964): 243-251.

0734. Hampson, Robert G. "Conrad, Guthrie, and *The Arabian Nights.*" *Conradiana* 18.2 (1986): 141-143.

0735. Handelman, Susan. "Freud's Midrash: The Exile of Interpretation." *Intertextuality: New Perspectives in Criticism.* Eds. Jeanine P. Plottel and Hanna Charney. New York Literary Forum 2. New York: Literary Forum, 1978. 99-112.

0736. Handley, Graham. "Mrs. Gaskell's Reading: Some Notes on Echoes and Epigraphs in *Mary Barton.*" *Durham University Journal* 28 (1967): 131-138.

0737. Hanne, Michael. "Significant Allusions in Vittorini's *Conversazione in Sicilia.*" *Modern Language Review* 70 (1975): 75-83.

0738. Hanning, R. W. "Roasting a Friar, Mis-Taking a Wife, and Other Acts of Textual Harrassment in Chaucer's *Canterbury Tales.*" *Studies in the Age of Chaucer* 7 (1985): 3-21.

0739. Hansen-Loeve, Aage A. "Intermedialitaet und Intertextualitaet: Probleme der Korrelation von Wort- und Bildkunst am Beispiel der russischen Moderne." *Dialog der Texte: Hamburger Kolloquium zur Intertextualitaet.* Eds. Wolf Schmid and Wolf-Dieter Stempel. Wiener Slawistischer Almanach Sonderband 11. Wien, 1983. 291-360.

0740. Harder, Kelsie B. "Chaucer's Use of the Mystery Plays in the 'Miller's Tale.'" *Modern Language Quarterly* 17 (1956): 193-198.

0741. Harding, Davis P. *The Club of Hercules: Studies in the Classical Background of Paradise Lost.* Illinois Studies in Language and Literature 50. Urbana, Ill.: University of Illinois Press, 1962.

0742. Harlow, C. G. "The Old English *Advent VII* and the 'Doubting of Mary' Tradition." *Leeds Studies in English* 16 (1985): 101-117.

0743. Harris, Brice. "Some Seventeenth-Century Chaucer-Allusions." *Philological Quarterly* 18 (1939): 395-405.

0744. Harris, Joseph. "*Beowulf* in Literary History." *Pacific Coast Philology* 17 (1982): 16-23.

0745. Harris, William. "The Thematic Importance of Skelton's Allusion to Horace in *Magnyfycence*." *Studies in English Literature* 3 (1963): 9-18.

0746. Harrison, Keith. "Allusions in *Under the Volcano*: Function and Pattern." *Studies in Canadian Literature* 9 (1984): 224-232.

0747. -----. "Lowry's Allusions to Melville in *Lunar Caustic*." *Canadian Literature* 94 (1982): 180-184.

0748. Harrison, Richard Clarence. "Walt Whitman and Shakespeare." *Publications of the Modern Language Association* 44 (1929): 1201-1238.

0749. Hartman, Charles Matthew. "Language and Allusion in the Poetry of Han Yu: The 'Autumn Sentiments.'" Diss. Indiana University, 1975.

0750. Harty, E. R. "Text, Context, Intertext." *Journal for Literary Studies* 1.2 (1985): 1-13.

0751. Harty, Kevin J. "Archetype and Popular Lyric in Joyce Carol Oates's 'Where Are You Going, Where Have You Been?'" *Pennsylvania English* 8 (1980-81): 26-28.

0752. Harward, Vernon. "Hary's *Wallace* and Chaucer's *Troilus and Criseyde*." *Studies in Scottish Literature* 10 (1972): 48-50.

0753. Harweg, Roland. "Einige Besonderheiten von Zitaten in linguistischer Rede." *Zeitschrift fuer vergleichende Sprachforschung* 84 (1970): 288-298.

0754. Hatten, Robert S. "The Place of Intertextuality in Music Studies." *American Journal of Semiotics* 3.4 (1985): 69-82.

0755. Haulica, Cristina. *Textul ca intertextualitate: Pornind de la Borges*. Bucaresti, Rumania: Eminescu, 1981.

0756. Havens, Raymond Dexter. *The Influence of Milton on English Poetry*. 1922; New York: Russell & Russell, 1961.

0757. Haverkamp, Anselm. "Lauras Metamorphosen (Eichs 'Lauren'): Dekonstruktion einer lyrischen Figur in der Prosa der *Maulwuerfe*." *Deutsche Vierteljahrsschrift fuer Literaturwissenschaft und Geistesgeschichte* 58 (1984): 317-346.

0758. -----. "Laura's Metamorphoses: Eich's 'Lauren.'" *Comparative Literature* 36 (1984): 312-327.

0759. Hawkins, Peter S. "Resurrecting the Word: Dante and the Bible." *Religion and Literature* 16.3 (1984): 59-71.

0760. -----. "Transfiguring the Text: Ovid, Scripture and the Dynamics of Allusion." *Stanford Italian Review* 5 (1985): 115-139.

0761. Hawthorne, Mark D. "Thomas Wolfe's Use of the Poetic Fragment." *Modern Fiction Studies* 11 (1965): 234-244.

0762. Haynes, John. "Okigbo's Technique in 'Distances.'" *Research in African Literatures* 17 (1986): 73-84.

0763. Haywood, Lynn. "Historical Notes for *This Side of Paradise.*" *Resources for American Literary Study* 10 (1980): 191-208.

0764. Healey, James. "Pop Music and Joyce Carol Oates' 'Where Are You Going, Where Have You Been?'" *Notes on Modern American Literature* 7.1 (1983): Item 5.

0765. Heath, Stephen. "Structuration of the Novel-Text." *Signs of the Times: Introductory Readings in Textual Semiotics.* Ed. St. Heath. Cambridge, UK: Granta, 1971. 52-78.

0766. Heffner, Ray, Mason, E. Dorothy, and Frederick M Paddleford. "Spenser Allusions in the Sixteenth and Seventeenth Centuries." *Studies in Philology* 68.5 (1971) and 69.5 (1972) [Special issues].

0767. Heilman, Robert B. "Three Modern Chaucer Allusions." *Notes and Queries* 176 (1939): 117.

0768. Hein, Juergen. "Der anthologische Nestroy: Notizen und Bibliographie." *Nestroyana* 6 (1984-85): 67-78.

0769. Heissenbuettel, Helmut. "Die Konsequenzen der konservativen Gesinnung: Zum 75. Geburtstag Ezra Pounds am 30. Oktober 1960." H. Heissenbuettel. *Ueber Literatur.* Olten, Freiburg, W. Germany: Walter, 1966. 32-35.

0770. Helbig, Louis Ferdinand. *Das Geschichtsdrama Georg Buechners: Zitatprobleme und historische Wahrheit in Dantons Tod.* Bern, Switzerland: Lang, 1973.

0771. Heller, Lane. "Quelques allusions à Epictète dans les *Pensées* de Pascal." *Dixseptième Siècle* 96 (1972): 3-10.

0772. Henkel, Arthur. "Zitat-Spiele Goethes." *Antike Traditionen und neuere Philologien: Symposium zu Ehren des 75. Geburtstags von Rudolf Suehnel.* Ed. H. J. Zimmermann. Heidelberg, W. Germany: Winter, 1984. 107-125.

0773. Henning, Sylvie D. "Samuel Beckett's *Film* and *La dernière bande*: Intratextual and Intertextual Doubles." *Symposium* 35 (1981): 131-153.

0774. Herget, Winfried. "Joyce Carol Oates' Re-imaginationen." *Theorie und Praxis im Erzaehlen des 19. und 20. Jahrhunderts: Studien zur englischen und amerikani-*

schen Literatur zu Ehren von Willi Erzgraeber. Eds. W. Herget, K. P. Jochum, and I. Weber. Tuebingen, W. Germany: Narr, 1986. 359-371.

0775. Hernadi, Paul. "More Questions Concerning Quotations." *Journal of Aesthetics and Art Criticism* 39 (1981): 271-273.

0776. Herrero, Javier. "La metáfora del libro en Cervantes." *Actas del séptimo congreso de la Asociación Internacional de Hispanistas.* Ed. Guiseppe Bellini. Roma: Bulzoni, 1982. 579-584.

0777. Herron, Dale. "Poetic Vision in Two Sonnets of Milton." *Milton Quarterly* 2 (1968): 23-28.

0778. Herron, Don. "The Biggest Horror Fan of Them All." *Discovering Stephen King.* Ed. Darrell Schweitzer. Starmont Studies in Literary Criticism 8. Mercer Island, Wash.: Starmont, 1985. 26-40.

0779. Herzog, Urs. "'... mit dem grossen Poeten Jacobo Balde': Balde-Zitate in Matthias Heimbachs, S. J., 'Neuer Schau-Buehne des Todes' (1716)." *Jacob Balde und seine Zeit. Akten des Ensisheimer Kolloquiums 15.- 16. Oktober 1982.* Ed. Jean-Marie Valentin. Bern, Switzerland: Lang, 1986. 271-283.

0780. Heumann, Karl F. "Forms for Literature Citations." *Science* 120 (1954): 1038-1041.

0781. Heuston, Edward F. "The Chaucer Sprig in Wordsworth's *Liberty.*" *Notes and Queries* 209 (1964): 20-21.

0782. Heyndels, Ralph. "Intertexte, institution, pédagogié." *Neohelicon* 10 (1983): 301-309.

0783. Hickey, Leo. "El valor de la alusión en literatura." *Revista de Occidente* 88 (1970): 49-60.

0784. Hieatt, A. Kent. *Chaucer-Spenser-Milton: Mythopoetic Continuities and Transformations.* Montreal: McGill-Queen's University Press, 1975.

0785. Hieatt, Constance B. "Dream Frame and Verbal Echo in *The Dream of the Rood.*" *Neuphilologische Mitteilungen* 72 (1971): 251-263.

0786. Higdon, David L. "The Sense of Tradition in Margaret Drabble's Novels." *Conference of College Teachers of English of Texas Proceedings* 50 (1985): 25-31.

0787. -----. "A *Ulysses* Allusion to Karl Marx." *James Joyce Quarterly* 22 (1985): 316-319.

0788. Hightower, James R. "Allusion in the Poetry of T'ao Ch'ien." *Harvard Journal of Asiatic Studies* 31 (1971): 5-27.

0789. Hildebrand, Karl-Gustaf. *Bibeln i nutida svensk lyrik*.
Stockholm, Sweden: Svenska Kyrkans Diakonistyrelses
Bokfoerlag, 1939.

0790. Hill, D. M. "Allusion and Meaning in Herbert's 'Jordan
I.'" *Neophilologus* 56 (1972): 344-351.

0791. Hill, James S. "Carlyle's 'Shooting Niagara: And After?'" *Explicator* 36.4 (1978): 20.

0792. ----- "Faulkner's Allusion to Virginia Woolf's *A Room
of One's Own* in *The Wild Palms*." *Notes on Modern
American Literature* 4 (1980): Item 10.

0793. Hill, Thomas D. "Two Notes on Exegetical Allusion in
Langland: *Piers Plowman* XI, 161-167, and B, I, 115-
124." *Neuphilologische Mitteilungen* 75 (1974): 92-97.

0794. Hilton, Nelson, "An Original Story." *Unnam'd Forms:
Blake and Textuality*. Eds. Nelson Hilton and Thomas A.
Vogler. Berkeley, Cal.: University Press, 1986. 69-
104.

0795. Hindus, Milton, "Literary Echoes in Whitman's 'Passage
to India.'" *Walt Whitman Review* 7 (1961): 52-53.

0796. -----. "Whitman and Poe: A Note." *Walt Whitman Review*
3 (1957): 5-6.

0797. Hines, Susan Laurel. "The Metaphorical Use of Mythological and Historical Allusions in Plautus." Diss.
University of Minnesota, 1973.

0798. Hinkle, James. "Some Unexpected Sources for *The Sun
Also Rises*." *Hemingway Review* 2 (Fall 1982): 26-42.

0799. Hinman, Willis S. "Literary Quotation and Allusion in
the Rhetoric, Poetics and Nicomachean Ethics of Aristotle." Diss. Columbia University, New York, 1935.

0800. Hiriart, Rosario. *Las alusiones literarias en la obra
narrativa de Francisco Ayala*. Torres Library of
Literary Studies 16. New York: Torres, 1971.

0801. Hirschi, Andrée. "Les allusions esthétiques dans les
romans." *La Revue des Lettres Modernes* 285-289 (1972):
37-60.

0802. Hirsh, A. "Truffaut's Subversive Siren: Intertextual
Narrative in *Mississippi Mermaid*." *Film Criticism* 4
(1979): 81-88.

0803. Hirstein, James S. "La Rome de Virgile et celle du
seizième siècle dans 'Ad Janum Avansonimu apud summum
pont. oratorem regium, Tyberis' de Joachim Du Bellay."
*Acta Conventus Neo-Latini Sanctandreani: Proceedings
of the Fifth International Congress of Neo-Latin
Studies*. Ed. J. D. McFarlane. Binghamton, N.Y.: Medieval & Renaissance Texts & Studies, 1986. 351-358.

0804. Hodgson, Richard G. "Intertextuality, Sexuality, and Literary Convention in the French Baroque Novel." *Papers on French Seventeenth Century Literature* 22 (1985): 71-85.

0805. Hoehler, Gertrud. *Unruhige Gaeste: Das Bibelzitat in Wilhelm Raabes Roman*. Bonn, W. Germany: Bouvier, 1969.

0806. Hoek, Leo H. *La Marque du titre: Dispositifs sémiotique d'une pratique textuelle*. Approaches to Semiotics 60. LaHaye, New York: Mouton, 1981.

0807. Hoffman, Arthur W. "Allusion and the Definition of Themes in Congreve's *Love for Love*." *The Author In His Work: Essays on a Problem in Criticism*. Eds. Louis L. Martz and Aubrey Williams. London, New Haven, Conn.: Yale University Press, 1978. 283-296.

0808. Hoffman, Nancy. "*The Great Gatsby*: Troilus and Criseyde Revisited?" *Fitzgerald/Hemingway Annual* (1971): 148-158.

0809. Hoffmann, Richard L. "Two Notes on Chaucer's Arcite." *English Language Notes* 4 (1967): 172-175.

0810. Holdsworth, R. V. "Sexual Allusions in *Love's Labour's Lost, The Merry Wives of Windsor, Othello, The Winter's Tale*, and *Two Noble Kinsmen*." *Notes and Queries* 33 (1986): 351-353.

0811. Holland, Michael. "De l'intertextualité: Métacritique." *Texte* 2 (1983): 177-192.

0812. Hollander, John. *The Figure of Echo: A Mode of Allusion in Milton and After*. Berkeley, Cal.: University of California Press, 1981.

0813. -----. "The Footing of His Feet: On a Line of Milton's." *On Poetry and Poetics*. Ed. Richard Waswo. Swiss Papers in English Language and Literature 2. Tuebingen, W. Germany: Narr, 1985. 11-30.

0814. Holter, Karin. "Simon Citing Simon: A Few Examples of Limited Intertextuality." *Orion Blinded: Essays on Claude Simon*. Eds. Randi Birn and Karen Gould. Lewisburg, Pa.: Bucknell University Press, 1981. 133-147.

0815. Horn, Pierre L. "On a Whitman Quotation in *Les Caves du Vatican*." *French American Review* 1 (1976): 95.

0816. Horne, R. C. "Two Unrecorded Contemporary References to Shakespeare." *Notes and Queries* 31 (1984): 218-220.

0817. Hornstein, Lillian Herlands. "Some Chaucer Allusions by Sir Edward Coke." *Modern Language Notes* 60 (1945): 483-486.

0818. Horrent, Jules. "Galans a Roncasvals: Nouvel examen de l'allusion à la geste sur la bataille de Roncevaux

faite   dans   le   fragment   occitan   de   la   *Canso
d'Antiocha.*" *Romania* 102 (1981): 18-45.

0819. Houppermans, Sjef. "Raymond Roussel et l'intertextualité." *Le plaisir de l'intertexte: Formes et fonctions de l'intertextualité (roman populaire, surréalisme, André Gide, nouveau roman).* Eds. Raimund Theis
and Hans T. Siepe. Bern, Switzerland: Lang, 1986. 111-
131.

0820. Householder, Fred Walter. *Literary Quotation and Allusion in Lucian.* New York: King's Crown Press, 1941.

0821. Houston, John Porter. "Sexual Allusions and Scholarship: Observations on Rimbaud Studies." *Nineteenth
Century French Studies* 15 (1986-1987): 162-172.

0822. Howarth, Herbert. "Voices of the Past in Dickens and
Others." *University of Toronto Quarterly* 41 (1972):
151-162.

0823. Howes, George Edwin. "Homeric Quotations in Plato and
Aristotle." *Harvard Studies in Classical Philology* 6
(1895): 153-237.

0824. Hruby, Antonin. "Die Behandlung der Zitate im *Acker-
mann aus Boehmen.*" *Dichtung, Sprache und Gesellschaft.*
Eds. Victor Lange and Hans-Gert Roloff. Frankfurt, W.
Germany: Athenaeum, 1971. 91-97.

0825. Hubert, Renée Riese. "The Illustrated Book: Text and
Image." *Intertextuality: New Perspectives in Criticism.* Eds. Jeanine P. Plottel and Hanna Charney. New
York Literary Forum 2. New York: Literary Forum, 1978.
177-195.

0826. Huerkamp, Josef. "*Das Gedaechtnis der Menschheit*:
Fragen zum Zitatismus im Werk Arno Schmidts." *Text und
Kritik* 20-20a (1986): 119-134.

0827. Hughes, Peter. "Allusion and Expression in Eighteenth
Century Literature." *The Author In His Work: Essays on
a Problem in Criticism.* Eds. Louis L. Martz and Aubrey
Williams. London, New Haven, Conn.: Yale University
Press, 1978. 297-317.

0828. -----. "Knowing the Signs: Allusion and Poetic In-
sight." *Poetic Knowledge: Circumference and Centre.
Papers From the Wuppertal Symposium 1978.* Eds. Roland
Hagenbuechle and Joseph T. Swann. Bonn, W. Germany:
Bouvier, 1980. 51-57.

0829. Hulbert, James. "Diderot in the Text of Hegel: A Question of Intertextuality." Diss. Yale University, New
Haven, Conn., 1981.

0830. -----. "Diderot in the Text of Hegel: A Question of
Intertextuality." *Studies in Romanticism* 22 (1983):
267-291.

0831. Hurry, David. "Style, Allusion, and the Manipulation of Viewpoint." *Critical Quarterly* 23 (1981): 61-71.

0832. Hurwitz, Harold. "*The Great Gatsby* and *Heart of Darkness*: The Confrontation Scene." *Fitzgerald/Hemingway Annual* (1969): 27-34.

0833. Idt, Geneviève. "Intertextualité, 'transposition,' critique des sources." *Nova Renascenca* 13 (1984): 5-20.

0834. Imbert, Patrick. "De l'influence à l'intertexte: La littérature canadienne-française et la littérature québécoise face à Balzac." *Canadian Review of Comparative Literature* 13 (1986): 35-63.

0835. Ingelby, C. M., et al. *Shakespeare Allusion-Book*. London: The New Shakespeare Society, 1874.

0836. Ingold, Felix Philipp. "Das Buch im Buche: Versuch ueber Edmond Jabès." *Akzente* 26 (1979): 632-636.

0837. *Intertextualitaet: Formen, Funktionen, anglistische Fallstudien*. Eds. Ulrich Broich and Manfred Pfister. Tuebingen, W. Germany: Niemeyer, 1985.

0838. "Intertextualitate." *Studii si Cercetari Lingvistice* 36.1 (1985) [Special issue].

0839. "Intertextualité." *Sémiotique & Bible* 15 (1979) [Special issue].

0840. "L'intertextualité: Intertexte, autotexte, intratexte." *Texte* 2 (1983) [Special issue].

0841. "L'intertextualité dans la théorie de Mikhail Bakhtin." *Sémiotique & Bible* 15 (1979): 4-22.

0842. "Intertextualités." *Poétique* 27 (1976) [Special issue].

0843. "Intertextualités au XVIIème siècle." *Littérature* 55 (1984) [Special issue].

0844. "Intertextualités médiévales." *Littérature* 41 (1981) [Special issue].

0845. "Intertextuality." *American Journal of Semiotics* 3.4 (1985) [Special issue].

0846. *Intertextuality: New Perspectives in Criticism*. Eds. Jeanine P. Plottel and Hanna Charney. New York Literary Forum 2. New York: Literary Forum, 1978.

0847. *Intertextuality in Faulkner*. Eds. Michel Gresset and Noel Polk. Jackson, Miss.: University Press of Mississippi, 1985.

0848. Ioli, Giovanna. "Autocitazione: Il gioco intertestuale dell'ultimo Montale." *L'arte dell'interpretare: Studi critici offerti a Giovanni Getto.* Cuneo, Italy: Arciere, 1984. 821-835.

0849. Isaacs, Neil D. "Image, Metaphor, Irony, Allusion, and Moral: The Shifting Perspective of *The Seafarer.*" *Neuphilologische Mitteilungen* 67 (1966): 266-282.

0850. Issacharoff, Michael. "Intertextual Interlude: Jarry's *Léda.*" *L'Esprit Créateur* 24.4 (1984): 67-74.

0851. -----. "Labiche et l'intertextualité comique." *Cahiers de l'Association Internationale des Etudes Françaises* 35 (1983): 169-182.

0852. Ivanov, Viach V. "The Significance of M. M. Bakhtin's Ideas on Sign, Utterance, and Dialogue for Modern Semiotics." *Semiotics and Structuralism: Readings from the Soviet Union.* Ed. Henryk Baran. White Plains, N.Y.: International Arts and Sciences Press, 1974. 310-367.

0853. Ivanova, T. F. "Priemy tsitirovaniia v. leninskikh tekstakh." *Russkaia Rech* 4 (1986): 11-16.

0854. Jack, Ian. "Novels and Those 'Necessary Evils': Annotating the Brontës." *Essays in Criticism* 32 (1982): 321-337.

0855. Jackson, Dennis. "Literary Allusions in *Lady Chatterley's Lover.*" *D. H. Lawrence's 'Lady': A New Look at Lady Chatterley's Lover.* Eds. Michael Squires and Dennis Jackson. Athens, Ga.: University of Georgia Press, 1985. 170-196.

0856. Jackson, Heather J. "Sterne, Burton, and Ferriar: Allusions to the *Anatomy of Melancholy* in Volumes Five to Nine of *Tristram Shandy.*" *Philological Quarterly* 54 (1975): 457-470.

0857. Jackson, Holly. "Ovid's *Metamorphoses* and Milton's *Paradise Lost*: The Pattern of Allusions." Diss. Stanford University, Stanford, Cal., 1975.

0858. Jackson, MacD. P. "An Allusion to Marlowe's *The Jew of Malta.*" *Notes and Queries* 29 (1982): 132-133.

0859. Jacobson, Manfred R. "The Narrator's Allusions to Art and Ambiguity: A Note on C. F. Meyer's *Der Heilige.*" *Seminar* 10 (1974): 265-273.

0860. Jacobus, Lee A. "'Lycidas' in the 'Nestor' Episode." *James Joyce Quarterly* 19 (1982): 189-194.

0861. Jacomuzzi, Angelo. "La citazione come procedimento letterario: Appunti e considerazioni." *L'arte dell'interpretare: Studi critici offerti a Giovanni Getto.* Cuneo, Italy: Arciere, 1984. 3-15.

0862. Jaen, Didier T. "The Esoteric Tradition in Borges' 'Tloen, Uqbar, Orbis Tertius.'" *Studies in Short Fiction* 21 (1984): 25-39.

0863. Jambeck, Thomas J. "The Canvas-Tossing Allusion in the *Secunda pastorum.*" *Modern Philology* 76 (1978-79): 49-54.

0864. James, Trevor. "Allen Curnow: Theologian Manqué." *Poetry of the Pacific Region: Proceedings of the CRNLE/SPACLALS Conference.* Ed. Paul Sharrad. Adelaide, Australia: CRNLE, 1984. 57-64.

0865. Jameson, Frederic. "The Ideology of the Text." *Salmagundi* 31-32 (1976): 204-246.

0866. Janssen, Anke. "A Hitherto Unnoticed Allusion to Francis Godwin's *The Man in the Moone* in Swift's *The Battle Between the Ancient and the Modern Books.*" *Notes and Queries* 32 (1985): 200-201.

0867. Janssen, J. D. "Tekstinterpretatie via een Onderzoek van de Co - en Intertekstuele Relaties in de 'Roman van Walewein.'" *Spiegel der Letteren* 24 (1982): 81-95.

0868. Japp, Uwe. "Das Buch im Buch: Eine Figur des literarischen Hermetismus." *Neue Rundschau* 86 (1975): 651-670.

0869. Jaquillard, Pierre. "Note sur Proust, ses citations et le Petit Larousse." *Bulletin de la Société des Amis de Marcel Proust et des Amis de Combray* 10 (1960): 262-267.

0870. Jarrell, Mackie L. "Joyce's Use of Swift's *Polite Conversations* in the 'Circe' Episode of *Ulysses.*" *Publications of the Modern Language Association* 72 (1957): 545-554.

0871. Jean, Raymond. "Le mariage des livres." *Sur Aragon: Le libertinage.* Aix-en-Provence, France: Université de Provence, 1986. 11-18.

0872. Jeanneret, Michel. "Polyphonie de Rabelais: Ambivalence, antithèse et ambiguité." *Littérature* 55 (1984): 98-111.

0873. Jefferson, Ann. "Intertextuality and the Poetics of Fiction." *Contemporary Criticism* 2 (1980): 235-250.

0874. Jeffrey, David L. "Tolkien as Philologist." *Seven* 1 (1980): 47-61.

0875. Jeffrey, Lloyd N. "A Concordance to the Biblical Allusions in *Moby Dick.*" *Bulletin of Bibliography* 21 (1956): 223-229.

0876. Jenny, Laurent, "Le discours du carneval." *Littérature* 16 (1974): 19-36.

0877. -----. "Sémiotique du collage intertextuel, ou la littérature à coups de ciseaux." *Revue d'Esthétique* 3-4
(1978): 165-182.

0878. -----. "La stratégie de la forme." *Poétique* 27 (1976):
257-281. [Engl. trans. by R. Carter: "The Strategy of
Form." *French Literary Theory Today: A Reader.* Ed.
Tzvetan Todorov. Cambridge, UK: Cambridge University
Press, 1982. 34-63.]

0879. Jensch, Fritz. *Wilhelm Raabes Zitatenschatz.* Wolfen-
buettel, W. Germany: Heckner, 1925.

0880. Jensen, Svend B. "Kulturanalyse og Intertekstualitet."
Litteratur og Samfund 35 (1982): 17-29.

0881. Johannessen, Harald. *On Quoting: An Essay on the
Ontology of Words.* Trondheim, Norway: Universitetsfor-
laget, 1976.

0882. Johnson, Anthony L. "Allusion in Poetry." *PTL: A Journal for Descriptive Poetics and Theory of Literature* 1
(1976): 579-587.

0883. Johnson, Barbara. "Les fleurs du mal armé: Réflexions
sur l'intertextualité." *Discours et pouvoir.* Ed. Ross
Chambers. Michigan Romance Studies 2. Ann Arbor,
Mich.: Michigan Romance Studies, 1982. 87-99. [Engl.
trans.: "Les fleurs du mal armé: Some Reflections on
Intertextuality." *Lyric Poetry: Beyond New Criticism.*
Eds. Chavia Hosek and Patricia Parker. Ithaca, N.Y.:
Cornell University Press, 1985. 264-280.]

0884. Johnson, Beatrice. "Classical Allusions in the Poetry
of Donne." *Publications of the Modern Language Association* 43 (1928): 1098-1109.

0885. Johnson, D. Barton. "Text and Pre-Text in Nabokov's
The Defense or 'Play It Again, Sasha.'" *Modern Fiction
Studies* 30 (1984): 278-287.

0886. Johnson, Glen. "The Moral Structure of Cheever's
Falconer." *Studies in American Fiction* 9.1 (1981): 21-
31.

0887. Johnson, James "Identifying Chaucer Allusions, 1953-
1980: An Annotated Bibliography." *Chaucer Review* 19
(1984): 62-86.

0888. Johnson, Oakley C. "Allusion and Style." *Fred Newton
Scott Anniversary Papers.* Chicago, Ill.: University of
Chicago Press, 1929. 189-198.

0889. -----. "Literary Allusion and Reference in Contemporary American Literature." Diss. University of
Michigan, Ann Arbor, Mich., 1928.

0890. Johnson, Patricia. "Quote, Unquote: Direct Quotation
as Anti-Literary Device in *L'étranger.*" *Research Stud-*

ies 47 (1979): 45-48.

0891. Johnson, Theodore. "La place de Vittore Carpaccio dans l'oeuvre de Marcel Proust." *Mélanges à la mémoire de Franco Simone: France et Italie dans la culture européenne, III: XIIe et XXe siècle.* Geneva, Switzerland: Slatkine, 1984. 673-687.

0892. Johnston, Kenneth. "Our History and Our Institutions: Truisms, Proverbs, Clichés, and Quotations Touching the Value of Literature." *College Literature* 5 (1978): 139-143.

0893. Jones, H. W. "Thomas Hobbes and the Bible: A Preliminary Enquiry." *Arts du spectacle et histoire des idées.* Tours, France: Centre d'Etudes Supérieures de la Renaissance, 1984. 271-285.

0894. Jones, Malcolm V. "Dostoevsky, Rousseau, and Others." *Dostoevsky Studies* 4 (1983): 81-93.

0895. Jones, Stanley. "A Hazlitt Quotation Applied to Charles Matthews." *Notes and Queries* 23 (1976): 455.

0896. Jones, Tobin H. "Mythic Vision and Ironic Allusion: Barbusse's *Le feu* and Zola's *Germinal.*" *Modern Fiction Studies* 28 (1982): 215-228.

0897. Jones-Davies, Margaret. "Paroles intertextuelles: Lecture intertextuelle de parolles." *All's Well That Ends Well: Nouvelles perspectives critiques.* Eds. Jean Fuzier and François Laroque. Montpellier, France: Publication de l'Université de Paul Valery, 1985. 65-80.

0898. Joost, Nicholas, and Alan Brown. "T. S. Eliot and Ernest Hemingway: A Literary Relationship." *Papers on Language and Literature* 14 (1978): 425-449.

0899. Jordan, Peter R. "Allusions in Two Early Seventeenth-Century Plays." *Notes and Queries* 31 (1984): 330-331.

0900. Joseph, George. "Rhetoric, Intertextuality, and Genre in Marot's 'Elegies déploratives.'" *Romanic Review* 72 (1981): 13-25.

0901. Joseph, Gerhard. "The Labyrinth and the Library: A View From the Temple in *Martin Chuzzlewit.*" *Dickens Studies Annual* 15 (1986): 1-22.

0902. Joseph, Jean R. "'Marcel Proust,' ou les métamorphoses du portrait." *Romanic Review* 75 (1984): 492-503.

0903. Jost, David. "The Reading Program of the Middle English Dictionary: Evaluation and Instructions." *Dictionaries* 6 (1984): 113-127.

0904. Juergens, Heiko. "Die Funktion der Kirchenvaeterzitate in der Heidelberger Disputation Luthers (1518)." *Ar-*

chiv fuer Reformationsgeschichte 66 (1975): 71-78.

0905. Kadir, Djelal. "Nostalgia or Nihilism: Pop Art and the New Spanish American Novel." *Journal of Spanish Studies: Twentieth Century* 2 (1974): 127-135.

0906. Kadish, Doris Y. "'Alissa dans La Vallée': Intertextual Echoes of Balzac in Two Novels by Gide." *French Forum* 10 (1985): 67-83.

0907. Kaempfert, Manfred. *Saekularisation und neue Heiligkeit: Religioese und religionsbezogene Sprache bei Friedrich Nietzsche.* Berlin, W. Germany: Schmidt, 1971. [Diss. Bonn, W. Germany, 1968.]

0908. Kaiser, Gerhard R. "'Doktor Faust, sind Sie des Teufels?': Eine Notiz zu Heinrich Heines *Seegespenst.*" *Euphorion* 78 (1984): 188-197.

0909. -----. "Goethes *Faust* und die Bibel." *Deutsche Vierteljahrsschrift fuer Literaturwissenschaft und Geistesgeschichte* 58 (1984): 391-413.

0910. -----. *Proust, Musil, Joyce: Zum Verhaeltnis von Literatur und Gesellschaft am Paradigma des Zitat.* Frankfurt, W. Germany: Athenaeum, 1972. [Diss. Mainz, W. Germany, 1971.]

0911. Kaiser, Leo M. "Latin Quotation in Cotton Mather." *Early American Literature* 13 (1978): 296-298.

0912. Kapp, Volker. "Intertextualité et rhétorique des citations." *Recherches sur l'histoire de la poétique.* Ed. Marc M. Muench. Nancy, France: Lang, 1984. 237-254.

0913. Kappel, Andrew J. "The Reading and Writing of a Modern *Paradiso*: Ezra Pound and the Books of Paradise." *Twentieth Century Literature* 27 (1981): 223-246.

0914. Karahka, Urpu-Liisa. "Studier i Johannes Edfelts stilutveckling fran *Gryningroester* till *Hoegmaessa.*" *Perspektiv pa Johannes Edfelt.* Eds. Ulla-Britta Lagerroth and Goesta Loewendahl. Stockholm, Sweden: Raben & Sjoegren, 1969. 185-207.

0915. Karbusicky, Vladimir. "Intertextualitat in der Musik." *Dialog der Texte: Hamburger Kolloquium zur Intertextualitaet.* Eds. Wolf Schmid and Wolf-Dieter Stempel. Wiener Slawistischer Almanach Sonderband 11. Wien, 1983. 361-398.

0916. Karrer, Wolfgang. "Intertextualitaet als Elementen- und Struktur-Reproduktion." *Intertextualitaet: Formen, Funktionen, anglistische Fallstudien.* Eds. U. Broich and M. Pfister. Tuebingen, W. Germany: Niemeyer, 1985. 98-116.

0917. Kaske, R. E. "*The Canticum Canticorum* in the *Miller's Tale.*" *Studies in Philology* 59 (1962): 479-500.

0918. -----. "The Summoner's Garleek, Oynons, and eek Lekes." *Modern Language Notes* 74 (1959): 481-484.

0919. Kaufmann, Vincent. "Contrats sans paroles (Sur Louis-René des Forêts)." *Texte* 2 (1983): 35-47.

0920. Kean, P. M. "Chaucer's Dealings with a Stanza of *Il filostrato* and the Epilogue of *Troilus and Criseyde*." *Medium Aevum* 33 (1964): 36-46.

0921. Keller, Luzius. "L'autocitation chez Proust." *Modern Language Notes* 95 (1980): 1033-1048.

0922. Kellett, Ernest Edward. *Literary Quotation and Allusion*. 1933; Port Washington, N.Y.: Kennikat Press, 1969.

0923. Kelley, Alice van Buren. "Von Aschenbach's *Phaedrus*: Platonic Allusion in *Der Tod in Venedig*." *Journal of English and Germanic Philology* 75 (1976): 228-240.

0924. Kelly, Douglas. "Les inventions ovidiennes de Froissart: Réflexions intertextuelles comme imaginations." *Littérature* 41 (1981): 82-92.

0925. Kelly, Kathleen. "Berryman's 'His Toy, His Dream, His Rest.'" *Explicator* 42.3 (1984): 56.

0926. Kelly, Lionel. "Personal History in *The Cantos*." *Pound and History*. Ed. Marianne Korn. Orono, Me.: University of Maine, 1985. 119-133.

0927. Kelly, Robert. "Allusion to the Vulgate Cycle in *Sir Gawain and the Green Knight*." *Literary and Historical Perspectives of the Middle Ages: Proceedings of the 1981 SEMA Meeting*. Eds. Patricia W. Cummins et al. Morgantown, W. Va.: West Virginia University Press, 1982. 183-199.

0928. Kennedy, Angus J. "Christine de Pizan and Maximianus." *Medium Aevum* 54 (1985): 282-283.

0929. Kennedy, Elspeth. "Merlin and the Role of Allusions in the First Part of the Prose *Lancelot*." *Bulletin Bibliographique de la Société Internationale Arthurienne* 12 (1960): 126-127.

0930. Kennedy, Richard F. "Another Chaucer Allusion." *Notes and Queries* 31 (1984): 156.

0931. -----. "Byron and Petrarch." *Byron Journal* 11 (1983): 52-53.

0932. Kerner, M. "Randbemerkungen zur *Institutio Traiani*." *The World of John of Salisbury*. Ed. Michael Wilks. Studies in Church History, Subsidia 3. Oxford, UK: Blackwell, 1984. 203-206.

0933. Kibéda-Varga, A.. "Pour une histoire intertextuelle de la littérature." *Degrés* 12 (1984): g1-g10.

0934. Kilworth-Mason, Wendy. "Hobbes' Vision of the Kingdom of God and the 'Leviathan': A Consideration of the Religious Allusions in and the Religious Implications of Hobbes' *Leviathan*." Diss. Florida State University, Tallahassee, Fla, 1985.

0935. Kinsley, William. "'Allusion' in the Eighteenth Century: The Disinherited Critic." *Man and Nature/L'homme et la nature*. III, 1984. Edmonton, Alberta: Academic Prints and Publishing, 1984. 23-45.

0936. Kirby, Ian J. *Biblical Quotation in Old Icelandic-Norwegian Religious Literature I*. 2 Vols. Reykjavik, Iceland: Stofnun Arna Magnussonar, 1976-1980.

0937. Kirby, Thomas A. "Carlyle on Chaucer." *Modern Language Notes* 61 (1946): 184-185.

0938. -----. "Further Seventeenth-Century Chaucer Allusions." *Modern Language Notes* 64 (1949): 81-82.

0939. -----. "J. Q. Adams and Chaucer." *Modern Language Notes* 61 (1946): 185-186.

0940. -----. "Theodore Roosevelt on Chaucer and a Chaucerian." *Modern Language Notes* 68 (1953): 34-37.

0941. Kisseleff, Natalia. "Literary Allusions and Themes in *The First Circle*." *Canadian Slavonic Papers* 8 (1971): 219-233.

0942. Klein, Alfons. "Aesthetisches Rollenspiel: Zum Motiv der 'gelebten Literatur' in Oscar Wildes *The Picture of Dorian Gray*." *Gelebte Literatur in der Literatur: Studien zu Erscheinungsformen und Geschichte eines literarischen Motivs*. Ed. Theodor Wolpers. Goettingen, W. Germany: Vandenhoeck & Ruprecht, 1986. 272-297.

0943. Kleinert, Annemarie. "Ein Modejournal des 19. Jahrhunderts und seine Leserin: 'La Corbeille' und Madame Bovary." *Romanische Forschungen* 90 (1978): 458-477.

0944. -----. "Vorsicht Literatur! Eine literarische Lektion vom gefaehrlichen Lesen." *Germanisch-Romanische Monatsschrift* 33 (1983): 94-100.

0945. Kleinherz, Christopher. "Dante and the Bible: Intertextual Approaches to the *Divine Comedy*." *Italica* 63 (1986): 225-236.

0946. Klemp, P. J. "'Sunke in that dead sea of life': Fulke Greville in Jonson's Cary-Morison Ode." *Sidney Newsletter* 5.2 (1984): 10-16.

0947. Klingel, Joan E. "Dickens's First Epistle to the Utilitarians." *Dickens Quarterly* 3 (1986): 124-128.

0948. Kloepfer, Rolf. "Grundlagen des 'dialogischen Prin-
zips' in der Literatur." *Dialogizitaet*. Ed. Renate
Lachmann. Muenchen, W. Germany: Fink, 1982. 85-106.

0949. Klotz, Alfred. "Die Plautuscitate Varros." *Philologus:
Zeitschrift fuer das klassische Altertum* 96 (1944):
18-27.

0950. Klotz, Volker. "Zitat und Montage in neuerer Literatur
und Kunst." *Sprache im technischen Zeitalter* 60
(1976): 259-277.

0951. Knauer, Georg Nicolaus. *Die Aeneis und Homer: Studien
zur poetischen Technik Vergils mit Listen der Homer-
zitate in der Aeneis*. Goettingen, W. Germany: Vanden-
choek & Ruprecht, 1964.

0952. -----. "Psalmenzitate in Augustins Konfessionen."
Diss. Hamburg, W. Germany, 1952.

0953. Kneale, J. Douglas. "Wordsworth and Milton." *Ap-
proaches to Teaching Wordsworth's Poetry*. Eds. Spencer
Hall and Jonathan Ramsey. New York: Modern Language
Association of America, 1986. 119-123.

0954. Knee, Robin. "Claude Ollier's *Le jeu d'enfant*: An
Intertextual Reading." Diss. University of Pennsylvania, 1983.

0955. -----. "Unmuddling Claude Ollier's *Fuzzy Sets*: An
Intra/Intertextual Essay." *Symposium* 38 (1984-85):
311-320.

0956. Kneif, Tibor. "Zur Semantik des musikalischen Zitats."
Neue Zeitschrift fuer Musik 134 (1973): 3-9.

0957. Knoepflmacher, M. C. "Irony Through Scriptural Allusion: A Note on Chaucer's Prioresse." *Chaucer Review* 4
(1970): 180-183.

0958. Knorr, Walter L. "Doctorow and Kleist: 'Kohlhaas' in
Ragtime." *Modern Fiction Studies* 22 (1976): 224-227.

0959. Koester, Patricia. "Hagar 'The Egyptian': Allusions
and Illusions in *The Stone Angel*." *Ariel: A Review of
International English Literature* 16.3 (1985): 41-52.

0960. Kohn, Wila. "The Faust Complex in the Fiction of Micha
Joseph Berdyczewski." Diss. University of California
Los Angeles, Cal., 1985.

0961. Koller, Kathrine. "A Chaucer Allusion." *Modern Language Notes* 52 (1937): 568-570.

0962. Komar, Kathleen L. "*The Death of Vergil*: Broch's
Reading of Vergil's *Aneid*." *Comparative Literature
Studies* 21 (1984): 255-269.

0963. Koopmann, Helmut. "Joseph und sein Vater: Zu den bi-

blischen Anspielungen in Schillers *Raeubern.*" *Herkom-
men und Erneuerung: Essays fuer Oskar Seidlin.* Eds.
Gerald Gillespie and Edgar Lohner. Tuebingen, W. Germany: Niemeyer, 1976. 150-167.

0964. Kopper, Edward Anthony. "A Study of the Catholic Allusions in *Finnegans Wake.*" Diss. Temple University,
Philadelphia, Pa., 1963.

0965. Kosny, Witold. "Bedeutung und Funktion der literarischen Zitate in A. P. Cechovs *Tri Sestry.*" *Welt der
Slawen* 16 (1971): 126-150.

0966. Kraettli, Anton. "'Leben im Zitat': Zu Max Frischs
'Montauk.'" *Schweizer Monatshefte* 55 (1975): 653-656.

0967. Krance, Charles. "Montaigne's Last Krapp." *Intertextuality: New Perspectives in Criticism.* Eds.
Jeanine P. Plottel and Hanna Charney. New York
Literary Forum 2. New York: Literary Forum, 1978. 45-
67.

0968. Krause, Wilhelm. "Versuch einer allgemeinen Theorie
des Zitats." Wilhelm Krause. *Die Stellung der frueh-
mittelalterlichen Autoren zur heidnischen Literatur.*
Wien: Herder, 1958. 51-58.

0969. Kristeva, Julia. "Bakhtine, le mot, le dialogue et le
roman." *Critique* 239 (1967): 438-465. [Repr. in *Séméi-
otikè: Recherches pour une sémanalyse.* Paris: Seuil,
1969. 143-173. Engl. trans. by Thomas Gora, Alice Jar-
dine, and Léon S. Roudiez: "Word, Dialogue, and
Novel." Julia Kristeva. *Desire in Language: A Semiotic
Approach to Literature and Art.* Ed. Léon S. Roudiez.
New York: Columbia University Press, 1980. 64-91;
"Word, Dialogue and Novel." *The Kristeva Reader.* Ed.
Toril Moi. Oxford, UK: Blackwell, 1986. 34-61].

0970. -----. "Narration et transformation." *Semiotica* 1
(1969): 422-448.

0971. -----. "Poésie et négativité." Julia Kristeva. *Séméiotikè: Recherches pour une sémanalyse.* Paris: Seuil,
1969. 246-278.

0972. -----. "Une poétique ruinée." Preface to Mikhaïl
Bakhtine. *La poétique de Dostoïevski.* Paris: Seuil,
1970. 5-27. [Engl. trans. by Vivienne Mylne: "The Ruin
of a Poetics." *Twentieth Century Studies* 7-8 (1972):
102-119.]

0973. -----. "Problèmes de la structuration du texte."
Théorie d'ensemble. Paris: Seuil, 1968. 297-317.

0974. -----. "La productivité dite texte." *Communications* 11
(1968): 59-83.

0975. -----. *La révolution du langage poétique.* Paris:
Seuil, 1974. [Engl. trans. by Margaret Walker: *Revolu-*

tion in Poetic Language. New York: Columbia University
Press, 1984.]

0976. -----. *Séméiotikè: Recherches pour une sémanalyse*.
Paris: Seuil, 1969.

0977. -----. "Le texte clos." *Langages* 12 (1966): 103-125.
[Repr. in *Séméiotikè: Recherches pour une sémanalyse*.
Paris: Seuil, 1969. 113-142. Engl. trans. by Thomas
Gora, Alice Jardine, and Léon S. Roudiez: "The Bounded
Text." Julia Kristeva. *Desire in Language: A Semiotic
Approach to Literature*. Ed. Léon S. Roudiez. New York:
Columbia University Press, 1980. 36-63.]

0978. -----. *Le texte du roman: Approche sémiologique d'une
structure discursive transformationelle*. The Hague,
Holland: Mouton, 1970.

0979. Kronfeld, Chana. "Allusion: An Israeli Perspective."
Prooftexts 5 (1985): 137-163.

0980. Kropholler, P. F. "Notes to 'The Nether World.'"
Gissing Newsletter 22.2 (1986): 21-25.

0981. Krummacher, Hans-Henrik. "Bibelwort und hymnisches
Sprechen bei Klopstock." *Jahrbuch der deutschen Schil-
lergesellschaft* 13 (1969): 155-179.

0982. Kruse, Margot. "'Gelebte Literatur' im *Don Quijote*."
*Gelebte Literatur in der Literatur: Studien zu Er-
scheinungsformen und Geschichte eines literarischen
Motivs*. Ed. Theodor Wolpers. Goettingen, W. Germany:
Vandenhoeck & Ruprecht, 1986. 30-71.

0983. Krysinski, Wladimir. "L'intertexte du roman et
l'espace comparatif." *Canadian Review of Comparative
Literature* 11 (1984): 469-477.

0984. -----. "Le 16 Juin 1904 et après ..." *Texte* 2 (1983):
61-84.

0985. Kuberski, Philip. "Ego, Scriptor: Pound's Odyssean
Writing." *Paideuma* 14 (1985): 31-51.

0986. Kuehn, Clemens. "Bernd Alois Zimmermann: 'Photopto-
sis': Ein Blick auf das Zitat in der Kunst der Gegenwart." *Musik und Bildung: Zeitschrift fuer Theorie und
Praxis der Musikerziehung* 65 (1974): 109-115.

0987. -----. *Das Zitat in der Musik der Gegenwart - mit
Ausblicken auf bildende Kunst und Literatur*. Hamburg,
W. Germany: Wagner, 1972.

0988. Kuhn, Reinhard. "Traces in the Sand: Gide and Novalis
with the Enigmatic Child." *Intertextuality: New
Perspectives in Criticism*. Eds. Jeanine P. Plottel and
Hanna Charney. New York Literary Forum 2. New York:
Literary Forum, 1978. 77-85.

0989. Kunitzsch, Paul. "Das Abu Ma'sar Zitat im Rosenroman."
      Romanische Forschungen 82 (1970): 102-111.

0990. Kurata, Marilyn J. "Italians with White Mice Again:
      Middlemarch and *The Woman in White*." *English Language
      Notes* 22.4 (1985): 45-47.

0991. Kurihaha, Takehiko. "The Syntax and Semantics of Quo-
      tation Reconsidered." *Language and Culture* 7 (1985):
      67-89.

0992. Kurth-Voigt, Lieselotte E. "The Art of Allusion: Les-
      sing's *Vademecum Duplik* and Anti-Goeze." *Aufnahme* –
      *Weitergabe: Literarische Impulse um Lessing und
      Goethe. Festschrift fuer Heinz Moekemeyer zum 68.
      Geburtstag*. Eds. John A. McCarthy and Albert A. Kipa.
      Hamburg, W. Germany: Buske, 1982. 108-124.

0993. Kurz, Josef. *Die Redewiedergabe: Methoden und Moeg-
      lichkeiten*. Leipzig, E. Germany: Karl Marx Universi-
      taet, 1966.

0994. La Cassagnère, Christian. "Image picturale et image
      littéraire dans le nocturne romantique: Essai poétique
      intertextuelle." *Romantisme* 49 (1985): 47-65.

0995. LaCharité, Raymond C. "Rabelais and the Silenic Text:
      The Prologue to *Gargantua*." *Rabelais's Incomparable
      Book: Essays on His Art*. Ed. Raymond C. LaCharité.
      Lexington, Ky.: French Forum, 1986. 72-86.

0996. -----. "Réflexion-divertissement et intertextualité:
      Rabelais   et   l'Ecolier   limousin."   *Textes   et
      intertextes: Etudes sur le XVIe siècle pour Alfred
      Glauser*. Eds. Floyd Gray and Marcel Tetel. Paris:
      Nizet, 1979. 93-104.

0997. Lachmann, Renate. "Ebenen des Intertextualitaetsbe-
      griffs." *Das Gespraech*. Eds. Karlheinz Stierle and
      Rainer Warning. Poetik und Hermeneutik 11. Muenchen,
      W. Germany: Fink, 1984. 133-138.

0998. -----. "Intertextualitaet als Sinnkonstitution: Andrej
      Belyjs 'Petersburg' und die 'fremden' Texte." *Poetica*
      15 (1983): 66-107.

0999. -----. "Intertextualitaet in der Lyrik (zu Maja-
      kovskijs 'Oda Revoljucii')." *Wiener Slawistischer
      Almanach* 5 (1980): 5-23.

1000. -----. "Intertextuelle Strukturen in Vladimir Kazakovs
      'Osibka Zivych.'" *Text – Symbol – Weltmodell: Johannes
      Holthusen zum 60. Geburtstag*. Eds. Johanna-Renate
      Doering-Smirnov,   Peter   Rehder,   and   Wolf   Schmid.
      Muenchen, W. Germany: Sagner, 1984. 345-364.

1001. -----. "Zur Frage einer dialogischen Poetizitaetsbe-
      stimmung bei Roman Jakobson." *Poetica* 14 (1982): 278-
      293.

1002. ------. "Zur Semantik metonymischer Intertextualitaet."
       Das Gespraech. Eds. Karlheinz-Stierle and Rainer War-
       ning. Poetik und Hermeneutik 11. Muenchen, W. Germany:
       Fink, 1984. 517-523.

1003. Lackey, Kris. "Additional Biblical Allusions in *Moby
       Dick.*" *Melville Society Extracts* 54 (1983): 12.

1004. ------. "The Holy Guide-Book and the Sword of the Lord:
       How Melville Used the Bible in *Redburn* and *White-
       Jacket.*" *Studies in the Novel* 17 (1985): 241-254.

1005. Ladriere, James C. "Sarmoni Propius: A Study of the
       Horatian Theory of the Epistle and of Dryden's Allu-
       sion to It in the Preface of 'Religio Laici.'" Diss.
       University of Michigan, Ann Arbor, Mich., 1938.

1006. Laermann, Klaus. "Vom Sinn des Zitierens." *Merkur* 38
       (1984): 672-681.

1007. Lafay, Henry. "Les animaux malades de la peste: Essai
       d'analyse d'intertextualité." *Romanische Zeitschrift
       fuer Literaturgeschichte* 1 (1977): 40-49.

1008. Lams, Victor J. "Ruth, Milton, and Keats's 'Ode to a
       Nightingale.'" *Modern Language Quarterly* 34 (1973):
       417-435.

1009. "Land of Lost Allusion." *Atlantic Monthly* 129 (Febru-
       ary 1922): 279-281.

1010. Landrum, Grace Warren. "Chaucer's Use of the Vulgate."
       Publications of the Modern Language Association 39
       (1924): 75-100.

1011. ------. "Spenser's Use of the Bible and His Alleged
       Puritanism." *Publications of the Modern Language Asso-
       ciation* 41 (1926): 517-544.

1012. Lane, Lauriat. "Robert Lowell: The Problems and Power
       of Allusion." *Dalhousie Review* 60 (1980-81): 697-702.

1013. Lang, G. M. "From the Pictograph to the Metapoem:
       Realms of Concrete Literary Reference in Brazilian
       Concrete Poetry." *Revista Canadiense de Estudios
       Hispanicos* 3 (1979): 101-120.

1014. Lang, Helmer. "Under manen vaetebomben: Karlfeldt och
       Artur Lundkvist." H. Lang. *Dikt att Foerklara*. Lund,
       Sweden: Lang, 1971. 270-279.

1015. Lange, Henrik. "Saekularisierte Bibelreminiszenzen in
       Kleists 'Michael Kohlhaas.'" *Kopenhagener germa-
       nistische Studien* 1 (1969): 213-226.

1016. Lank, Edith. "'Lop't and Crop't.'" *Persuasions* 7
       (1985): 20.

1017. Lapp, John C. "Montaigne et le nouveau monde: Style,

thématique et mythe." *Textes et intertextes: Études sur le XVIe siécle pour Alfred Glauser.* Eds. Floyd Gray and Marcel Tetel. Paris: Nizet, 1979. 105-122.

1018. Larbaud, Valery. "Des citations." Valery Larbaud. *Sous l'invocation de Saint Jerome.* Paris: Gallimard, 1946. 215-219.

1019. Larrea, María Isabel. "Los epígrafes en 'Los pasos perdidos' de Alejo Carpentier." *Estudios Filológicos* 21 (1986): 91-109.

1020. Larson, Janet. *Dickens and the Broken Scripture.* Athens, Ga.: University of Georgia Press, 1985.

1021. Larson, Mildred L. *The Functions of Reported Speech in Discourse.* Dallas, Tex.: Inst. of Linguistics, 1978.

1022. -----. "Quotation, A Translation Problem." *Notes on Translation* 82 (1981): 2-15.

1023. Lascelles, Mary. "Johnson's Last Allusion to Mary, Queen of Scots." *Review of English Studies* 8 (1957): 32-37.

1024. Lasine, Stuart. "Kafka's *The Trial.*" *Explicator* 43.3 (1985): 34-36.

1025. Latour, Helen Elizabeth. "A Study of the Quotations in *Ecbasis captivi.*" Diss. University of North Carolina, Chapel Hill, N. C., 1972.

1026. Lattimore, David. "Allusion and T'ang Poetry." *Ariel: A Review of International English Literature* 2 (1971): 28-50.

1027. Laub, Roger M. "The Poetics of Literary Allusion in the Early Fictions of William Makepeace Thackeray." Diss. University of Kansas, Lawrence, Kans., 1978.

1028. Lauer, Reinhard. "Die literarischen Folien in A. P. Cechovs fruehem Drama *Platonov.*" *Gelebte Literatur in der Literatur: Studien zu Erscheinungsformen und Geschichte eines literarischen Motivs.* Ed. Theodor Wolpers. Goettingen, W. Germany: Vandenhoeck & Rupp-recht, 1986. 255-271.

1029. -----. "Realistisches Wiedererzaehlen und 'gelebte Literatur': Zur intertextuellen Struktur von Laza Lazarevics 'Verter.'" *Gelebte Literatur in der Literatur: Studien zu Erscheinungsformen und Geschichte eines literarischen Motivs.* Ed. Theodor Wolpers. Goettingen, W. Germany: Vandenhoeck & Ruprecht, 1986. 231-254.

1030. Laurette, Pierre. "A l'ombre du pastiche la ré-écriture: Automatisme et contingence." *Texte* 2 (1983): 113-134.

1031. La Valée-Williams, Marthe. "Biblical Allusions in *La chute.*" *Agora* 2 (1970): 13-31.

1032. Lawler, Traugott. "'Wafting Vapours From the Land of Dreams': Virgil's Fourth and Sixth Eclogues and the Dunciad." *Studies in English Literature* 14 (1974): 373-386.

1033. Lea, Henry A. "The Specter of Romanticism: Hauptmann's Use of Quotations." *Germanic Review* 49 (1974): 267-283.

1034. Le Blanc, Alonzo. "Ronfard: Dérive organisée et conflit des cultures." *Etudes Littéraires* 18 (1985): 123-141.

1035. Lecercle, Francois. "Le texte comme langue: Cicéronianisme et Pétrarquisme." *Littérature* 55 (1984): 45-53.

1036. Le Coat, Gérard. "Literary and Musical Syntax of the Eighteenth Century." *Intertextuality: New Perspectives in Criticism.* Eds. Jeanine P. Plottel and Hanna Charney. New York Literary Forum 2. New York: Literary Forum, 1978. 159-176.

1037. Le Comte, Edward. *Sly Milton: The Meaning Lurking in the Contexts of His Quotations.* East Meadow, N.Y.: English Studies Collections, 1976.

1038. *Lecteur et la lecture dans l'oeuvre: Actes du colloque international de Clermont-Ferrand.* Ed. Alain Montandon. Clermont-Ferrand, France: Association des Publications de la Faculté des Lettres, 1982.

1039. Lee, Guy. *Allusion, Parody and Imitation: The St. John's College Cambridge Lecture 1970-71.* Hull, UK: University of Hull, 1971.

1040. Legge, M. D. "Quelques allusions littéraires." *Mélanges de langue et de littérature médiévales offerts à Pierre Le Gentil, Professeur à la Sorbonne, par ses collègues, ses élèves et ses amis.* Paris: S.E.D.E.S. et C.D.U. Réunion, 1973. 479-483.

1041. Leggett, B. J. "The Miltonic Allusions in Housman's 'Terence, This is Stupid Stuff.'" *English Language Notes* 5 (1968): 202-207.

1042. Lehmann, Hans-Thies. "Mueller/Hamlet/Grueber/Faust: Intertextualitaet als Problem der Inszenierung." *Studien zur Aesthetik des Gegenwartstheaters.* Ed. Ch. W. Thomsen. Heidelberg, W. Germany: Winter, 1985. 33-45.

1043. Leibfried, Erwin. "Goethes Werther als Leser von Lessings *Emilia Galotti.*" *Text-Leser-Bedeutung.* Ed. Herbert Grabes. Grossen-Linden, W. Germany: Hoffmann, 1977. 145-156.

1044. Leigh, John. "Shepard, Pound, and Bertran de Born."

Paideuma 14 (1985): 331-339.

1045. Lejeune, Rita. "L'allusion à Tristan chez le trouba-
dour Cercamon." *Romania* 83 (1962): 183-209.

1046. -----. "Les allusions à Merlin dans la littérature
occitane (XII - XIIIième siècle)." *Bulletin Bibliographique de la Société International Arthurienne* 12
(1960): 128.

1047. Lemke, Gerd. *Untersuchungen zu Zitat und Zitiermethode
im Werk des Literaturkritikers Albert Béguin.* Bern,
Switzerland: Lang, 1973.

1048. Lemke, J.L. "Ideology, Intertextuality, and the Notion
of Register." *Systemic Perspectives on Discourse.* Ed.
James D. Benson. Norwood, N. J.: Ablex, 1985. 1: 275-
294.

1049. Lense, Edward. "Pynchon's *V.*" *Explicator* 43.1 (1984):
60-61.

1050. Lensing, Leo A. "Goethe's *Torquato Tasso* in *Lord Jim*:
A Note on Conrad's Use of Literary Quotation." *English
Literature in Transition* 19 (1976): 101-104.

1051. Lenz, Bernd. "Intertextualitaet und Gattungswechsel:
Zur Transformation literarischer Gattungen." *Intertextualitaet: Formen, Funktionen, anglistische Fallstudien.* Eds. U. Broich and M. Pfister. Tuebingen, W.
Germany: Niemeyer, 1985. 158-178.

1052. Lepow, Laureen. "Daw's Tennis Ball: A Topical Allusion
in the *Secunda pastorum.*" *English Language Notes* 22.2
(1984): 5-8.

1053. Leps, Marie-Christine. "For an Intertextual Method of
Analyzing Discourse: A Case Study of Presuppositions."
Europa 3 (1979-80): 89-103.

1054. Lerner, Laurence. "Romantik, Realismus und negierte
Intertextualitaet." *Intertextualitaet: Formen, Funktionen, anglistische Fallstudien.* Eds. U. Broich and
M. Pfister. Tuebingen, W. Germany: Niemeyer, 1985.
278-296.

1055. LeVay, John. "De la Mare's 'Please to Remember.'" *Explicator* 42.3 (1984): 38-39.

1056. Levi, A. H. T. "Histoire littéraire, intertextualité
et civilization." *Etudes françaises en Europe non
francophone.* Ed. Jozef Heistein. Warsaw, Poland: Nau-
kowe, 1981. 148-156.

1057. Levin, G. "An Allusion to Tasso in Conrad's *Chance.*"
Nineteenth-Century Fiction 13 (1958): 145-151.

1058. Levin, Harry. "The Female Quixote." *Madame Bovary and
the Critics.* Ed. B. F. Bart. New York: New York Uni-

versity Press, 1966. 106-131.

1059. Levine, Herbert J. "The Marriage of Allegory and Realism in *Daniel Deronda*." *Genre* 15 (1982): 421-445.

1060. Levine, Suzanne J. "Writing as Translation: *Three Trapped Tigers* and *A Cobra*." *Modern Language Notes* 90 (1975): 265-277.

1061. Levinson, Marjorie. "Spiritual Economics: A Reading of Wordsworth's 'Michael.'" *ELH: A Journal of English Literary History* 52 (1985): 707-731.

1062. LeVot, A. E. "*Our Mutual Friend* and *The Great Gatsby*." *Fitzgerald Newsletter*. Ed. Matthew J. Bruccoli. Washington, D. C.: Microcard, 1969. 105-107.

1063. Levy, Michele F. "Of Time and the River: Lorca's *La casa de Bernarda Alba* and Chekhov's *Try sestry* (*Three Sisters*)." *La Chispa '85: Selected Proceedings*. Ed. Gilbert Paolini. New Orleans, La.: Tulane University, 1985. 203-212.

1064. Levy, Raphael. "L'allusion à la sodomie dans *Eneas*." *Philological Quarterly* 27 (1948): 372-376.

1065. Levy, Robert Allen. "Dryden's Translation of Chaucer: A Study of the Means of Recreating Literary Models." Diss. University of Tennessee, 1973.

1066. Lewalski, Barbara. "Biblical Allusion and Allegory in *The Merchant of Venice*." *Shakespeare Quarterly* 13 (1962): 327-343.

1067. Liao, Ping Hui, and Jonathan Hall. "Intersection and Juxtaposition of Wor(l)ds." *Tamkang Review* 14.1-4 (1983-84): 395-415.

1068. Liebman, Sheldon. "Hawthorne's *Comus*: A Miltonic Source for 'The Maypole of Merry Mount.'" *Nineteenth-Century Fiction* 27 (1972): 345-351.

1069. Lienhard, Martin. "Una intertextualidad 'indoamericana' y *Moriencia* de Augusto Roa Bastos." *Revista Iberoamericana* 50 (1984): 505-523.

1070. Lim, C. S. "Dr. Johnson's Quotation from *Macbeth*." *Notes and Queries* 33 (1986): 518.

1071. Lindberger, Oerjan. "Dolda allusioner. Gunnar Ekeloef: Helvetets-Brueghel, detalj." *Att lasa poesi*. Eds. O. and Reidar Ekner. Stockholm: Bonniers, 1955. 121-129.

1072. Lindboe, Berit R. "'O Shakespear, Had I Thy Pen!': Fielding's Use of Shakespeare in *Tom Jones*." *Studies in the Novel* 14 (1982): 303-315.

1073. Linderman, Deborah. "Narrative Surplus: The 'Blow-Up' as Metarepresentation and Ideology." *American Journal of Semiotics* 3.4 (1985): 99-118.

1074. Lindley, David. "A Downland Allusion in Herbert's 'Grief.'" *Notes and Queries* 31 (1984): 238-239.

1075. Lindner, Monika. "Integrationsformen der Intertextualitaet." *Intertextualitaet: Formen, Funktionen, anglistische Fallstudien.* Eds. U. Broich and M. Pfister. Tuebingen, W. Germany: Niemeyer, 1985. 116-135.

1076. Link, Juergen. "Interdiscourse, Literature, and Collective Symbols: Theses Towards a Theory of Discourse and Literature." *Enclitic* 8.1-2 (1984): 157-165.

1077. Linthicum, M. C. "Three Chaucer Allusions in Sixteenth-Century Libraries." *Philological Quarterly* 12 (1933): 409-410.

1078. Lissa, Zofia. "Aesthetische Funktionen des musikalischen Zitats." *Musikforschung* 19 (1966): 364-378.

1079. "Literary Allusion." *The Nation* (December 13, 1906): 503-504.

1080. Little, Thomas Alexander. "Literary Allusions in the Writings of Herman Melville." Diss. University of Nebraska, Lincoln, Nebr., 1948.

1081. Littmann, Mark E., and Charles A. Schweighauser. "Astronomical Allusions, Their Meaning and Purpose, in *Ulysses.*" *James Joyce Quarterly* 2 (1965): 238-246.

1082. Livingston, Charles H. "Explication d'une allusion littéraire dans un texte du XIIIième siècle." *Romanic Review* 31 (1940): 112-113.

1083. Ljungerud, Ivar. "Froedings bibelkaennedom." *Arsskrift foer Modersmalslaerarnas Foerening* (1941): 13-43.

1084. Llorens, Vincente Castillo. *Don Quijote y los libros.* Universidad de Puerto Rico: Junta Editora, 1947.

1085. Lock, F. P. "A Jane Austen Quotation Identified." *Notes and Queries* 20 (1973): 289.

1086. Lockwood, John. "A Double-Barreled Literary Reference." *Mark Twain Journal* 20.2 (1980): 18-19.

1087. Loewenstein, Joseph. *Responsive Readings: Versions of Echo in Pastoral Epic, and the Jonsonian Masque.* Yale Studies in English 192. New Haven, Conn.: Yale University Press, 1984.

1088. Logan, Marie Rose. "L'intertextualité au carrefour de la philologie et de la poétique." *Littérature* 41 (1981): 47-49.

1089. Long, Anne Bowers. "The Relations Between Classical and Biblical Allusions in Milton's Later Poems." Diss.

University of Illinois, Urbana-Champaign, Ill., 1967.

1090. Long, Robert E. "The Allusion to Gilda Gray in *The Great Gatsby.*" *Fitzgerald/Hemingway Annual* (1972): 307-309.

1091. Lonsdale, Roger. "Gray and 'Allusion': The Poet as Debtor." *Studies in the Eighteenth Century IV: Papers Presented at the Fourth David Nichol Smith Memorial Seminar, Canberra, 1976.* Canberra, Australia: Australian National University Press, 1979. 31-55.

1092. Looper, Travis Dayton. "The Poetry of Lord Byron: A Compendium of Biblical Usage." Diss. Baylor University, Waco, Tex., 1976.

1093. Loucks, James Frederick. "'Scripture For His Purpose': A Study of Robert Browning's Use of Biblical Allusions in 'The Ring and the Book.'" Diss. Ohio State University, Columbus, Ohio, 1967.

1094. Lourenço, Eduardo. "O livro do desassossego: Texto suicida." *Actas do II. congresso internacional de estudos pessoanos.* Oporto, Portugal: Centro de Estudos Pessoanos, 1985. 347-361.

1095. Loverso, Marco Pietro. "Self-Knowledge and Sexual Allusion in the Works of Laurence Sterne." Diss. University of Alberta, Edmonton, Canada, 1976.

1096. Lowery, Robert G. "Music in the Autobiographies: An Index." *O'Casey Annual* 2 (1983): 27-69.

1097. Lucas, John, and William Myers. "*The Waste Land* Today." *Essays in Criticism* 19 (1969): 193-209.

1098. Luedtke, Luther. "J. D. Salinger and Robert Burns: *The Catcher in the Rye.*" *Modern Fiction Studies* 16 (1970): 198-201.

1099. Luetzeler, Paul Michael. "Nachweis der Vergil-Zitate aus *Der Tod des Vergil.*" *Materialien zu Hermann Brochs Der Tod des Vergil.* Ed. Paul Michael Luetzeler. Frankfurt, W. Germany: Suhrkamp, 1976. 306-363.

1100. Lund, Hans Peter. "Note sur *Toast funèbre* de Mallarmé et *La comédie de la mort* de Gautier." *Revue Romane* 18 (1983): 73-81.

1101. Luxton, Andrea Th. J. "Milton's Hermeneutics: An Intertextual Study of the Epistle to the Hebrews and *Paradise Lost.*" Diss. Catholic University of America, Washington, D. C., 1986.

1102. Lyles, Albert M. "A Note on Sidney's Use of Chaucer." *Notes and Queries* 198 (1953): 99-100.

1103. Mabbott, T. O. "Early Quotations and Allusions of Walt Whitman." *Notes and Queries* 150 (1926): 169-170.

1104. MacAdam, Alfred. "Euclides da Cunha y Mario Vargas
      Llosa: Meditaciones intertextuales." *Revista Ibero-
      americana* 50 (1984): 157-164.

1105. -----. "Mario Vargas Llosa and Euclides da Cunha: Some
      Problems of Intertextuality." *Proceedings of the Tenth
      Congress of the International Comparative Literature
      Association*. Ed. Anna Balakian. New York: Garland,
      1985. 3: 85-90.

1106. MacAleer, John J. "Biblical Analogy in the Leather-
      stocking Tales." *Nineteenth Century Fiction* 17 (1962-
      63): 217-235.

1107. McArthur, Murray G. "Language and History in Blake's
      Milton and Joyce's *Ulysses*." Diss. University of West-
      ern Ontario, London, Canada, 1985.

1108. McCall, Dan. "'The Self-Same Song That Found a Path':
      Keats and *The Great Gatsby*." *American Literature* 42
      (1971): 521-530.

1109. McDonald, Christie. "Dialogue and Intertextuality: The
      Posterity   of   Diderot's   *Neveu   de   Rameau*." *Pre-
      Text/Text/Context: Essays on Nineteenth-Century French
      Literature*. Ed. Robert L. Mitchell. Columbus, Ohio:
      Ohio State University Press, 1980. 257-266.

1110. MacDonald, D. L. "Eighteenth-Century Optimism as Meta-
      fiction in *Pale Fire*." *Nabokovian* 14 (1985): 26-32.

1111. McDonald, W. U. "Hazlitt's Use of *Don Quixote* Allu-
      sions." *Romance Notes* 2 (1960): 27-30.

1112. McEnerney, John. "The Poetic Quotations of Dio
      Chrysostom." Diss. University of Pennsylvania, 1950.

1113. McFarlane, I. D. "Les réseaux d'images dans l'oeuvre
      de Joachim Du Bellay." *Textes et intertextes: Etudes
      sur le XVIe siècle pour Alfred Glauser*. Eds. Floyd
      Gray and Marcel Tetel. Paris: Nizet, 1979. 123-146.

1114. Macfarlane, Keith H. "Baudelaire's Revaluation of the
      Classical Allusion." *Studies in Romanticism* 15 (1976):
      423-444.

1115. McGann, Jerome J. "Byron, Mobility and the Poetics of
      Historical Ventriloquism." *Romanticism Past and Pres-
      ent* 9 (1985): 67-82.

1116. -----. "The Idea of an Indeterminate Text: Blake's
      Bible of Hell and Dr. Alexander Geddes." *Studies in
      Romanticism* 25 (1986): 303-324.

1117. McGrady, Donald. "El redentor del Asterión de Borges."
      Revista Iberoamericana 52 (1986): 531-535.

1118. Machado, Arlindo. "Eisenstein: A Radical Dialogism."
      Dispositio 6 (1981): 119-130.

1119. McHenry, Robert. "'The Sons of Belial' in *Absalom and Achitophel*." *English Language Notes* 22.2 (1984): 27-30.

1120. Macht, David. "Biblical Allusions in Shakespeare's *The Tempest* in the Light of Hebrew Exegesis." *The Jewish Forum* (1955): 118-120.

1121. Mack, Maynard. "Wit and Poetry and Pope: Some Observations on His Imagery." *Pope and His Contemporaries: Essays Presented to George Sherburne*. Eds. James L. Clifford and Louis Landa. Oxford, UK: Clarendon, 1949. 20-40.

1122. Mack, Tom. "A Note on Biblical Analogues in Sarah Orne Jewett's 'Miss Tempy's Watchers.'" *American Literary Realism* 17 (1984): 225-227.

1123. McKeehan, Irene P. "Guillaume de Palerne: A Medieval 'Best Seller.'" *Publications of the Modern Language Association* 41 (1926): 785-809.

1124. McKenna, John J., and M. V. Peterson. "More Muddy Water: Wilson's Shakespeare in 'The Short Happy Life of Francis Macomber.'" *Studies in Short Fiction* 18 (1981): 82-85.

1125. Mackerness, E. D. "A Chaucer Allusion of 1598." *Notes and Queries* 194 (1949): 554.

1126. -----. "Two Chaucer Allusions of 1659." *Notes and Queries* 203 (1958): 197-198.

1127. McKinley, Mary B. *Words in a Corner: Studies in Montaigne's Latin Quotations*. Lexington, Ky.: French Forum Publishers, 1981.

1128. McKinney, Kitzie. "Diversions of Transformation in Pantagruel's Medlar Myth." *French Review* 59 (1986): 546-552.

1129. Macksey, Richard. "Reading Quotation: Last Words - The *Artes moriendi* and a Transtextual Genre." *Genre* 16 (1983): 493-516.

1130. McLauchlan, Juliet. "Allusion in *The Waste Land*." *Essays in Criticism* 19 (1969): 454-460.

1131. McMahon, Robert. "Narcissus and the Problem of Interpretation: Dante's Theory of Reading in the *Commedia*." Diss. University of California, Santa Cruz, 1986.

1132. McMullen, Kim. "Necessary Fictions: Fictional Reflexivity in Works by Vladimir Nabokov, Flann O'Brien, Gilbert Sorrentino, and John Barth." Diss. Duke University, Durham, N. C., 1986.

1133. McWhir, Anne. "The Wolf in the Fold: John Gay in *The Shepherd's Week* and *Trivia*." *Studies in English Liter-

ature 1500–1900 23 (1983): 413-423.

1134. Maddox, Donald, and Sara Sturm-Maddox. "Intertextual Discourse in the William Cycle." *Olifant: A Publication of the Société Rencesvals* 7 (1979): 131-148.

1135. Maeno, Shigeru. *The Sources of Melville's Quotations.* Tokyo, Japan: Kaibunsha, 1981.

1136. Magné, Bernard. "Boulevard écrit." *Revue Romane* 17.2 (1982): 75-88.

1137. Magoun F. P., Jr. "The Chaucer of Spenser and Milton." *Modern Philology* 25 (1927): 129-136.

1138. Magureanu, Anca. "Intertextualitate si comunicare." *Studii si Cercetari Lingvistice* 36 (1985): 10-17.

1139. Maher, Susan N. "Order in Paradise: An Examination of Nineteenth and Twentieth Century Robinsonades." Diss. University of Wisconsin, 1985.

1140. Maier, Hans Albert. "Zu drei Goethe-Anspielungen in Uebersetzungen von J. D. Gries." *Monatshefte* 53 (1961): 1-8.

1141. Malcuzynski, M. Pierette. "Critique de la (dé)raison polyphonique." *Etudes Françaises* 20 (1984): 45-56.

1142. Malkoff, Karl. "Allusion as Irony: Pound's Use of Dante in *Hugh Selwyn Mauberley*." *Minnesota Review* 7 (1967): 81-88.

1143. Mancing, Howard. "The Art of Literary Allusion in Juan Rulfo." *Modern Fiction Studies* 23 (1977): 242-244.

1144. Manea, Dana. "O delimitare a conceptului de 'intertextualitate.'" *Studii si Cercetari Lingvistice* 36 (1985): 18-24.

1145. Manning, Gilian. "Some Quotations From Rochester in Charles Blount's *Philostratus*." *Notes and Queries* 33 (1986): 38-40.

1146. Manning, Peter J. "Byron's *English Bards and Scotch Reviewers*: The Art of Allusion." *Keats-Shelley Memorial Bulletin* 31 (1970): 7-11.

1147. Manning, Walter J. "Athletic Allusions in *Finnegans Wake*." Diss. Temple University, Philadelphia, Pa., 1972.

1148. Mantel, Herman E. "Mythological Allusion in Horace." Diss. New York University, 1916.

1149. Manzalaoui, Mahoud. "George Wither and Chaucer's *Troilus and Criseyde*, I, 813 ff." *Notes and Queries* 209 (1964): 92.

1150. Marcus, Philip E. "Three Irish Allusions in *Ulysses.*" *James Joyce Quarterly* 6 (1969): 299-305.

1151. Marino, Lucia Maria Silvana. "Allusion, Allegory, and Iconology in the 'Decamerone Cornice': Boccaccio's Allegorical Case For a Humanistic Theory of Literature." Diss. University of California Los Angeles, Cal., 1977.

1152. Marks, Elaine. "Lesbian Intertextuality." *Homosexuality and French Literature: Cultural Contexts/Critical Texts.* Eds. George Stambolian and Elaine Marks. Ithaca, N.Y.: Cornell University Press, 1979. 353-377.

1153. Marsyla, Sandra Lee. "The Unheroic Hero: A Study of Mythical Echoes and Their Effect Upon the Technically Ineffectual Heroes of Charles Dickens' Fiction." Diss. Kent State University, Kent, Ohio, 1972.

1154. Martin, John S. "Copperfield and Caulfield: Dickens in the Rye." *Notes on Modern American Literature* 4 (1980): Item 29.

1155. Martin, Leslie Howard. "The Source and Originality of Dryden's Melantha." *Philological Quarterly* 52 (1973): 746-753.

1156. Martin, Loy D. "Browning: The Activation of Influence." *Victorian Newsletter* 53 (1978): 4-9.

1157. Martin, Robert Paul. "Paul's Use of Old Testament Quotations in Romans." Diss. Southwestern Baptist Theological Seminary, 1983.

1158. Martin, W. R., and Warren Ober. "Hemingway and James: 'A Canary for One' and 'Daisy Miller.'" *Studies in Short Fiction* 22 (1985): 469-471.

1159. Martinho, Fernando. "Da intertextualidade como procedimento sinedoquico em As imaginaçoes pecaminosas de Autran Dourado." *Cadernos de Literatura* 15 (1983): 19-25.

1160. Mason, Barbara. "Quotations from *Sylvie* and *Description de San Marco* in Michel Butor's *Intervalle.*" *Kentucky Romance Quarterly* 32 (1985): 65-76.

1161. Mass, Roslyn. "A Linking of Legends: *The Great Gatsby* and *Citizen Kane.*" *Literature and Film Quarterly* 2 (1974): 207-215.

1162. Masson, Pierre. "Production - reproduction: L'intertextualité comme principe créateur dans l'oeuvre d'André Gide." *Le plaisir d l'intertexte: Formes et fonctions de l'intertextualité (roman populaire, surréalisme, André Gide, nouveau roman).* Eds. R. Theis and H. T. Siepe. Bern, Switzerl.: Lang, 1986. 209-226.

1163. Mathieu-Castellani, Gisèle. "Intertextualité et allusion: Le régime allusif chez Ronsard." *Littérature* 55 (1984): 24-36.

1164. Mathis, Gilles. "L'implicité dans le discours poétique." *L'implicité dans la littérature et la pensée anglaises.* Ed. Nadia Rigaud. Aix-en-Provence, France: PU de Provence, 1984. 1-23.

1165. -----. "Mémoire et création dans *Le paradis perdu.*" *Mémoire et création dans le monde anglo-américain aux XVIIième et XVIIIième siècles.* Strasbourg, France: Université de Strasbourg II, 1984. 147-167.

1166. Mathur, Durgalal. "Baudelaire a-t-il connu Keats?" *Bulletin Baudelairien* 8 (1973): 27.

1167. Mattenklott, Gert. "Gewinnen, nicht siegen: Kommentare zu zwei Texten von Kafka." *Merkur* 39 (1985): 961-967.

1168. Matthews, John T. "Intertextuality and Originality: Hawthorne, Faulkner, and Updike." *Intertextuality in Faulkner.* Eds. Michel Gresset and Noel Polk. Jackson, Miss.: University Press of Mississippi, 1985. 144-157.

1169. -----. "The Word as Scandal: Updike's *A Month of Sundays.*" *Arizona Quarterly* 39 (1983): 351-380.

1170. Matthews, R. E. "Political Allusions in Voltaire's *Les lois de Minos.*" *Nottingham French Studies* 12 (1973): 11-21.

1171. Maurer, Iris Sue. "Allusions to the Epistle to the Romans in *Paradise Lost*: A Comparison of Their Contexts in the Light of Reformation Theology." Diss. Catholic Univ. of America, Washington, D. C., 1981.

1172. Maurer, Karl. "Die literarische Uebersetzung als Form fremdbestimmter Textkonstitution." *Poetica* 8 (1976): 233-257.

1173. Mautner, Franz. "Die griechischen Anklaenge in Thomas Manns *Tod in Venedig.*" *Monatshefte* 44 (1952): 20-26.

1174. Mavrodin, Irina. "Voyage à travers l'espace-temps poétique." *Cahiers Roumains d'Etudes Littéraires* 4 (1980): 77-82.

1175. Maxwell, J. C. "'The Ancient Mariner' and 'The Squire's Tale.'" *Notes and Queries* 211 (1966): 224.

1176. -----. "An Echo of Chaucer in *The Kingis Quair.*" *Notes and Queries* 209 (1964): 172.

1177. Mays, Jack Thurston. "The Use of Quixote Figures and Allusions to *Don Quixote* in the Novels of Tobias Smollett." Diss. Ball State Univ., Muncie, Ind., 1974.

1178. Means, James A. "Faulkner's *The Sound and the Fury.*" *Explicator* 42.4 (1984): 42-43.

1179. Meerhoff, Kees. "Intertextualité, metadiscours, histoire littéraire de Guez de Balzac à Boileau." *La littérature et ses doubles*. Ed. Leo H. Hoek. Groningen, Holland, 1985. 127-146.

1180. Meijer, Jan M. "A Case of Quoting." *Slavia* 45 (1976): 187-191.

1181. Mertin, Ray-Guede. *Ariano Suassuna: Romance d'a Pedra do Reino: Zur Verarbeitung von Volks- und Hochliteratur im Zitat*. Koelner Romanistische Arbeiten 54. Genève, Switzerland: Droz, 1979.

1182. Metschies, Michael. *Zitat und Zitierkunst in Montaignes Essais*. Koelner Romanistische Arbeiten 37. Genève, Switzerland: Droz, 1966.

1183. Mettler, Darlene D. "Sound and Sense: Musical Allusion and Imagery in the Novels of Iris Murdoch as an Aid to Theme and Characteriziation." Diss. Georgia State University, Atlanta, Ga., 1986.

1184. Metzidakis, Stamos. "Picking Up Narrative Pieces in a Surrealist Poem." *Orbis Litterarum* 40 (1983): 317-326.

1185. Meyer, Herman. *Das Zitat in der Erzaehlkunst: Zur Geschichte und Poetik des europaeischen Romans*. 1960; Stuttgart, W. Germany: Metzler, 1967. [Engl. trans. by Theodore and Yetta Ziolkowski: *The Poetics of Quotation in the European Novel*. Princeton, N. J.: Princeton University Press, 1968.]

1186. -----. "Das Zitat als Gespraechselement in Theodor Fontanes Romanen." *Wirkendes Wort* 10 (1960): 221-238.

1187. Meyer, Karl Alfons. "Zitate und Plagiate." *Revue Internationale d'Ethique Professionelle - International Journal of Professional Ethics* 1 (1955): 54-58.

1188. Meyer, Reinhart. *Hamburgische Dramaturgie und Emilia Galotti: Studie zu einer Methodik des wissenschaftlichen Zitierens*. Wiesbaden, W. Germ.: Humanitas, 1973.

1189. Meyers, Kate B. "Jane Austen's Use of Literary Allusion in the Sotherton Episode of *Mansfield Park*." *Papers on Language and Literature* 22 (1986): 96-99.

1190. Michel, Paul. "Heinrich Seuse als Diener des goettlichen Wortes: Persuasive Strategien bei der Verwendung von Bibelzitaten im Dienste seiner pastoralen Aufgaben." *Das "Einig Ein": Studien zu Theorie und Sprache der deutschen Mystik*. Eds. Alois M. Haas and Heinrich Stirnimann. Freiburg, Switzerland: Universitaetsverlag, 1980. 281-367.

1191. Mieder, Wolfgang. "'Die Axt im Haus erspart den Zimmermann' (*Wilhelm Tell*, III,1): Vom Schiller-Zitat zum parodierten Sprichwort." *Sprachspiegel* 40 (1984): 137-142.

1192. -----. "Einer fehlt beim Gruppenbild: 'Gefluegelter' Abschied von Heinrich Boell." *Sprachdienst* 29 (1985): 167-172.

1193. -----. *Investigations of Proverbs, Proverbial Expressions, Quotations and Clichés: A Bibliography of Explanatory Essays Which Appeared in Notes and Queries (1849-1983).* Bern, Switzerland: Lang, 1984.

1194. -----. "'Nach Zitaten draengt, am Zitate haengt doch alles.'" *Muttersprache* 92 (1982): 76-98.

1195. -----. "'Sein oder Nichtsein'- und doch kein Ende: Zum Weiterleben des Hamlet-Zitats in unserer Zeit." *Sprachdienst* 23 (1979): 81-85.

1196. -----. "Das Sprichwort als volkstuemliches Zitat bei Thomas Mann." *Notes and Queries* 3.7 (1972): 50-53.

1197. -----. *Sprichwort, Redensart, Zitat: Tradierte Formelsprache in der Moderne.* Bern, Switzerland: Lang, 1985.

1198. -----. "'Zitate sind des Buergers Zierde': Zum Weiterleben von Schiller-Zitaten." *Muttersprache* 95 (1984-85): 284-306.

1199. Mihaila, Ecaterina. "Text si intertextualitate." *Studii si Cercetari Lingvistice* 36 (1985): 34-42.

1200. Mihaila, Rodica. "Titlul, metatext si intertext." *Studii si Cercetari Lingvistice* 36 (1985): 73-81.

1201. Miletich, John S. "Biblical Allusions in Mallea's *Diesta en Novembre.*" *Romance Notes* 16 (1975): 731-733.

1202. Milic, Louis T. "Allusion: Using Other Men's Flowers." *Unicorn* (Cleveland State Univ.) 15 (1974): 1-2.

1203. Militz, Hans-Manfred. "Sprichwoertliches in der Dichtung." *Sprachpflege* 34.7 (1985): 97-99.

1204. Miller, Dan. "Blake's Allusions: *Jerusalem* 86." *New Orleans Review* 13 (1986): 22-33.

1205. Miller, Norbert. "Die Rolle des Zitierens." *Sprache im technischen Zeitalter* 1 (1961-62): 165-169.

1206. Miller, Owen. "Intertextual Identity." *Identity of the Literary Text.* Eds. Owen Miller and Jonathan Culler. Toronto, Canada: University of Toronto Press, 1985. 19-40.

1207. Milward, Peter. *Biblical Influence in Shakespeare's Great Tragedies.* Tokyo, Japan: Renaissance Institute, Sophia University, 1985.

1208. -----. "Notes on the Religious Dimension of *King Lear.*" *English Literature and Language* 23 (1986): 5-27.

1209. Miner, Earl. "Allusion." *Princeton Encyclopedia of Poetry and Poetics*. Enlarged Edition. Ed. Alex Preminger. Princeton, N. J.: Princeton University Press, 1974. 18.

1210. -----. "Chaucer in Dryden's *Fables*." *Studies in Criticism and Aesthetics 1660-1800: Essays in Honor of Samuel Holt Monk*. Eds. Howard Anderson and John S. Shea. Minneapolis, Minn.: University of Minnesota Press, 1967. 58-72.

1211. Mintz, Alan. "On the Tel Aviv School of Poetics." *Prooftexts* 4 (1984): 215-235.

1212. Mitchell, P. Beattie. "An Allusion to Chaucer in the Seventeenth Century." *Modern Language Notes* 51 (1936): 437.

1213. -----. "A Chaucer Allusion in a 1644 Pamphlet." *Modern Language Notes* 51 (1936): 435-437.

1214. Mitchell, St. Gérard. "An Analysis of Plutarch's Quotations From Euripides." Diss. University of Southern California, 1968.

1215. Mitescu, Adriana. "Pour une lecture 'anachronique' d'Al. Philippide." *International Journal of Rumanian Studies* 4.1 (1984-86): 51-53.

1216. Mjoeberg, Joeran. "Karlfeldt och Georg Stiernhielm." *Svensk Litteraturtidskrift* 39 (1976): 4-13.

1217. Moelk, Ulrich. "Gustave Flaubert: *Madame Bovary. Moeurs de province*." *Gelebte Literatur in der Literatur: Studien zu Erscheinungsformen und Geschichte eines literarischen Motivs*. Ed. Theodor Wolpers. Goettingen, W. Germany: Vandenhoeck & Ruprecht, 1986. 217-230.

1218. Mogren, Jan. "Guldsand i diktens vag." *Arsskrift foer Modersmalslararnas Foerening* (1967): 100-116.

1219. Moler, Kenneth L. *Jane Austen's Art of Allusion*. Lincoln, Nebr.: University of Nebraska Press, 1968.

1220. Mommsen, Momme. "Traditionsbezuege als Geheimschicht in Hoelderlin's Lyrik." *Neophilologus* 51 (1967): 32-42, 156-168.

1221. Mon, Franz, and F. Loeffelholz. *Texte ueber Texte*. Neuwied, Berlin, W. Germany: Luchterhand, 1970.

1222. Montenegro, Nivia. "El juego intertextual de *Si te dicen que caí*." *Revista Canadiense de Estudios Hispánicos* 5 (1981): 145-155.

1223. Montero, Oscar Julia. "The French Intertext of 'De donde son los cantates.'" Diss. University of North Carolina, Chapel Hill, N. C., 1978.

1224. Moore, Edward. *Studies in Dante. First Series: Scrip-ture and Classical Authors in Dante*. 1896; Oxford, UK: Clarendon, 1969.

1225. Moore, Michael D. "Linguistic Aggression and Literary Allusion (Verbal Dueling)." *Western Folklore* 38 (1979): 259-266.

1226. Morawski, Stefan. "The Basic Functions of Quotation." *Sign, Language, Culture*. Eds. A. J. Greimas and Roman Jakobson. The Hague, Holland: Mouton, 1970. 690-705.

1227. Morgan, Thais E. "Is There an Intertext in This Text?: Literary and Interdisciplinary Approaches to Inter-textuality." *American Journal of Semiotics* 3.4 (1985): 1-40.

1228. Morier, Henri. "Allusion." Henri Morier. *Dictionnaire de poétique et de rhétorique*. Paris: Presses Univer-sitaires de France, 1981. 86-96.

1229. Morlang, Werner. "'Auch ein grosser Mann': Zitieren als essayistisches Verfahren." *Bargfelder Bote* 49 (1980): 3-9.

1230. Morley-Mower, G. F., and Joan Powell. "Cabell's Mode of Quotation." *Kalki: Studies in James Branch Cabell* 8 (1984): 244-252.

1231. Morris, Inez Robinson. "Dark Imagery - Allusion and Metaphor - in Lawrence's Fiction." Diss. University of Mississippi, 1979.

1232. Morrison, Kristin. "Neglected Biblical Allusions in Beckett's Plays: 'Mother Pegg' Once More." *Samuel Beckett: Humanistic Perspectives*. Ed. Morris Beja. Columbus, Ohio: Ohio State University Press, 1983. 91-98.

1233. Morrissette, Bruce. *Intertextual Assemblage in Robbe-Grillet: From Topology to The Golden Triangle*. Fredericton, N. B.: York Press, 1979.

1234. -----. "Intertextual Assemblage as Fictional Gener-ator: *Topologie d'une cité fantôme*." *International Fiction Review* 5 (1978): 1-14.

1235. Morton, Gerald W. "An Interesting Benlowes Allusion." *Notes and Queries* 33 (1986): 392.

1236. Moss, Leonhard. "Biographical and Literary Allusion in *After the Fall*." *Educational Theatre Journal* 18 (1966): 34-40.

1237. Motiramani, Mahesh. *Die Funktion der literarischen Zi-tate und Anspielungen in Aleksander Solzenicyns Prosa (1962-1968)*. Frankfurt, W. Germany: Lang, 1983.

1238. Mountford, James Frederick. *Quotation from Classical*

Authors in Medieval Latin Glossaries. New York: Longman's, Green & Co., 1925.

1239. Mourão, José Augusto. "Da intratextualidade: Citação e comentário nas *Viagens* de A. Garret." *Revista de Comunicações & Linguagens* 3 (1986): 99-112.

1240. Mourot, Jean. "Remarques sur les *Poésies* d'Isidor Ducass." *Au bonheur des mots: Mélanges en l'honneur de Gérald Antoine.* Nancy, France: Presses Universitaires de Nancy, 1984. 375-382.

1241. Moutote, Daniel. "Intertextualité et journal dans l'oeuvre d'André Gide." *Le plaisir de l'intertexte: Formes et fonctions de l'intertextualité (roman populaire, surréalisme, André Gide, nouveau roman).* Eds. Raimund Theis and Hans T. Siepe. Bern, Switzerland: Lang, 1986. 137-184.

1242. Muecke, Frances. "'Semo stati poeti ancora noi': Classical Allusion and Imitation in Francesco Berni." *Altro Polo: The Classical Continuum in Italian Thought and Letters.* Sydney, Australia: University of Sydney, 1984. 75-92.

1243. Mueller, Joachim. "Das Zitat im epischen Gefuege: Die Goethe-Verse in Raabes Erzaehlung *Die Akten des Vogelsangs.*" Joachim Mueller. *Epik, Dramatik, Lyrik.* Halle, E. Germany: Niemeyer, 1974. 64-77.

1244. Mueller, Wolfgang G. "The Erudite Detective: A Tradition in English and American Detective Fiction." *Sprachkunst* 17 (1986): 245-262.

1245. Mulhauser, Ruth. "The Historic Allusion Poems in the *Délie* of Maurice Scève." *Symposium* 16 (1962): 136-143.

1246. Muller, Marcel. "Proust et Flaubert: Une dimension intertextuelle de *A la recherche du temps perdu.*" *Proust et le texte producteur.* Eds. John D. Erickson and Irène Pagès. Guelph, Ont.: University of Guelph, 1980. 57-70.

1247. Munns, Jessica. "Does Otway Praise Rochester in *The Poet's Complaint*?" *Notes and Queries* 33 (1986): 40-41.

1248. Murphy, Clare M. "The Turkish Threat and Thomas More's *Utopia.*" *Acta Conventus Neo-Latini Bononiensis.* Ed. Richard J. Schoeck. Binghamton, N.Y.: Medieval & Renaissance Texts and Studies, 1985. 158-171.

1249. Murphy, Denis M. "*The Sound and the Fury* and Dante's *Inferno*: Fire and Ice." *Markham Review* 4 (1974): 71-78.

1250. Murphy, Mable Gant. "Nature Allusions in the Works of Clement of Alexandria." Diss. Catholic University of America, Washington, D. C., 1942.

1251. Murphy, Steve. "Bribes bonapartistes." *Parade Sauvage* 3 (1986): 50-60.

1252. Murtuza, Athar. "An Arabian Source for Poe's 'The Pit and the Pendulum.'" *Poe Studies* 5 (1972): 52.

1253. Mustard, W. P. "E. K.'s Classical Allusions." *Modern Language Notes* 34 (1919): 193-203.

1254. Myers, William. "Allusion in *The Waste Land*: A Reply." *Essays in Criticism* 20 (1970): 120-122.

1255. Nadel, Alan Mitchell. "Invisible Criticism: A Study in Allusion." Diss. Rutgers University, New Brunswick, N.J., 1981.

1256. -----. "Translating the Past: Literary Allusions as Covert Criticism." *Georgia Review* 36 (1982): 639-651.

1257. Naenny, Max. "The Oral Roots of Ezra Pound's Methods of Quotation and Abbreviation." *Paideuma* 8 (1979): 381-387.

1258. Nash, Stanley. "The Codes of Shofman: Allusions to Texts and Persons." *Modern Hebrew Literature* 9.1-2 (1983): 58-69.

1259. Nathan, Jacques. *Citations, références et allusions de Marcel Proust dans A la recherche du temps perdu*. Paris: Nizet, 1969.

1260. Neaman, Judith S. "Allusion, Image, and Associative Pattern: The Answers in Mansfield's 'Bliss.'" *Twentieth Century Literature* 32 (1986): 242-254.

1261. Nedergaard, Leif. "Omkring *Niels Lyhne* og udtrykket 'at do staende.'" *Danske Studier* 69 (1974): 152-156.

1262. Neel, Jasper Phillip. "'A Kind of Mungral Breed': The Allusive Method in Butler's *Hudibras*." Diss. University of Tennessee, 1975.

1263. Negus, Kenneth. "The Allusions to Schiller's *Der Geisterseher* in E.T.A. Hoffmann's *Das Majorat*: Meaning and Background." *German Quarterly* 32 (1959): 341-355.

1264. Nelles, William. "Saving the State in Lowell's 'For the Union Dead.'" *American Literature* 55 (1983): 639-642.

1265. Nellis, Marilyn K. "Peele's *Edward I*." *Explicator* 44.2 (1986): 5-8.

1266. Nelson, Carl. "The Ironic Allusive Texture of *Lord Jim*: Coleridge, Crane, Milton, and Melville." *Conradiana* 4 (1972): 47-59.

1267. Nelson, Lowrie. "Baudelaire and Virgil: A Reading of *Le cygne*." *Comparative Literature* 13 (1961): 332-345.

1268. Neptune, Patricia Mae. "Raymond Queneau's *Le chien-dent*: Novelistic Parody as *ré-écriture carnevalesque*." Diss. University of California, Berkeley, Cal., 1985.

1269. Net, Mariana. "Tensiunea textului si intertextualita-tea." *Studii si Cercetari Lingvistice* 36 (1985): 43-51.

1270. -----. "Towards a Pragmatics of Poetic Intertextual-ity." *Revue Roumaine de Linguistique* 28 (1983): 159-162.

1271. Neumann, Peter Horst. "Das Eigene und das Fremde: Ueber die Wuenschbarkeit einer Theorie des Zitierens." *Akzente* 27 (1980): 292-305.

1272. Neuschaefer, Hans-Joerg. "Intertextualité et genre littéraire: Le roman de moeurs dans le feuilleton de 1884." *Le plaisir de l'intertexte: Formes et fonctions de l'intertextualité (roman populaire, surréalisme, André Gide, nouveau roman)*. Eds. Raimund Theis and Hans T. Siepe. Bern, Switzerland: Lang, 1986. 46-63.

1273. New, Melvyn. "'At the backside of the door of purga-tory': A Note on Annotating *Tristram Shandy*." *Laurence Sterne. Riddles and Mysteries*. Ed. Valerie G. Myer. London: Vision, 1984. 15-23.

1274. Newlyn, Lucy. *Coleridge, Wordsworth, and the Language of Allusion*. Oxford, UK: Clarendon Press, 1986.

1275. -----. "'In City Pent': Echo and Allusion in Wordsworth, Coleridge, and Lamb, 1797-1801." *Review of English Studies* 32 (1981): 408-428.

1276. -----. "Parodic Allusion: Coleridge and the 'Nehemiah Higginbottom' Sonnets, 1797." *Charles Lamb Bulletin* 56 (1986): 255-259.

1277. Nicolaisen, W. I. H. "Names as Intertextual Device." *Onomastica Canadiana* 68 (1986): 58-66.

1278. Nihom, M. "Notes of the Origin of Some Quotations in the Sekoddesatika of Nadapada." *Indo-Iranian Journal* 27 (1984): 17-26.

1279. Noakes, Susan. "Intertextuality and Dante's Anti-thetical Hypersign." *Semiotics 1984: Proceedings of the Ninth Annual Meeting of the Semiotic Society of America*. Ed. John Deely. Lanham, Md. : University Press of America, 1985. 95-103.

1280. Nordberg, Arne. "Petrus Laestadius, citaternas als-kare." *Svensk Litteraturtidskrift* 39 (1976): 20-36.

1281. Noreiko, Stephen F. "*La vie mode d'emploi*: Mode d'emploi." *Orbis Litterarum* 39 (1984): 148-159.

1282. Norris, Christine L. "Literary Allusion in the Tales

of Isak Dinesen." Diss. University of California, San Diego, Cal., 1982.

1283. North, Helen. "The Use of Poetry in the Training of the Ancient Orator." *Traditio* 8 (1952): 1-33.

1284. Noske, Frits R. "Musical Quotation as a Dramatic Device: The Fourth Act of *Le nozze di Figaro.*" *Music Quarterly* 54 (1968): 185-198.

1285. Nouvet, Claire. "Pour une économie de la dé-limitation: *La Prison amoureuse* de Jean Froissart." *Neophilologus* 70 (1986): 341-356.

1286. Novak, M. "Zitatuebersetzungen?" *Lebende Sprachen* 20 (1975): 65-66.

1287. Novak, Marian Harrison. "Saints' Lives and Legends and Their Influence on Early English and Continental Literature." Diss. Washington State University, 1985.

1288. Noyer-Weidner, Alfred. "Zu Tassos 'binnenpoetischer' Auseinandersetzung mit Bembo." *Italien und die Romania in Humanismus und Renaissance.* Eds. Klaus W. Hempfer and Enrico Straub. Wiesbaden, W. Germany: Steiner, 1983. 177-196.

1289. Noyes, Robert Gale. *The Neglected Muse: Restoration and Eighteenth Century Tragedy in the Novel (1740-1780).* Providence, R.I.: Brown University Press, 1958.

1290. -----. *The Thespian Mirror: Shakespeare in the Eighteenth Century Novel.* 1953; Westport, Conn.: Greenwood, 1974.

1291. Nunes, Clare H. "Classical Allusion in the *Rambler* Essays of Samuel Johnson." Diss. Princeton University, Princeton, N. J., 1979.

1292. Nykrog, Per. "In the Ruins of the Past: Reading Samuel Beckett Intertextually." *Comparative Literature* 36 (1984): 289-311.

1293. Nyquist, Mary. "The Father's Word/Satan's Wrath." *Publications of the Modern Language Association* 100 (1985): 187-202.

1294. O'Connor, John J. "The Astrological Background of the *Miller's Tale.*" *Speculum* 31 (1956): 120-125.

1295. O'Connor, Mary E. "Parodie et histoire littéraire: Lecture de 'The Love Song of J. Alfred Prufrock' de T. S. Eliot." *Etudes Littéraires* 19 (1986): 125-138.

1296. O'Donnell, Patrick. "The Disappearing Text: Philip Roth's *The Ghost Writer.*" *Contemporary Literature* 24 (1983): 365-378.

1297. Ogden, James. "Allusions to Shakespeare in *Mary Bar-*

ton." *Notes and Queries* 31 (1984): 488-489.

1298. Ogunsanwo, Olatubosun. "George Meredith and F. Scott Fitzgerald: Literary Affinities, Narrative Indirectness and Realism." *Neohelicon* 8 (1981): 191-216.

1299. Ohashi, Kenzaburo. "'Motion' and Intertextuality in Faulkner's Fiction." *Intertextuality in Faulkner.* Eds. Michel Gresset and Noel Polk. Jackson, Miss.: University Press of Mississippi, 1985. 158-167.

1300. O'Keefe, Timothy. "Ironic Allusion in the Poetry of Wilfred Owen." *Ariel: A Review of International English Literature* 3 (1972): 72-81.

1301. O'Leary, Daniel Edwin. "Harmony and Ritualistic Allusion in the Tornabuoni Chapel in Santa Maria Novella." Diss. University of Michigan, Ann Arbor, Mich., 1983.

1302. Olive, W. "A Chaucer Allusion in Jonson's *Bartholomew Fair.*" *Modern Language Quarterly* 13 (1952): 21-22.

1303. Oliver, Andrew. "Introduction." *Texte* 2 (1983): 5-11.

1304. -----. "Michel, Job, Pierre, Paul: Intertextualité de la lecture dans *L'immoraliste* de Gide." *Archives des Lettres Modernes* 183 (1979): 3-68.

1305. Oliver, Anna. "Chaucer Allusions in Eighteenth Century Minor Poetry." *Notes and Queries* 174 (1938): 97-98.

1306. Oliver, H. J. "Literary Allusions in Jacobean Drama." *Renaissance Studies in Honor of Carroll Camden.* Ed. J. A. Ward. Houston, Tex.: Rice University, 1974. 131-140.

1307. Olmert, Michael. "Troilus in *Piers Plowman*: A Contemporary View of Chaucer's *Troilus and Crisyede.*" *Chaucer Newsletter* 2 (1980): 13-14.

1308. Olmstead, William. "The Palimpsest of Memory: Recollection and Intratextuality in Baudelaire's 'Spleen' II." *Romanic Review* 77 (1986): 359-367.

1309. Olson, Paul A. "Poetic Justice in the *Miller's Tale.*" *Modern Language Quarterly* 24 (1963): 227-236.

1310. Oppenheimer, Fred Eugene. "Literary Allusion in the Novels of Theodor Fontane." Diss. University of Wisconsin, 1961.

1311. Oras, Ants. "Surrey's Technique of Phonetic Echoes: A Method and Its Background." *Journal of English and Germanic Philology* 50 (1951): 289-308.

1312. Orkin, Martin R. "A Cluster of Proverb Allusions in *Julius Caesar.*" *Notes and Queries* 31 (1984): 195-196.

1313. Orr, Leonard. "Intertextuality and the Cultural Text

in Recent Semiotics." *College English* 48 (1986): 811-823.

1314. O'Sullivan, Maurice J. "The Mask of Allusion in Robert Hayden's 'The Diver.'" *College Language Association Journal* 17 (1973): 85-92.

1315. Ott, Norbert H. "Komplikation und Zitat in Weltchronik und Kathedralikonographie." *Geschichtsbewusstsein in der deutschen Literatur des Mittelalters.* Ed. Christoph Gerhardt. Tuebingen, W. Germany: Niemeyer, 1985. 119-135.

1316. Otto, Eberhard. "Wert und Fragwuerdigkeit des Zitats." *Kulturwarte* 4 (1958-59): 254-257.

1317. Otto, Regine. "Ein Herder-Zitat im Jahre 1938: Zur Herder-Rezeption Thomas Manns." *Herder-Kolloquium 1978: Referate und Diskussionsbeitraege.* Ed. Walter Dietze. Weimar, E. Germany: Boehlau, 1980. 265-271.

1318. Overesch, Lynne E. "The Neo-Baroque: Trends in the Style and Structure of the Contemporary Spanish Novel." Diss. University of Kentucky, 1981.

1319. Owen, John. "A Euphemistic Allusion to the *Reeve's Tale.*" *Modern Language Notes* 69 (1954): 43-44.

1320. Owen, W. J. B. "Literary Echoes in *The Prelude.*" *Wordsworth Circle* 3 (1972): 3-16.

1321. Ower, John. "A Thematic Reference to *The Rubaiyat of Omar Khayyam* in *The Great Gatsby.*" *Fitzgerald/ Hemingway Annual* (1975): 103-105.

1322. Pabst, Walter. "*Fuerst Galeotto* oder die Macht der erfundenen Werke." *Deutsche Beitraege* 3 (1949): 168-181.

1323. -----. "'Victimes du livre': Versuch über eine literarische Konstante." *Filologica y didactica hispanica: Homenaje al Profesor Hans-Karl Schneider.* Ed. José M. Navarro. Hamburg, W. Germany: Buske, 1975. 497-525.

1324. Pache, Walter. "Blake's seltsame Poesien: Bildzitat und Bildwirkung in Thomas Manns *Doktor Faustus.*" *Arcadia* 8 (1973): 138-155.

1325. Pacheco, Carlos. "La intertextualidad y el compilador: Nuevas claves para una lectura de la polifonía en *Yo el supremo.*" *Revista de Crítica Literaria Latino-Americana* 10 (1984): 47-72.

1326. Packman, David. "The Cryptogrammic Paper Chase." *Intertextuality: New Perspectives in Criticism.* Eds. Jeanine P. Plottel and Hanna Charney. New York Literary Forum 2. New York: Literary Forum, 1978. 15-22.

1327. Padhi, Shanti. "Hamlet's Satirical Rogue." *Hamlet Studies* 6.1-2 (1984): 68-71.

1328. Pafford, J. H. P. "Pigrogromitus: *Twelfth Night* II, iii, 23." *Notes and Queries* 33 (1986): 358.

1329. Paganini, Maria. "Intertextualité et stratégie du désir: La mélancolique villégiature de Mme de Breyves (*Les plaisirs et les jours*)." *Proust Research Association Newsletter* 19 (Spring 1978): 25-29.

1330. -----. "Intertextuality and the Strategy of Desire: Proust's 'Mélancolique villegiature de Mme de Breyves.'" *Yale French Studies* 57 (1979): 136-163.

1331. Palgen, Rudolf. "Due particolarità dello stile epico di Dante: La nomenclatura pseudoclassica e le metafore allusive." *Convivium* 31 (1963): 10-18.

1332. Palm, Anders. *Kristet, indiskt och antikt i Hjalmar Gullberg diktning.* Stockholm, Sweden: Norstedt & Soeners, 1976.

1333. Panzer, Friedrich. "Vom mittelalterlichen Zitieren." *Sitzungsberichte der Heidelberger Akademie der Wissenschaften, Philosophisch-Historische Klasse* (1950): 5-43.

1334. Parfitt, George. "Some Notes on the Classical Borrowings in *Volpone*." *English Studies* 55 (1974): 127-132.

1335. Parker, John. "Intertext, Interpretant, and Ideology in Luiz Vilela's *Entre amigos*." *Portuguese Studies* 2 (1986): 185-195.

1336. Parsons, Terence. "What Do Quotation Marks Name? Frege's Theories of Quotations and *That*-Clauses." *Philosophical Studies* 42 (1982): 315-328.

1337. Partee, Barbara Hall. "The Syntax and Semantics of Quotation." *A Festschrift for Morris Halle*. Eds. Paul Kiparsky and Stephen Anderson. New York: Holt, Rinehart, Winston, 1973. 410-418.

1338. Pasco, Allan H. "Marcel, Albertine, and Balbec in Proust's Allusive Complex." *Romanic Review* 62 (1971): 113-126.

1339. -----. "A Study of Allusion: Barbey's Stendhal in *Le rideau cramoisi*." *Publications of the Modern Language Association* 88 (1973): 461-471.

1340. Pasquali, Giorgio. "Arte allusiva." Giorgio Pasquali. *Pagine stavaganti*. Firenze, Italy: Sansoni, 1968. 2: 275-282.

1341. Passmann, Dirk, "An Allusion to Mandeville in *Gulliver's Travels*: The 'Air of Truth' Polluted." *Notes and Queries* 32 (1985): 205-207.

1342. Paterson, Alan K. G. "*Sutileza del pensar* in a Quevedo
       Sonnet." *Modern Language Notes* 81 (1966): 131-142.

1343. Patten, Robert L. "Pinocchio Through the Looking-
       Glass: Jerome Charyn's Portrait of the Artist as a
       Mytholept." *Novel* 17 (1983): 67-76.

1344. Patterson, J. Daniel. "Taylor's 'Preparatory Medi-
       tation' 2.1." *Explicator* 43.1 (1984): 22-23.

1345. Patterson, Mark. "Thoreau Quotations." *American Notes
       and Queries* 19 (1981): 150-151.

1346. Paul, Fritz. "Kierkegaards Verfuehrer, Don Juan und
       Faust." *Gelebte Literatur in der Literatur: Studien zu
       Erscheinungsformen und Geschichte eines literarischen
       Motivs.* Ed. Theodor Wolpers. Goettingen, W. Germany:
       Vandenhoeck & Ruprecht, 1986. 198-216.

1347. Peacock, Alan J. "Ben Jonson: Superannuated Lover."
       Etudes Anglaises: Grande-Bretagne, Etats-Unis 39
       (1986): 308-316.

1348. Pearce, Howard D. "Witchcraft Imagery and Allusion in
       James's *Bostonians.*" *Studies in the Novel* 6 (1974):
       236-247.

1349. Pearcy, Lee T. "A Case of Allusion: Stanza 18 of
       Spenser's 'Epithalamion' and Catullus 5." *Classical
       and Modern Literature* 1 (1981): 243-254.

1350. Pearcy, Roy J. "Chaucer, Deschamps, and *Le roman de
       Brut.*" *Arts: Journal of the Sidney University Arts
       Association* 12 (1984): 35-59.

1351. Percival-Kaye, George. "Chaucer in Fiction." *Notes and
       Queries* 180 (1941): 233.

1352. Perlina, Nina. "The Role and Function of Quotation in
       F. M. Dostoevsky's Works." *Forum* 3 (1980): 33-47.

1353. -----. *Varieties of Poetic Utterances: Quotation in
       The Brothers Karamasov.* Lanham, Md.: University Press
       of America, 1985. [Diss. Brown University, 1978.]

1354. Perri, Carmela. "Allusion Studies: An International
       Annotated Bibliography, 1921-1977." *Style* 13 (1979):
       178-225.

1355. -----. "Knowing and Playing: The Literary Text and the
       Trope Allusion." *American Imago* 41 (1984): 117-128.

1356. -----. "On Alluding." *Poetics* 7 (1978): 289-307.

1357. -----. "The Poetics of Dew: A Study of Milton's
       Sonnets." Diss. City University of New York, 1977.

1358. Perrone-Moises, Leyla. "L'intertextualité critique."
       Poétique 27 (1976): 372-384.

1359. Perry, Marvin B. Jr. "Keats and the Poets, 1815-1848:
Studies in His Early Vogue as Reflected in the Verse
Tributes and Allusions of His Contemporaries." Diss.
Harvard University, Cambridge, Mass., 1950.

1360. Peterfreund, Stuart. "Between Desire and Nostalgia:
Intertextuality in Shelley's *Alastor* and Two Shorter
Poems from the *Alastor* Volume." *Romanticism Past and
Present* 9 (1985): 47-66.

1361. Pétillon, Corentin L. *Allusions littéraires*. 2 Vol.
Chang-Hai: Mission Catholique, 1895-1898. [Kraus Re-
print, 1975.]

1362. Petrey, Sandy. "Must History Be Lost in Translation?"
Translation Perspectives: Selected Papers, 1982-1983.
Ed. Marilyn Rose. Binghamton, N.Y., 1984. 86-94.

1363. Pfeffer, J. Alan. "Das biblische Zitat im Volksmund
der Germanen und Romanen." *Teilnahme und Spiegelung:
Festschrift fuer Horst Ruediger*. Eds. Beda Allemann,
Erwin Koppen, and Dieter Gutzen. Berlin, W. Germany:
de Gruyter, 1975. 99-111.

1364. Pfister, Manfred. "Imitation und Intertextualitaet bei
Robert Lowell." *Intertextualitaet: Formen, Funktionen,
anglistische Fallstudien*. Eds. U. Broich and M.
Pfister. Tuebingen, W. Germ.: Niemeyer, 1985. 311-322.

1365. -----. "Konzepte der Intertextualitaet." *Intertextualitaet: Formen, Funktionen, anglistische Fallstudien*. Eds. U. Broich and M. Pfister. Tuebingen, W.
Germany: Niemeyer, 1985. 1-30.

1366. -----. "Zur Systemreferenz." *Intertextualitaet:
Formen, Funktionen, anglistische Fallstudien*. Eds. U.
Broich and M. Pfister. Tuebingen, W. Germany: Nie-
meyer, 1985. 52-58.

1367. Pheifer, J. D. "Errour in Echidna in *The Faerie
Queene*: A Study in Literary Tradition." *Literature and
Learning in Medieval and Renaissance England: Essays
Presented to Fitzroy Pyle*. Ed. John Scattergood.
Dublin, Ireland: Irish Academy Press, 1984. 127-174.

1368. Pick, Robert. "The Use and Abuse of Quotation." *German
Life and Letters* 16 (1962-63): 274-277.

1369. Pierce, Marvin. "Another Chaucer Allusion: 1672."
Notes and Queries 202 (1957): 2-3.

1370. Pilecki, Gerard A. "Hopkins' 'Spring and Fall' and
Modes of Knowing." *Victorian Poetry* 24 (1986): 88-91.

1371. Piquet, François. "Blake, l'intertexte de *Jerusalem* et
les tribulations d'Albion." *Romantisme* 49 (1985): 35-
45.

1372. Pitavy, François. "Forgetting Jerusalem: An Ironical

Chart for *The Wild Palms.*" *Intertextuality in Faulkner.* Eds. Michel Gresset and Noel Polk. Jackson,
Miss.: University Press of Mississippi, 1985. 114-127.

1373. Pitcher, Edward W. R. "'To Die Laughing': Poe's Allusion to Sir Thomas More in 'The Assignation.'"
Studies in Short Fiction 23 (1986): 197-200.

1374. Piwinski, David J. "Yeats's 'Her Courtesy.'" *Explicator* 42.1 (1983): 32-33.

1375. Pizer, Donald. "Stephen Crane's 'The Monster' and
Tolstoy's *What To Do*: A Neglected Allusion." *Studies
in Short Fiction* 20 (1983): 127-129.

1376. Pizzorusso, Arnaldo. "L'allusion biographique dans une
lettre d'Obermann." *Cahiers de l'Association Internationale des Etudes Françaises* 19 (1967): 129-142.

1377. *Le plaisir de l'intertexte: Formes et fonctions de
l'intertextualité (roman populaire, surréalisme, André
Gide, nouveau roman).* Eds. Raimund Theis and Hans T.
Siepe. Bern, Switzerland: Lang, 1986.

1378. Plett, Bettina. *Die Kunst der Allusion: Formen literarischer Anspielungen in den Romanen Theodor Fontanes.* Koelner Germanistische Studien 23. Koeln, W. Germany: Boehlau, 1986.

1379. Plett, Heinrich F. "Sprachliche Konstituenten einer
intertextuellen Poetik." *Intertextualitaet: Formen,
Funktionen, anglistische Fallstudien.* Eds. U. Broich
and M. Pfister. Tuebingen, W. Germany: Niemeyer, 1985.
78-98.

1380. Plottel, Jeanine P. "Introduction." *Intertextuality:
New Perspectives in Criticism.* Eds. Jeanine P. Plottel
and Hanna Charney. New York Literary Forum 2. New
York: Literary Forum, 1978. XI-XX.

1381. -----. "Semioschizocomicobuttonanalysis." *Intertextuality: New Perspectives in Criticism.* Eds.
Jeanine P. Plottel and Hanna Charney. New York Literary Forum 2. New York: Literary Forum, 1978. 281-287.

1382. Poeckl, Wolfgang. "Zitiertes Mittelalter in der deut-
schen Gegenwartsliteratur." *Mittelalter-Rezeption: Ein
Symposium.* Ed. Peter Wapnewski. Stuttgart, W. Germany:
Metzler, 1986. 531-546.

1383. -----. "Zur Uebersetzung von Zitiertem (Mit Beispielen
von Peter Handke)." *Textlinguistik und Semantik: Akten
der vierten Arbeitstagung oesterreichischer Linguisten
1975.* Innsbruck, Austria, 1976. 191-197.

1384. *Poems in Their Place: The Intertextuality and Order of
Poetic Collections.* Ed. Neil Fraistat. Chapel Hill,
N.C.: University of North Carolina Press, 1986.

1385. Poirion, Daniel. "Ecriture et ré-écriture au Moyen Age." *Littérature* 41 (1981): 109-118.

1386. Polk, Noel. "The Space Between *Sanctuary.*" *Intertextuality in Faulkner.* Eds. Michel Gresset and Noel Polk. Jackson, Miss.: University Press of Mississippi, 1985. 16-35.

1387. Pollak, Vivian R. "Emily Dickinson's Literary Allusions." *Essays in Literature* 1 (1974): 54-68.

1388. Pollin, Burton R. *Dictionary of Names and Titles in Poe's Collected Works.* New York: Da Capo, 1968.

1389. -----. "Edgar Allan Poe and John G. Chapman: Their Treatment of the Dismal Swamp and the Wissahickon." *Studies in the American Renaissance* (1983): 245-274.

1390. -----. "Poe's Mystification: Its Source in Fay's *Norman Leslie.*" *Mississippi Quarterly* 25 (1972): 111-130.

1391. -----. "Poe's 'The Conqueror Worm.'" *Explicator* 40.3 (1982): 25-28.

1392. -----. "Shakespeare in the Works of Edgar Allan Poe." *Studies in the American Renaissance* (1985): 157-186.

1393. Poole, Adrian. "Hidden Affinities in *Daniel Deronda.*" *Essays in Criticism* 33 (1983): 294-311.

1394. Pop-Cornis, Marcel. "Lumea ca spatiu intertextual sau despre cronotopul romanului modern." *Viata Romaneasca* 34 (1981): 120-126.

1395. Porter, William M. "Dancing Around Milton's Allusions." *Approaches to Teaching Milton's Paradise Lost.* Ed. Galbraith Crump. New York: Modern Language Association of America, 1986. 165-175.

1396. -----. "Milton and Horace: The Post-Bellum Muse." *Comparative Literature* 35 (1983): 351-361.

1397. Portz, John. "Allusion and Structure in Hemingway's 'A Natural History of the Dead.'" *Tennessee Studies in Literature* 10 (1965): 27-41.

1398. Pouilliart, Raymond. "Jeux d'intertextualité chez Hugo: La 'Preface' des *Burgraves.*" *Les Lettres Romanes* 35 (1981): 343-351.

1399. Pratt, Robert A. "Two Chaucer Allusions: 1819 and 1899." *Modern Language Notes* 63 (1948): 55-56.

1400. Prawer, Siegbert. "'Bless Thee, Bottom! Bless Thee! Thou Art Translated': Typographical Parallelism, Word-Play, and Literary Allusion in Arno Schmidt's *Zettels Traum.*" *Essays in German and Dutch Literature.* Ed. Scott W. D. Robson. Publications of the Institute of

Germanic Studies 15. London: University of London, 1973. 156-191.

1401. Preisendanz, Wolfgang. "Die Muse Belesenheit: Trans-textualitaet in Wielands 'Neuem Amadis.'" *Modern Language Notes* 99 (1984): 539-553.

1402. Prendergast, Christopher. "Flaubert: Quotation, Stupidity and the Cretan Liar Paradox." *French Studies* 35 (1981): 261-277.

1403. Prescott, Joseph. "Local Allusions in Joyce's *Ulysses.*" *Publications of the Modern Language Association* 68 (1953): 1223-1228.

1404. Preston, Thomas K. "Homeric Allusion in *A Journey to the Western Islands of Scotland.*" *Eighteenth-Century Studies* 5 (1972): 545-558.

1405. Preussner, Arnold W. "Chapman's Anti-Festive Comedy: Generic Subversion and Classical Allusion in *The Widow's Tears.*" *Iowa State Journal of Research* 59 (1985): 263-272.

1406. Price, Ruby V. "Christian Allusions in the Novels of Thomas Pynchon." Diss. Rice University, Houston, Tex., 1979.

1407. Prigozy, Ruth. "'Poor Butterfly': F. Scott Fitzgerald and Popular Music." *Prospects* 2 (1976): 41-67.

1408. Primmer, Adolf. "Das Dichterzitat in Sen. dial. 10, 2, 2." *Wiener Studien* 19 (1985): 151-157.

1409. Proffitt, Edward. "Allusion in Adrienne Rich's 'A Valediction Forbidding Mourning.'" *Concerning Poetry* 15 (1982): 21-24.

1410. Promies, Wolfgang. "Das Buch als Erzieher: Literarische Zitate in Buechern fuer Kinder." *Helft den Buechern, helft den Kindern.* Ed. Peter Haertling. Muenchen, W. Germany: Hanser, 1985. 63-71.

1411. Pruitt, Pamela Ann P. "The Biblical Allusions in the Theatre of Marguerite de Navarre." Diss. University of Georgia, Athens, Ga., 1984.

1412. Puccini, Dario. "Borges: Dos aspectos de su escritura." *Insula* 469 (1985): 5-6.

1413. Pugh, Mildred Elizabeth. "Homer 'Shadow'd and Heighten'd Carefully': A Study of Political Allusion in Alexander Pope's Translation of the *Iliad.*" Diss. Vanderbilt University, Nashville, Tenn., 1980.

1414. Purdie, Edna. "Herder's Quotations from Shakespeare." Edna Purdie. *Studies in German Literature of the Eighteenth Century: Some Aspects of Literary Affiliation.* London: Athlone, 1965. 1-30.

1415. Purdy, Dwight H. *Joseph Conrad's Bible*. Norman, Okla.: University of Oklahoma Press, 1984.

1416. Quirk, Tom. "Fitzgerald and Cather: *The Great Gatsby*." *American Literature* 54 (1982): 576-591.

1417. Rabinowitz, Peter J. "'What's Hecuba to Us?' The Audience's Experience of Literary Borrowing." *The Reader in the Text: Essays on Audience and Interpretation*. Eds. Susan R. Suleiman and Inge Crosman. Princeton, N.J.: Princeton University Press, 1980. 241-263.

1418. Raghavan, E., and B. Wood. "Thoreau's Hindu Quotations in *A Week*." *American Literature* 51 (1979): 94-98.

1419. Rahman, Mojibur. *Allusions and References in Persian Poetry*. Calcutta, India: Anwar Book Department, 1974.

1420. Raizis, M. Byron. "Nikos Kazantzakis and Chaucer." *Comparative Literature Studies* 6 (1969): 141-147.

1421. Rand, Nicholas. "Texte passeur: Dialogies intra-textuelles dans *La légende de Saint Julien L'Hospitalier* de Flaubert." *Romanic Review* 77 (1986): 42-55.

1422. Randall, Dale B. J. "A 1613 Chaucer Allusion." *Philological Quarterly* 39 (1960): 131-132.

1423. Randel, Mary Gaylord. "Reading the Pastoral Palimpsest: *La Galatea* in Góngora's *Soledad primera*." *Symposium* 36 (1982): 71-91.

1424. Rasmussen, Egil. "Det intertekstuelle menneske eller Den solidariske tekst. Noen bemerkninger om Svend Age Madsens poetikk." *Vinduet* 40 (1986): 24-28.

1425. Rau, Wilhelm. *Die vedischen Zitate im Vyakarana-Mahabhasya*. Abhandlungen der geistes- und sozialwissenschaftlichen Klasse/Akademie der Wissenschaften und Literatur 1985/4. Stuttgart, W. Germany: Steiner-Wiesbaden, 1985.

1426. Rauch, Beda M. "Philologie und philologische Anspielung im Werk Wilhelm Raabes." Diss. Muenchen, W. Germany, 1971.

1427. Ray, Robert Henry. "George Herbert in the Seventeenth Century: Allusions to Him, Collected and Annotated." Diss. University of Texas, Austin, Tex., 1967.

1428. Rea, Joanne E. "Joyce and 'Master François Somebody.'" *James Joyce Quarterly* 18 (1981): 445-450.

1429. Rees, John. "A Reading of *The Purple Land*." *Kansas Quarterly* 14 (1982): 135-148.

1430. -----. "Spenserian Analogues in *Moby Dick*." *ESQ: Journal of the American Renaissance* 18 (1972): 174-178.

1431. Regalado, Nancy F. "'Des contraires choses': La fonction poétique de la citation et des *exempla* dans le
Roman de la rose de Jean de Menn." *Littérature* 41
(1981): 62-81.

1432. Reichler, Claudia. "On the Notion of Intertextuality:
The Example of the Libertine Novel." *Diogenes* 113-114
(1981): 205-215.

1433. Reinert, Harro. "Zitate - falsch zitiert." *Muttersprache* 67 (1957): 357-358.

1434. Reis, Carlos. "Intertextualité et lecture critique."
Canadian Review of Comparative Literature 12 (1985):
46-55.

1435. Reising, Russell J. "Yeats, the Rhymer's Club, and
Pound's *Hugh Selwyn Mauberley.*" *Journal of Modern
Literature* 12 (1985): 179-192.

1436. Reiss, Edmund. "Biblical Parody: Chaucer's 'Distor-
tions' of Scripture." *Revue de l'Université d'Ottawa*
53 (1983): 309-323.

1437. Reitsma-La Brujeere, Cora. "Récit et métaécrit, texte
et intertexte dans *Les géorgiques* de Claude Simon."
French Forum 9 (1984): 225-235.

1438. Resnick, Robert B. "The Wit of Biblical Allusion and
Imagery in Thomas Fuller." *Greyfriar Siena Studies in
Literature* 10 (1968): 16-24.

1439. Reuter, O. R. "Some Notes on Thomas Deloney's In-
debtedness to Shakespeare." *Neuphilologische Mitteilungen* 87 (1986): 255-261.

1440. Reynolds, William. "Literature, Latin, and Love:
Dorothy L. Sayers *Gaudy Night.*" *Clues* 6.1 (1985): 67-
78.

1441. Rhodes, Pamela, and Richard Godden. "*The Wild Palms*:
Degraded Culture, Devalued Texts." *Intertextuality in
Faulkner*. Eds. Michel Gresset and Noel Polk. Jackson,
Miss.: University Press of Mississippi, 1985. 87-113.

1442. Ribner, Irving. "A 1576 Allusion to Chaucer." *Notes
and Queries* 195 (1950): 24.

1443. Ricardou, Jean. "Claude Simon: Textuellement." *Claude
Simon: Analyse, théorie*. Paris: U.G.E., 1975. 7-38.

1444. -----. *Nouveaux problèmes du roman*. Paris: Seuil,
1978.

1445. -----. *Pour une théorie du nouveau roman*. Paris:
Seuil, 1971.

1446. -----. "Le prisme d'epsilon." *Degrés* 1.2 (1973): d1-
d9.

1447. -----. "Le texte survit à l'excité." *Texte* 2 (1983): 193-215.

1448. Richards, I. A. "The Allusiveness of Modern Poetry." I. A. Richards. *Principles of Literary Criticism.* London: Routledge & Kegan Paul, 1924. 215-219.

1449. Richey, Clarence W. "'The Riverrun': A Note Upon a Joycean Quotation in Wright Morris' *In Orbit.*" *Notes on Contemporary Literature* 2 (1972): 14-15.

1450. Rickman, John. "On Quotations." *International Journal of Psycho-Analysis* 10 (1929): 242-248.

1451. Ricks, Christopher. "Allusion: The Poet as Heir." *Studies in the Eighteenth Century, III.* Eds. R. F. Brissenden and J. C. Eade. Canberra, Australia: Australian National University Press, 1976. 209-240.

1452. Ridden, Geoffrey M. "*An Apology* and Bishop Longchamp." *Milton Quarterly* 18 (1984): 68.

1453. -----. "Winstanley's Allusion to Milton." *Notes and Queries* 31 (1984): 321-323.

1454. Riddle, Florence K. "Allusions to Job in the 'Wreck of the Deutschland.'" *Cithara* 13 (1974): 57-68.

1455. Ridenour, George M. "Source and Allusion in Some Poems of Coleridge." *Studies in Philology* 60 (1963): 73-95.

1456. Riese, Gerd. "Die alttestamentlichen Zitate im Roemerbrief: Eine Untersuchung zur paulinischen Schriftauslegung." Diss. Muenchen, W. Germany, 1978.

1457. Riffaterre, Michael. "All-Purpose Words: The Case of the French Buttons." *Intertextuality: New Perspectives in Criticism.* Eds. Jeanine P. Plottel and Hanna Charney. New York Literary Forum 2. New York: Literary Forum, 1978. 247-255.

1458. -----. "Descriptive Imagery." *Yale French Studies* 61 (1981): 107-125.

1459. -----. "Flaubert's Presuppositions." *Diacritics* 11.4 (1981): 2-11.

1460. -----. "Generating Lautréamont's Text." *Textual Strategies: Perspectives in Post-Structuralist Criticism.* Ed. Josué V. Harari. Ithaca, N. Y.: Cornell University Press, 1979. 404-420.

1461. -----. "Hermeneutic Models." *Poetics Today* 4 (1983): 7-16.

1462. -----. "The Interpretant in Literary Semiotics." *American Journal of Semiotics* 3.4 (1985): 41-55.

1463. -----. "Interpretation and Descriptive Poetry: A Read-

ing of Wordsworth's 'Yew Trees.'" *New Literary History*
4 (1972/73): 229-256.

1464. -----. "Interpretation and Undecidability." *New
Literary History* 12 (1981): 227-242.

1465. -----. "L'intertexte inconnu." *Littérature* 41 (1981):
4-7.

1466. -----. "Intertextual Representation: On Mimesis as
Interpretive Discourse." *Critical Inquiry* 11 (1984):
141-162.

1467. -----. "Intertextual Scrambling." *Romanic Review* 67
(1977): 197-206.

1468. -----. "Intertextualité surréaliste." *Melusine* 1
(1980): 27-37.

1469. -----. "Lecture intertextuelle du poème." *Au bonheur
des mots: Mélanges en l'honneur de Gérald Antoine*.
Nancy, France: Presses de Nancy, 1984. 403-417.

1470. -----. "The Making of a Literary Sign: *Miroirs sans
tain*." *French Forum* 2 (1977): 160-167.

1471. -----. "On the Prose Poem's Formal Features." *The
Prose Poem in France: Theory and Practice*. Eds. Mary
Ann Caws and Hermine Riffaterre. New York: Columbia
University Press, 1983. 117-132.

1472. -----. "Paradigm and Significance." *Semiotext(e)* 2
(1975): 72-87.

1473. -----. "The Poetic Functions of Intertextual Humor."
Romanic Review 65 (1974): 278-293.

1474. -----. "Poetic Words." *Semiotica* [Special supplement]
(1981): 47-57.

1475. -----. "Ponge intertextuel." *Etudes Françaises* 17
(1981): 73-85.

1476. -----. "Production du roman: L'intertexte du *Lys dans
la vallée*." *Texte* 2 (1983): 23-33.

1477. -----. "The Referential Fallacy." *Columbia Review* 57
(1978): 21-35.

1478. -----. "The Self-Sufficient Text." *Diacritics* 3
(1973): 39-45.

1479. -----. "Sémanalyse de l'intertexte." *Texte* 2 (1983):
171-175.

1480. -----. "Semantic Overdetermination in Poetry." *PTL: A
Journal For Descriptive Poetics and Theory of
Literature* 2 (1977): 1-19.

1481. ------. *Semiotics of Poetry*. Bloomington, Ind.: Indiana University Press, 1978.

1482. ------. "Sémiotique intertextuelle: L'interprétant." *Revue d'Esthétique* 1-2 (1979): 128-150.

1483. ------. "Sur la sémiotique de l'obscurité en poésie." *French Review* 55 (1982): 625-632.

1484. ------. "La syllepse intertextuelle." *Poétique* 40 (1979): 496-501.

1485. ------. "Syllepsis." *Critical Inquiry* 6 (1980): 625-638.

1486. ------. *Text Production*. New York: Columbia University Press, 1983.

1487. ------. "Textuality: W. H. Auden's 'Musée des beaux arts.'" *Textual Analysis: Some Readers Reading*. Ed. Mary Ann Caws. New York: Modern Language Association of America, 1986. 1-13.

1488. ------. "Le tissu du texte: Du Bellay, *Songe*, VII." *Poétique* 34 (1978): 193-203.

1489. ------. "La trace de l'intertexte." *La Pensée* 215 (1980): 4-18.

1490. ------. "Trollope's Metonymies." *Nineteenth Century Fiction* 37 (1982): 272-292.

1491. Rigolot, Carol. "L'Amérique de Saint-John Perse: Référentielle oú intertextuelle?" *Colloque 1980: Saint-John Perse et les Etats-Unis*. Espaces de Saint-John Perse 1980/3. Aix-en-Provence, France: Université de Provence, 1981. 87-98.

1492. ------. "Victor Hugo et Saint-John Perse: 'Pour Dante.'" *French Review* 57 (1984): 794-801.

1493. Rigolot, M. François. "La 'Conjointure' du 'Pantagruel': Rabelais et la tradition mediévale." *Littérature* 41 (1981): 93-104.

1494. ------. "L'intertexte du dizain scévien: Pétrarque et Marot." *Cahiers de l'Association Internationale des Etudes Françaises* 32 (1980): 91-106.

1495. ------. "Référentialité, intertextualité, autotextualité dans les *Essais* de Montaigne." *Oeuvres et Critiques* 8 (1983): 87-101.

1496. ------. "Rhétorique de la métamorphose chez Ronsard." *Textes et intertextes: Etudes sur le XVIe siècle pour Alfred Glauser*. Eds. Floyd Gray and Marcel Tetel. Paris: Nizet, 1979. 147-160.

1497. Riha, Karl. *Cross-Reading and Cross-Talking: Zitat-*

Collagen als poetische und satirische Technik. Stuttgart, W. Germany: Metzler, 1971.

1498. -----. "'Heiraten' in der Fackel: Zu einem Zeitungs-Zitat-Typus bei Karl Kraus." *Karl Kraus.* Ed. Heinz Ludwig Arnold. Muenchen, W. Germany: Text und Kritik, 1975. 116-126.

1499. Ringler, William. "An Early Chaucer Allusion Restored." *Notes and Queries* 174 (1938): 120.

1500. Rissman, Leah. "Homeric Allusion in the Poetry of Sappho." Diss. University of Michigan, 1980.

1501. Ritzel, Wolfgang. "Ein Aristoteles-Zitat in 'Frau Jenny Treibel.'" *Neue Zuercher Zeitung* (June 20, 1971): 51.

1502. -----. "Zur Hermeneutik literarischer Anklaenge." *Kulturwissenschaften: Festgabe fuer Wilhelm Perpeet zum 65. Geburtstag.* Eds. Heinrich Luetzeler, Gerhard Pfafferott, and E. Strohmaier. Bonn, W. Germany: Bouvier, 1980. 354-370.

1503. Robbins, Rossell H. "A Late-Sixteenth-Century Chaucer Allusion (Douce MS. 290)." *Chaucer Review* 2 (1967): 135-137.

1504. Roberts, Marjorie. "Understanding Literary Allusions in Literature." *Research in the Teaching of English* 3 (1969): 160-165.

1505. -----. "Understanding of Allusions Possessed by Ninth-Grade Students." Diss. University of Missouri, 1967.

1506. Robertson, Stuart. "Chaucer and Wordsworth." *Modern Language Notes* 43 (1928): 104-105.

1507. Robichez, Jacques. "L'usage de l'allusion dans le théâtre de Giraudoux." *Cahiers de l'Association Internationale des Etudes Françaises* 34 (1982): 237-244.

1508. Roche, Anne. "Intertextualité et paragrammatisme dans *Talismano* d'Abdelwahab Meddeb: Traces d'un dialogue entre cultures?" *Peuples Méditerranéens* 30 (1985): 23-31.

1509. Rodi, Frithjof. "Anspielungen: Zur Theorie der kulturellen Kommunikationseinheiten." *Poetica* 7 (1975): 115-134.

1510. Rodriguez-Briseño, Armando. "*Terciopelo violeta.*" *La Palabra y el Hombre* 59-60 (1986): 125-129.

1511. Roell, Walter. "Zum Zitieren als Kunstmittel in der aelteren deutschen Lyrik." *Beitraege zur Geschichte der deutschen Sprache und Literatur* 105 (1983): 66-79.

1512. Roelleke, Heinz. "Brentano-Zitate bei Wilhelm Raabe."

Jahrbuch des Freien Deutschen Hochstifts (1981): 365-369.

1513. -----. "Ein Eichendorff-'Zitat' in den *Kinder- und Hausmaerchen* der Brueder Grimm." *Aurora: Jahrbuch der Eichendorff-Gesellschaft* 42 (1982): 239-240.

1514. -----. "Ein Grimm-'Zitat' in Hofmannsthals 'Maerchen der 672. Nacht.'" *Wirkendes Wort* 34 (1984): 65-66, 168.

1515. -----. "Zwei Volksliedzitate in Brentanos Drama 'Aloys und Imelde.'" *Jahrbuch des Freien Deutschen Hochstifts* (1976): 211-215.

1516. Roettger, Jakob. "Das Zitat bei Platon." Diss. Tuebingen, W. Germany, 1961.

1517. Rogal, Samuel. "Scriptural Quotation in Wesley's *Earnest Appeal*." *Research Studies* 47 (1979): 181-188.

1518. Rogers, Pat. "Allusions in Pope's Correspondence." *Notes and Queries* 30 (1983): 36-38.

1519. -----. "Literary Allusions in Chesterfield's Letters." *Notes and Queries* 31 (1984): 45-48.

1520. -----. "Satiric Allusions in John Gay's 'Welcome to Mr. Pope.'" *Papers on Language and Literature* 10 (1974): 427-432.

1521. Rohrkemper, John. "The Allusive Past: Historical Perspective in *The Great Gatsby*." *College English* 12 (1985): 153-162.

1522. Rolle, Dietrich. "Titel und Ueberschrift: Zur Funktion eines literarischen Elementes." *Gutenberg Jahrbuch* 61 (1986): 281-294.

1523. Roloff, Volker. "Lecture et intertextualité - A propos de l'evolution du discours esthétique dans les cahiers et dans *A la recherche du temps perdu*." *Bulletin d'Informations Proustiennes* 13 (1982): 37-41.

1524. -----. "Der Moerder als Erzaehler: Existentialismus und Intertextualitaet bei Sartre, Camus, Cela und Sábato." *Romanistische Zeitschrift fuer Literaturgeschichte* 10 (1986): 197-218.

1525. -----. "Zur Thematik der Lektuere bei Gustave Flaubert *Madame Bovary: Moeurs de province*." *Germanisch-Romanische Monatsschrift* 25 (1975): 322-337.

1526. Ronconi, Alessandro. "Per Dante interprete dei poeti latini." *Studi Danteschi* 41 (1964): 5-44.

1527. Rosenblum, Joseph. "'The Immortal': Jorge Luis Borges' Rendition of T. S. Eliot's *The Waste Land*." *Studies in Short Fiction* 18 (1981): 183-186.

1528. Rosenmeier, Rosamond R. "The Wounds Upon Bathsheba: Anne Bradstreet's Prophetic Art." *Puritan Poets and Poetics: Seventeenth-Century American Poetry in Theory and Practice*. Eds. Peter White and Harrison T. Meserole. University Park, Pa.: Pennsylvania State University Press, 1985. 129-146.

1529. Rosenplenter, Lutz. *Zitat und Autoritaetenberufung im Renner Hugos von Trimberg: Ein Beitrag zur Bildung des Laien im Spaetmittelalter*. Frankfurt, W. Germany: Lang, 1982.

1530. Ross, Alan S. C. "An Estonian Quotation in *Castle Rackrent*." *Notes and Queries* 22 (1975): 26.

1531. Ross, Jacqueline Renée. "The Magnetic Chain: Preternatural Allusions in the Writings of Nathaniel Hawthorne." Diss. University of Wisconsin, 1976.

1532. Ross, Margaret C., and B. K. Martin. "Narrative Structures and Intertextuality in *Snorra Edda*: The Example of Thørr's Encounter with Geirrøthr." *Structure and Meaning in Old Norse Literature*. Eds. John Lindow, Lars Loennroth, and Gerd W. Weber. Odense, Denmark: Odense University Press, 1986. 56-72.

1533. Ross, Stephanie. "Art and Allusion." *Journal of Aesthetics and Art Criticism* 40 (1981): 59-70.

1534. Ross, Stephen M. "Oratory and the Dialogical in *Absalom, Absalom!*" *Intertextuality in Faulkner*. Eds. Michel Gresset and Noel Polk. Jackson, Miss.: University Press of Mississippi, 1985. 73-86.

1535. Rothe, Arnold. *Der literarische Titel: Funktionen, Formen, Geschichte*. Das Abendland N. S. 16. Frankfurt, W. Germany: Klostermann, 1986.

1536. Rothe, Hans. "Quotations in Dostoyevsky's *A Raw Youth*." *Modern Language Review* 79 (1984): 131-141.

1537. Rothfield, Lawrence. "From Semiotic to Discursive Intertextuality: The Case of *Madame Bovary*." *Novel* 19 (1985): 57-81.

1538. Rothstein, Eric. "Allusion and Analogy in the Romance of *Caleb Williams*." *University of Toronto Quarterly* 37 (1967): 18-30.

1539. Roudiez, Léon. "History and Fiction in Claude Simon's Novels." *Review of Contemporary Fiction* 5 (1985): 47-55.

1540. Roulston, Robert. "*This Side of Paradise*: The Ghost of Rupert Brooke." *Fitzgerald/Hemingway Annual* (1975): 117-130.

1541. -----. "Traces of *Tono Bungay* in *The Great Gatsby*." *Journal of Narrative Technique* 10 (1980): 68-76.

1542. Roventa, Daniela. "Intratextuel-intertextuel dans une
      lecture pragmatique du texte littéraire." *Degrés* 28
      (1981): g1-g6.

1543. -----. "A Pragmatic Reading of Literary Texts." *Revue
      Roumaine de Linguistique* 31 (1986): 41-47.

1544. Rubin, David Lee. *Higher, Hidden Order: Design and
      Meaning in the Odes of Malherbe*. University of North
      Carolina Studies in Romance Languages and Literatures
      117. Chapel Hill, N. C.: University of North Carolina
      Press, 1972.

1545. Rudat, Wolfgang E. H. "Allusive Technique in Pope's
      Early *Rota Virgilii* Poetry." *Antike und Abendland* 22
      (1976): 70-99.

1546. -----. "Another Look at the Limits of Allusion: Pope's
      Rape of the Lock and the Virgilian Tradition." *Durham
      University Journal* 71 (1978): 27-34.

1547. -----. "Belinda's 'Painted Vessel': Allusive Technique
      in *The Rape of the Lock*." *Tennessee Studies in
      Literature* 19 (1974): 49-55.

1548. -----. "Brett's Problem: Ovidian and Other Allusions
      in *The Sun Also Rises*." *Style* 19 (1985): 317-325.

1549. -----. "Dickinson and Immortality: Virgilian and
      Miltonic Allusions in 'Of Death I Try to Think Like
      This.'" *American Notes and Queries* 16 (1978): 85-87.

1550. -----. "Heresy and Springtime Ritual: Biblical and
      Classical Allusions in *The Canterbury Tales*." *Revue
      Belge de Philologie et d'Histoire* 54 (1976): 823-836.

1551. -----. *The Mutual Commerce: Masters of Classical Allu-
      sion in English and American Literature*. Heidelberg,
      W. Germany: Winter, 1985.

1552. -----. "The 'Mutual Commerce' in *The Rape of the Lock*:
      Pope and the Virgilian Tradition." *Etudes Anglaises* 29
      (1976): 534-544.

1553. -----. "Pope and the Classical Tradition: Allusive
      Technique in *The Rape of the Lock* and *The Dunciad*."
      Anglia 100 (1982): 435-441.

1554. -----. "Pope's Mind at Work: Virgil and the Road to
      the Lock." Diss. University of California, San Diego,
      Cal., 1972.

1555. -----. "Pope's 'Mutual Commerce': Allusive Manip-
      ulation in *January and May* and *The Rape of the Lock*."
      Durham University Journal 77 (1984): 19-24.

1556. -----. "Spenser's 'Angry Ioue': Vergilian Allusion in
      the First Canto of *The Faerie Queene*." *Classical and
      Modern Literature* 3 (1983): 89-98.

1557. -----. "T. S. Eliot's Allusive Technique: Chaucer, Virgil, Pope." *Renascence* 35 (1983): 167-182.

1558. Rude, Donald. "An Unreported Allusion to Chaucer in *The Female Tatler*." *American Notes and Queries* 23 (1985): 129-130.

1559. -----. "An Unreported Allusion to *Macbeth*." *American Notes and Queries* 24 (1985): 7-8.

1560. -----. "Two Additional Allusions to Chaucer in the Work of Stephen Hawes." *American Notes and Queries* 16 (1978): 82-83.

1561. -----. "Two Unreported Allusions to Shakespeare and Jonson." *American Notes and Queries* 23 (1985): 99.

1562. Ruderman, Judith. "Milton's Choices: Styron's Use of Robert Frost's Poetry in *Lie Down in Darkness*." *College Language Association Journal* 27 (1983): 141-151.

1563. Rule, Philip C. "The Function of Allusion in *Jane Eyre*." *Modern Language Studies* 15 (1985): 165-171.

1564. Rummel, E. "Quoting Poetry Instead of Scripture: Erasmus and Eucherius on *Contemptus mundi*." *Bibliothèque d'Humanisme et Renaissance* 45 (1983): 503-509.

1565. Runyon, Randolph. "Trumpet Variations on an Original Air: Self-Referential Allusion in Montaigne's 'Apology.'" *Romanic Review* 77 (1986): 195-208.

1566. Ruprecht, Hans-Georg. "Aspects logiques de l'intertextualité: Pour une approche sémiotique de la poésie de Julián del Casal." *Dispositio* 2 (1977): 1-27.

1567. -----. "Conditions sémiotiques d'un intertexte: Le modernisme de Julián del Casal." *Revue de l'Université de Bruxelles* 3-4 (1979): 366-394.

1568. -----. *Du formant intertextuel: Remarques sur un objet éthnosémiotique.* Documents de recherche du Groupe de Recherches Sémiolinguistiques III/21. Paris, 1981.

1569. -----. "Intertextualité." *Texte* 2 (1983): 13-22.

1570. -----. "L'intertexte isotope: 'Horridum somnium' de Julián del Casal." *Northsouth/Nordsud: Canadian Journal of Latin American Studies* 2 (1977): 223-249.

1571. Rusinko, Elaine. "Intertextuality: The Soviet Approach to Subtext." *Dispositio* 4 (1979): 213-235.

1572. Russotto, Márgara. "Intertextualidad y memoria (en la primera novela de Graciliano Ramos: *Caetés*)." *Escritura* 8.15 (1983): 133-146.

1573. Ryan, Mari-Laure. "When 'Je' is 'Un autre': Fiction,

Quotation, and the Performative Analysis." *Poetics Today* 2 (1981): 127-155.

1574. Saal-Losq, Christine. "Literary Allusion in Anton Chekhov's Short Stories (1889-1904)." Diss. Stanford University, Stanford, Cal., 1978.

1575. Sacerio-Gari, Enrique. "Borges: Una literatura inter-textual." Diss. Yale University, New Haven, Conn., 1978.

1576. -----. "Detectives North and South." *Proceedings of the Tenth Congress of the International Comparative Literature Association.* Ed. Anna Balakian. New York: Garland. 1985. 3: 91-97.

1577. Sackton, Alexander H. "A Note on Keats and Chaucer." *Modern Language Quarterly* 13 (1952): 37-40.

1578. Safer, Elaine B. "The Allusive Mode, the Absurd, and Black Humor in William Gaddis' *The Recognitions.*" *Studies in American Humor* 1 (1982): 103-118.

1579. -----. "The Allusive Mode and Black Humor in Barth's *Giles Goat-Boy* and Pynchon's *Gravity's Rainbow.*" *Renascence* 32 (1980): 89-104.

1580. -----. "The Allusive Mode and Black Humor in Barth's *Sot-Weed Factor.*" *Studies in the Novel* 13 (1981): 424-438.

1581. Sager, Olof. "Quotations in English Book-Titles." *Moderna Sprak* 45 (1951): 40-48.

1582. Said, Edward. "The Problem of Textuality: Two Exemplary Positions." *Critical Inquiry* 4 (1978): 673-714.

1583. Saint-John, Raymond Alvin. "Biblical Quotation in Edward Taylor's Preparatory Meditations." Diss. University of North Carolina, Chapel Hill, N. C., 1975.

1584. Sammarcelli, Françoise. "La chambre aux echoes: Notes sur l'intertextualité restreinte dans *Letters* de John Barth." *Delta* 21 (1985): 105-125.

1585. Samuray, Patrick. "Searching for Jason Richmond Compson: A Question of Echolalia and a Problem of Palimpsest." *Intertextuality in Faulkner.* Eds. Michel Gresset and Noel Polk. Jackson, Miss.: University Press of Mississippi, 1985. 178-209.

1586. Sanchez, M. E. "Intersexual and Intertextual Codes in the Poetry of Bernice Zamora." *Melus* 7 (1980): 55-68.

1587. Sandler, Florence. "*The Faerie Queene*: An Elizabethan Apocalypse." *The Apocalypse in English Renaissance Thought and Literature: Patterns, Antecedents and Repercussions.* Eds. C. A. Patrides and Joseph Wittreich. Ithaca, N.Y.: Cornell University Press, 1984. 148-174.

1588. Sankey, Margaret. "Meaning Through Intertextuality: Isomorphism of Defoe's *Robinson Crusoe* and Tournier's *Vendredi ou Les limbes du Pacifique.*" *Australian Journal of French Studies* 18 (1981): 77-88.

1589. Sankovitch, Tilde. "Inventing Authority of Origin: The Difficult Enterprise." *Women in the Middle Ages and the Renaissance: Literary and Historical Perspectives.* Ed. Mary Beth Rose. Syracuse, N. Y.: Syracuse University Press, 1986. 227-243.

1590. Sattelmeyer, Robert. "'Interesting but Tough': *Huckleberry Finn* and the Problem of Tradition." *One Hundred Years of Huckleberry Finn: The Boy, His Book, and American Culture.* Eds. R. Sattelmeyer et al. Columbia, Mo.: University of Missouri Press, 1985. 354-370.

1591. Satterfield, Leon. "Robinson's 'An Evangelist's Wife.'" *Explicator* 41.3 (1983): 36-37.

1592. Saulnier, Verdun Louis. "Une étrange promesse de gloire: L'exhortation de François Demoulins au futur François 1er (1513)." *Textes et intertextes: Etudes sur le XVIe siècle pour Alfred Glauser.* Eds. Floyd Gray and Marcel Tetel. Paris: Nizet, 1979. 161-172.

1593. Saunders, Judith P. "Frost's 'Once by the Pacific.'" *Explicator* 39.4 (1981): 29-31.

1594. -----. "Mortal Stain: Literary Allusion and Female Sexuality in 'Mrs. Dalloway in Bond Street.'" *Studies in Short Fiction* 15 (1978): 139-144.

1595. Scanlan, Timothy. "A Biblical Allusion in Rousseau's *Emile.*" *Language Quarterly* 14 (1975): 13-14.

1596. Schaar, Claes. *The Full Voic'd Quire Below: Vertical Context Systems in Paradise Lost.* Lund, Sweden: CWK Gleerup, 1982.

1597. -----. "Linear Sequence, Spatial Structure, Complex Sign, and Vertical Context System." *Poetics* 7 (1978): 377-388.

1598. -----. "Vertical Context Systems." *Style and Text: Studies Presented to Nils E. Enkvist.* Ed. Hakan Ringbom. Stockholm, Sweden: Sprakfarlaget, 1975. 146-157.

1599. Schabert, Ina. "Interauktorialiaet." *Deutsche Vierteljahrsschrift fuer Literaturwissenschaft und Geistesgeschichte* 57 (1983): 679-701.

1600. Schadewaldt, Wolfgang. "Hoelderlin und Homer. Erster Teil." *Hoelderlin-Jahrbuch* 4 (1950): 2-27.

1601. -----. "Hoelderlin und Homer. Zweiter Teil." *Hoelderlin-Jahrbuch* 7 (1953): 1-53.

1602. Schakel, Peter J. *The Poetry of Jonathan Swift: Allu-*

sion and the Development of a Poetic Style. Madison,
Wis.: University of Wisconsin Press, 1978.

1603. -----. "Swift's 'Dapper Clerk' and the Matrix of
Allusions in *Cadenus and Vanessa*." *Criticism* 17
(1975): 246-261.

1604. -----. "Virgil and the Dean: Christian and Classical
Allusion in *The Legion Club*." *Studies in Philology* 70
(1973): 427-438.

1605. Scharrer, Walther. *Wilhelm Raabes literarische Symbo-
lik dargestellt an Prinzessin Fisch*. Muenchen, W. Germany: Knorr & Hirth, 1927.

1606. Scherer, Olga. "A Polyphonic Insert: Charles' Letter
to Judith." *Intertextuality in Faulkner*. Eds. Michel
Gresset and Noel Polk. Jackson, Miss.: University
Press of Mississippi, 1985. 168-177.

1607. Schick, Ursula. "Erzaehlte Semiotik oder intertextuelles Verwirrspiel? Umberto Ecos *Il nome della rosa*."
Poetica 16 (1984): 138-161.

1608. Schier, Rudolf D. "Buechner und Trakl: Zum Problem der
Anspielungen im Werk Trakls." *Publications of the
Modern Language Association* 87 (1972): 1052-1064.

1609. Schlack, Beverly Ann. *Continuing Presences: Virginia
Woolf's Use of Literary Allusions*. University Park,
Pa.: Penn State University Press, 1979. [Diss. New
York University, 1974.]

1610. Schleifer, Ronald. "George Moore's Turning Mind: Di-
gression and Autobiographical Art in *Hail and
Farewell*." *Genre* 12 (1979): 473-503.

1611. Schlicher, John J. "The Moods of Indirect Quotation."
American Journal of Philology 26 (1905): 60-88.

1612. Schmeling, Manfred. *Métathéâtre et intertexte: Aspects
du théâtre dans le théâtre*. Paris: Lettres Modernes,
1982.

1613. -----. "Textuelle Fremdbestimmung und literarischer
Vergleich." *Neohelicon* 12 (1985): 231-239.

1614. Schmid, Wolf. "Diegetische Realisierung von Sprich-
woertern, Redensarten und semantischen Figuren in
Puškins 'Povesti Belkina.'" *Wiener Slawistischer Almanach* 10 (1982): 163-195.

1615. -----. "Intertextualitaet und Komposition in Puškins
Novellen 'Der Schuss' und 'Der Posthalter.'" *Poetica*
13 (1981): 82-132.

1616. -----. "Sinnpotentiale der diegetischen Allusion:
Aleksander Puškins Posthalternovelle und ihre Prae-
texte." *Dialog der Texte: Hamburger Kolloquium zur In-*

tertextualitaet. Eds. Wolf Schmid and Wolf-Dieter Stempel. Wiener Slawistischer Almanach Sonderband 11. Wien, 1983. 141-187.

1617. -----. *Der Textaufbau in den Erzaehlungen Dostoev-skijs*. Muenchen, W. Germany: Fink, 1973.

1618. -----. "Three Diegetic Devices in Pushkin's *Tales of Belkin*." *Language and Literary Theory in Honor of Ladislav Matejka*. Eds. Benjamin A. Stolz, I. R. Titunik, and Lubomir Dolezel. Ann Arbor, Mich.: University of Michigan Press, 1984. 505-525.

1619. Schmidt, Paul Gerhard. "Das Zitat in der Vaganten-dichtung." *Antike und Abendland* 20 (1974): 74-87.

1620. Schmidt, Roderich. "a e i o u: Die mittelalterlichen 'Vokalspiele' und das Salomon-Zitat des Reinbot von Durne." *Zeiten und Formen in Sprache und Dichtung: Festschrift fuer Fritz Tschirch zum 70. Geburtstag*. Eds. Karl-Heinz Schirmer and Bernhard Sowinski. Koeln, W. Germany: Boehlau, 1972. 113-133.

1621. Schmidt-Henkel, Gerhard. "Zitate und Wunschbilder als Mittel politischer Werbung." *Sprache im technischen Zeitalter* 8 (1963): 634-649.

1622. Schneider, Michael. "Allusionen, Plagiate und Schmidt: Einige Nachweise." *Bargfelder Bote* 49 (1980): 10-17.

1623. Schneider, Ulrich. *Die Funktion der Zitate im Ulysses von James Joyce*. Bonn, W. Germany: Bouvier, 1970.

1624. Schoeck, R. J. "Autour de l'intertextualité chez Bodin." *Jean Bodin: Actes du colloque interdisci-plinaire d'Angers, 24 au 27 Mai 1984*. Angers, France: Presse de l'Université d'Angers, 1985. 215-221.

1625. -----. *Intertextuality and Renaissance Texts*. Bamber-ger Schriften zur Renaissance-Forschung 12. Bamberg, W. Germany: Kaiser, 1984.

1626. Schoenau, Walter. *Sigmund Freuds Prosa: Literarische Elemente seines Stils*. Stuttgart, W.G.: Metzler, 1968.

1627. Schoenberger, Otto. "Ein griechisch-roemisches Zitat bei Goethe." *Goethe-Jahrbuch* 99 (1982): 282-283.

1628. Schoepp, Joseph C. "'Endmeshed in endtanglements': In-tertextualitaet in Donald Barthelmes The Dead Father." *Intertextualitaet: Formen, Funktionen, anglistische Fallstudien*. Eds. U. Broich and M. Pfister. Tuebingen, W. Germany: Niemeyer, 1985. 332-348.

1629. -----. "Multiple 'Pretexts': Raymond Federmans zer-ruettete Autobiographie." *Arbeiten aus Anglistik und Amerikanistik* 6 (1981): 41-55.

1630. Scholtz, Nini. "Nagra Dante reminiscenser hos Hjalmar

Gullberg." *Svensk Litteraturtidskrift* 36 (1973): 21-
26.

1631. Schonhorn, Manuel. "Heroic Allusion in *Tom Jones*:
Hamlet and the Temptations of Jesus." *Studies in the
Novel* 6 (1974): 218-227.

1632. -----. "*The Sun Also Rises*: The Jacob Allusion II:
Parody as Meaning." *Ball State University Forum* 16
(1975): 49-55.

1633. Schork, R. J. "Stendhal's *Latinitas*." *Classical and
Modern Literature* 6 (1985). 23-38.

1634. Schrader, Carl G. "Literary and Mythological Allusions
in the Poetry of George Meredith." Diss. Texas Tech.
University, Lubbock, Tex., 1974.

1635. Schricker, Gale C. "The Case of Cress: Implications of
Allusion in *Paterson*." *William Carlos Williams Review*
11.2 (1985): 16-29.

1636. Schubert, Werner. "Sprichwort oder Zitat? Zur lateini-
schen Rede im 'Baeuerischen Machiavellus' von Christian Weise." *Weimarer Beitraege* 15 (1969): 148-166.

1637. Schuler, Robert M. "Jonson's Alchemists, Epicures, and
Puritans." *Medieval and Renaissance Drama in England* 2
(1985): 171-208.

1638. Schulte-Middelich, Bernd. "Funktionen intertextueller
Sinnkonstitution." *Intertextualitaet: Formen, Funktionen, anglistische Fallstudien*. Eds. U. Broich and M.
Pfister. Tuebingen, W. Germany: Niemeyer, 1985. 197-
242.

1639. Schultz, Hartwig. "Quellenverwandlung, Zitat oder
Kopie." *Jahrbuch des Freien Deutschen Hochstifts*
(1986): 242-256.

1640. Schultz, J. R. "Sir Walter Scott and Chaucer." *Modern
Language Notes* 28 (1913): 246-247.

1641. Schulz, Georg-Michael. "'fort aus Kannitverstan': Bemerkungen zum Zitat in der Lyrik Paul Celans." *Text
und Kritik* 53-54 (1977): 26-41.

1642. Schutte, William M. *Joyce and Shakespeare: A Study in
the Meaning of Ulysses*. New Haven, Conn.: Yale University Press, 1957.

1643. Schwanitz, Dietrich. "Intertextualitaet und Aequiva-
lenzfunktionalismus: Vorschlaege zu einer vergleichen-
den Analytik von Geschichten." *Dialog der Texte: Hamburger Kolloquium zur Intertextualitaet*. Eds. Wolf
Schmid and Wolf-Dieter Stempel. Wiener Slawistischer
Almanach Sonderband 11. Wien, 1983. 27-51.

1644. Schwartz, Nessel. "Themes, *Ecriture*, and Authorship in

Paisajes después de la batalla." *Hispanic Review* 52 (1984): 477-490.

1645. Schwartz, Paul. "The Unifying Structures of George Perec's Suspended Memoirs." *International Fiction Review* 12 (1985): 71-73.

1646. Schweikert, Rudi. "'Ko Bate!': Kurd Lasswitz' Roman *Auf zwei Planeten* im Werk Arno Schmidts. Nebst einigen Anmerkungen zur Schmidtschen Zitierkunst und zu seinem Realitaetsverstaendnis." *Bargfelder Bote* 26 (1977): 3-23.

1647. -----. "'Merlin and Vivien': Zitate aus Alfred Lord Tennysons 'Idyll of the King' in Arno Schmidts *Zettels Traum* - Teil 1." *Bargfelder Bote* 58-60 (1980): 3-11.

1648. -----. "'Wir leben alle wie in ei'm kolossal'n Roman': Zur Zitierkunst Arno Schmidts in der 'Schule der Atheisten.'" *Bargfelder Bote* 37 (1979): 3-11.

1649. Schweikle, Guenther. "Steckt im 'Summerlaten'-Lied Walthers von der Vogelweide ein Gedicht Reinmars des Alten?" *Zeitschrift fuer deutsche Philologie* [Special issue] 87 (1968): 131-153.

1650. Sciaroni, Elena. "Das Zitatrecht." Diss. Fribourg, Switzerland, 1970.

1651. Scott, Fred Newton. "A Substitute for the Classics." *The School Review* 16 (June 1908): 360-369.

1652. Scott, John A. "The Assumed Inferiority of Literary Borrowing." *The Classical Journal* 16 (1920): 114-115.

1653. Scruggs, Charles W. "Ralph Ellison's Use of *The Aeneid* in *Invisible Man.*" *College Language Association Journal* 17 (1974): 368-378.

1654. Seboek, Thomas A. "Enter Textuality: Echoes From the Extraterrestrial." *Poetics Today* 6 (1985): 657-663.

1655. Selig, Karl-Ludwig. "*Don Quixote* and *The Great Gatsby.*" *Revista Hispanica Moderna* 40 (1978-79): 128-129.

1656. -----. "*Il Gattopardo*: Observations on Enumeration and Some Other Aspects of the Text." *Teaching Language Through Literature* 26 (1986): 36-41.

1657. Selleck, Laura Jessie. "A Study of Conventions and Images of Historical Allusion in Spenser's *Faerie Queene.*" Diss. University of Toronto, Canada, 1978.

1658. Sermain, Jean-Paul. "Le travail de la citation dans le supplement manuscrit du *Dictionaire critique* de Féraud." *Autour de Féraud: La lexicographie en France de 1762 à 1835.* Ed. Simone Follet. Paris: Ecole Normale Supérieure de Jeunes Filles, 1986. 253-261.

1659. Servodidio, Mirella d'Ambrosio. "Oneiric Inter-
      textualities." *From Fiction to Metafiction: Essays in
      Honor of Carmen Martin-Gaite*. Eds. Mirela Servodidio
      and Marcia L. Welles. Lincoln, Nebr.: University of
      Nebraska Press, 1983. 117-127.

1660. -----. "Speculations on Intertextualities: Baroja and
      Valle-Inclán." *Hispania* 66 (1983): 11-16.

1661. Setaioli, Aldo. "Seneca e i poeti greci: Allusioni e
      traduzioni." *Giornale Italiano di Filologia* N. S. 16
      (1985): 161-200.

1662. Sgard, Jean. "L'explicit de la *Vie de Henry Brulard*."
      Revue d'Histoire Littéraire de la France 84 (1984):
      199-205.

1663. Shafer, Aileen. "Eliot Re-Donne: The Prufrockian
      Spheres." *Yeats Eliot Review* 5.2 (1978): 39-43.

1664. Shaked, Gershon, "Wie juedisch ist ein juedisch
      deutscher Roman? Ueber Joseph Roths *Hiob, Roman eines
      einfachen Mannes*." *Bulletin des Leo Baeck Instituts* 73
      (1986): 3-12.

1665. Shapiro, Norman Richard. "Topical Allusions in the
      Theatre of Georges Feydeau." Diss. Harvard University,
      Cambridge, Mass., 1958.

1666. Sherman, Carol, and Katherine Stephens. "Folkloric
      Intertexts in Voltaire's *Ingenu*." *Romance Notes* 21
      (1980): 193-199.

1667. Sherzer, Dina. "Lectures de *La Voie royale*." *Mélanges
      Malraux Miscellany* 16 (1984): 128-136.

1668. Shields, John C. "Jerome in Colonial New England:
      Edward Taylor's Attitude Toward Classical Paganism."
      Studies in Philology 81 (1984): 161-184.

1669. Shipps, Anthony W. "Quotations and Allusions in John
      Clarke's *Formulae oratoriae*." *Notes and Queries* 224
      (1979): 441-442.

1670. Shurr, William H. "American Drama and the Bible: The
      Case of O'Neill's *Lazarus Laughed*." *The Bible and
      American Arts and Letters*. Ed. Giles Gunn. Phila-
      delphia, Pa.: Fortress Press, 1983. 83-103.

1671. Sieburth, Richard. "*Gaspard de la nuit*: Prefacing
      Genre." *Studies in Romanticism* 24 (1985): 239-255.

1672. Siefken, Hinrich. "Emperor William II and His Loyal
      Subject - Montage and Historical Allusions in Heinrich
      Mann's Satirical Novel *Der Untertan*." *Trivium* 8
      (1973): 69-82.

1673. Siepe, Hans. "Mais tout cela, c'est de la littérature:
      Aspects de l'intertextualité chez Gaston Leroux." *Le

*plaisir de l'intertexte: Formes et fonctions de
l'intertextualité (roman populaire, sur-réalisme, André
Gide, nouveau roman)*. Eds. Raimund Theis und Hans T.
Siepe. Bern, Switzerland: Lang, 1986. 65-85.

1674. Siess, Juergen. *Zitat und Kontext bei Georg Buechner:
Eine Studie zu den Dramen Dantons Tod und Leonce und
Lena*. Goeppingen, W. Germany: Alfred Kuemmerle, 1975.

1675. Sigele, Rizel Louise. "El arte de la alusión en
Baroja: 'La mujer entre cristales' y la princesa de la
'Sonatina' de Rubén Darío." *Cuadernos Hispanoamerica-
nos* 314-315 (1976): 632-639.

1676. -----. "Baroja and Bécquer: The Anatomy of an Allusion." *Intertextuality: New Perspectives in Criticism*.
Eds. Jeanine P. Plottel and Hanna Charney. New York
Literary Forum 2. New York: Literary Forum, 1978. 87-
96.

1677. Simon, Hans-Ulrich. "Zitat." *Reallexikon der deutschen
Literaturgeschichte*. Second Edition. Eds. Klaus Kanzog
and Achim Masser. Berlin, W. Germany: Gruyter, 1984.
4: 1049-1081.

1678. Simons, John. "A Possible Reference to *Timon of Athens*
in *Paradise Lost*." *Notes and Queries* 31 (1984): 326-
327.

1679. Sims, James H. *Dramatic Uses of Biblical Allusions in
Marlowe and Shakespeare*. University of Florida Monographs: Humanities 24. Gainesville, Fla.: University
of Florida, 1966.

1680. Sjoeberg, Leif. "Allusions in the First Part of *En
Moelna-Elegi*." *Scandinavian Studies* 37 (1965): 293-
323.

1681. -----. "Allusions in the Last Part of *En Moelna-
Elegi*." *Germanic Review* 40 (1965): 132-149.

1682. Skinner, John F. "Semantic Play in the Poetry of
Howard Nemerov." *Literature in Performance* 6.2 (1986):
44-59.

1683. Slade, Leonard A. "The Use of Biblical Allusions in
The Grapes of Wrath." *College Language Association
Journal* 11 (1968): 241-247.

1684. Slatin, Myles. "'Mesmerism': A Study of Ezra Pound's
Use of the Poetry of Robert Browning." Diss. Yale University, New Haven, Conn., 1957.

1685. Sloane, William. "A Seventeenth-Century Chaucer Allusion." *Notes and Queries* 173 (1937): 226.

1686. Slott, Kathryn. "Le texte e(s)t son double: *Gaspard de
la nuit*: Intertextualité, parodie, auto-parodie."
French Forum 6 (1981): 28-35.

1687. Small, Julianne. "Classical Allusions in the Fiction of Herman Melville." Diss. University of Tennessee, 1974.

1688. Smirnov, Igor P. *Porozhdenie Interteksta*. Wiener Slawistischer Almanach Sonderband 17. Wien: Institut fuer Slawistik der Universitaet, 1985.

1689. -----. "Das zitierte Zitat." *Dialog der Texte: Hamburger Kolloquium zur Intertextualitaet*. Eds. Wolf Schmid and Wolf-Dieter Stempel. Wiener Slawistischer Almanach Sonderband 11. Wien, 1983. 273-290.

1690. Smith, Frederik. "Swift and Cannabis." *American Notes and Queries* 22 (1983): 37-39.

1691. Smith, Grover. *T. S. Eliot's Poetry and Plays: A Study in Sources and Meanings*. Chicago, Ill.: University of Chicago Press, 1956.

1692. Smith, James Penny. "Musical Allusions in James Joyce's *Ulysses*." Diss. University of North Carolina, Chapel Hill, N. C., 1968.

1693. Smith, Jonathan Clark. "Destiny Reversed: A Study of Biblical and Classical Allusion Patterns in Shakespeare's *Henry VI*." Diss. Indiana University, 1974.

1694. Smith, Paul Julian. "Allusive Context annd Literary Theory in the Love-Lyric of Quevedo." Diss. Cambridge, UK, 1984.

1695. -----. "A Case of Decorous Theft: Quevedo's Imitation of a Petrarchan Canzone." *Modern Language Review* 78 (1983): 573-587.

1696. -----. "Quevedo and the Sirens: Classical Allusion and Renaissance Topic in a Moral Sonnet." *Journal of Hispanic Philology* 9 (1984): 31-41.

1697. Smith, Philip E. "*Last Orders* and First Principles for the Interpretation of Aldiss's Enigmas." *Reflections on the Fantastic*. Ed. Michael R. Collings. New York: Greenwood, 1986. 69-78.

1698. Smith, Roland M. "Chaucer Allusions in the Letters of Sir Walter Scott." *Modern Language Notes* 65 (1950): 448-455.

1699. Smith, Stan. "Neither Callipe nor Apollo: Pound's Propertius and the Refusal of Epic." *English* 34 (1985): 212-231.

1700. -----. "Writing a Will: Yeats's Ancestral Voices in 'The Tower' and 'Meditations in Time of Civil War.'" *Irish University Review* 13 (1983): 14-37.

1701. Smyth, Mary Winslow. "Biblical Quotations in Middle English Literature Before 1350." Diss. Yale University, New Haven, Conn., 1910.

1702. Snow, Malinda. "Martin Luther King's 'Letter from Birmingham Jail' as Pauline Epistle." *Quarterly Journal of Speech* 71 (1985): 318-334.

1703. Sobel, Eli. "Sebastian Brant, Ovid, and Classical Allusions in the *Narrenschiff.*" *University of California Publications in Modern Philology* 36 (1952): 429-440.

1704. Sohn, Naomi Elizabeth H. "Allusive Methods: A Comparative Study of Biblical Elements of Joyce's *Ulysses* and Doeblin's *Berlin Alexanderplatz.*" Diss. Purdue University, Lafayette, Ind., 1979.

1705. Sokel, Walter H. "Quotation and Literary Echo as Structural Principles in Gabriele Wohmann's *Fruehherbst in Badenweiler.*" *Studies in Twentieth Century Literature* 5 (1980): 107-121.

1706. Solano, Seidy Araya, and Flora Ovares Ramírez. "Las manifestaciones intertextuales de *Bananos y hombres* de Carmen Lyra." *Kañina* 9 (1985): 103-108.

1707. Sonderegger, Stefan. "Eine althochdeutsche Paternoster-Uebersetzung der Reichenau: Versuch einer Rekonstruktion auf Grund der Zitate und entsprechender Formen aus den Reichenauer Denkmaelern." *Festschrift fuer Karl Bischoff zum 70. Geburtstag.* Eds. G. Bellmann, G. Eifler, and W. Kleiber. Koeln, W. Germany: Boehlau, 1975. 299-307.

1708. Sondrup, Steven P. "The Intertextual Landscape of Zola's *Germinal.*" *Symposium* 36 (1982): 166-181.

1709. Sonnenfeld, Albert. "Buttons and Beaux: James Joyce." *Intertextuality: New Perspectives in Criticism.* Eds. Jeanine P. Plottel and Hanna Charney. New York Literary Forum 2. New York: Literary Forum, 1978. 263-273.

1710. Speck, Gordon R. "Carbuncle, Christmas, and the Bloomsbury Tales: Holmes as Wise Man." *Baker Street Journal* 35 (1985): 228.

1711. Spector, Cheryl Ann. "Henry James and the Light of Allusion." Diss. Cornell University, Ithaca, N.Y., 1986.

1712. Speer, Mary B. "Intertextualités médiévales." *Modern Philology* 80 (1983): 294-299.

1713. -----. "The Prince's Baptism in the *Roman des sept sages*: Formal and Doctrinal Intertexts." *Medievalia et Humanistica* 14 (1986): 59-80.

1714. Spence, Sarah. "Et ades sera l'alba - 'Revelations' as Intertext for the Provencal 'Alba.'" *Romance Philology* 35 (1981): 212-217.

1715. Spencer, Michael. "Les citations ambiques de l'Oncle

Michel." *Australian Journal of French Studies* 20 (1983): 93-104.

1716. Spires, Robert C. "La autodestrucción creativa en *Reivindicación del Conde Don Julián.*" *Journal of Spanish Studies - Twentieth Century* 4 (1976): 191-202.

1717. -----. "Intertextuality in *El cuarto de atrás.*" *From Fiction to Metafiction: Essays in Honor of Carmen Martín-Gaite.* Eds. Mirella Servodido and Marcia Welles. Lincoln, Nebr.: University of Nebraska Press, 1983. 139-148.

1718. Spiro, Solomon Joseph. "A Study and Interpretation of the Judaic Allusions in *The Second Scroll* and *The Collected Poems* of A. M. Klein: Annotations and Commentary." Diss. McGill University, Montreal, 1980.

1719. Sprengel, Peter. "*Hamlet* in *Papa Hamlet*: Zur Funktion des Zitats im Naturalismus." *Literatur fuer Leser* (1984): 25-43.

1720. Spriet, Pierre. "A Retrospective Reading of *The Stone Angel* in the Light of *The Diviners.*" *World Literature Written in English* 24 (1984): 312-327.

1721. Springer, Marlene A. *Hardy's Use of Allusion.* London: Macmillan, 1983. [Diss. Indiana University, 1969.]

1722. -----. "Invention and Tradition: Allusions in *Desperate Remedies.*" *Colby Library Quarterly* 10 (1974): 475-485.

1723. Sprinker, Michael. "Textual Politics: Foucault and Derrida." *Boundary 2* 8 (1980): 75-98.

1724. Spurgeon, Caroline F. E. *Five Hundred Years of Chaucer Criticism and Allusion 1357-1900.* 3 Volumes. 1925; New York: Russell & Russell, 1960.

1725. Stackmann, Karl. "Ovid im deutschen Mittelalter." *Arcadia* 1 (1966): 231-254.

1726. Stahlenbrecher, Werner. "Die Dichterzitate in Ciceros Korrespondenz." Diss. Hamburg, W. Germany, 1957.

1727. Staiger, Emil. "Entstellte Zitate." Emil Staiger. *Die Kunst der Interpretation.* Zuerich, Switzerland: Atlantis, 1955. 161-179.

1728. Stanzel, Franz K. "Ein metapoetisches Experiment aus Kanada: Douglas Barbours und Stephen Scobies *The Pirates of Pen's Chance.*" *Arbeiten aus Anglistik und Amerikanistik* 10 (1985): 123-136.

1729. -----. "Zur poetischen Wiederverwertung von Texten: Found Poems, Metatranslation, Oberflaechenuebersetzung." *Literatur im Kontext: Festschrift fuer Helmut Schrey zum 65. Geburtstag am 6. 1. 1985.* Eds. Re-

nate Haas and Christine Klein-Braley. St. Augustin:
Richarz, 1985. 39-50.

1730. Stape, John H. "Myth, Allusion, and Symbol in E. M.
Forster's *The Other Side of the Hedge.*" *Studies in
Short Fiction* 14 (1977): 375-378.

1731. Staples, Hugh B. "Mr. Deasy and the 'French Celt.'"
James Joyce Quarterly 18 (1981): 199-201.

1732. Starobinski, Jean. "Bandello et Baudelaire: Le prince
et son bouffon." *Le mythe d'etiemble: Hommage, études
et recherches; inédits.* Paris: Didier, 1979. 251-259.

1733. -----. *Les mots sous les mots: Les anagrammes de
Ferdinand de Saussure.* Paris: Gallimard, 1971.

1734. -----. "Le texte dans le texte." *Tel Quel* 37 (1969):
3-33.

1735. Stauffacher, Werner. "Die Bibel als poetisches Bezugs-
system: Zu Alfred Doeblins *Berlin Alexanderplatz.*"
Sprachkunst 8 (1977): 35-40.

1736. Stearns, D. T. "E. K.'s Classical Allusions Recon-
sidered." *Studies in Philology* 39 (1942): 143-159.

1737. Steele, Peter. "*Scriptor ludens*: The Notion and Some
Instances." *Canadian Review of Comparative Literature*
12 (1985): 235-263.

1738. Stein, Edwin. "Wordsworth's Art of Allusion." Diss.
Yale University, New Haven, Conn., 1984.

1739. Steiner, Wendy. "Intertextuality in Painting." *American Journal of Semiotics* 3.4 (1985): 57-67.

1740. Stempel, Wolf-Dieter. "Intertextualitaet und Rezeption." *Dialog der Texte: Hamburger Kolloquium zur Intertextualitaet.* Eds. Wolf Schmid and Wolf-Dieter
Stempel. Wiener Slawistischer Almanach Sonderband 11.
Wien, 1983. 85-109.

1741. Stephany, William A. "Biblical Allusions to Conversion
in 'Purgatorio XXI.'" *Stanford Italian Review* 3
(1983): 141-162.

1742. Stern, Michael. "Tevye's Art of Quotation." *Prooftexts*
6 (1986): 79-96.

1743. Stern, Mirta E. "El espacio intertextual en la narrativa de Juan José Saer: Instancia productiva, refe-
rente y campo de teorización de la escritura." *Revista
Iberoamericana* 49 (1983): 965-981.

1744. Sternberg, Meir. "Proteus in Quotation-Land: Mimesis
and the Forms of Reported Discourse." *Poetics Today* 3
(1982): 107-156.

1745. Stetson, Erlene. "Literary Talk: Extended Allusion in
       Ulysses." *James Joyce Quarterly* 19 (1982): 178-181.

1746. Stevens, Bonnie Klomp. "Biblical Allusions in *Peter
       Bell*: The Story of Balaam's Ass." *English Language
       Notes* 14 (1977): 275-278.

1747. Stewart, Susan. *Nonsense: Aspects of Intertextuality
       in Folklore and Literature.* Baltimore, Md.: Johns
       Hopkins University Press, 1979. [Diss. University of
       Pennsylvania, 1978.]

1748. -----. "The Pickpocket: A Study in Tradition and Allu-
       sion." *Modern Language Notes* 95 (1980): 1127-1154.

1749. Stierle, Karlheinz. "Werk und Intertextualitaet." *Das
       Gespraech.* Eds. K. Stierle and Rainer Warning. Poetik
       und Hermeneutik 11. Muenchen, W. Germany: Fink, 1984.
       139-150.

1750. Stillinger, Jack. "*Kubla Khan* and Michelangelo's Glo-
       rious Boast." *English Language Notes* 23.1 (1985): 38-
       42.

1751. Stoddard, Eve M. "Dante's *Inferno* as Allusive Context
       for MacLeish's *Conquistador.*" *Notes on Modern American
       Literature* 6.3 (1982): Item 18.

1752. Stollmann, Samuel S. "Analogues and Sources for
       Milton's 'Great Task-Master.'" *Milton Quarterly* 6
       (1972): 27-32.

1753. Stolpe, Jan. "'Latrin och kraskisk': Det antika mate-
       rialet i Ekeloefs *En Moelna Elegi.*" *Rondo* 1 (1961):
       13-20.

1754. Stout, Janis. "Melville's Use of the Book of Job."
       Nineteenth Century Fiction 25 (1970): 69-83.

1755. Stovel, B. "*Waverley* and the *Aeneid*: Scott's Art of
       Allusion." *English Studies in Canada* 11 (1985): 26-39.

1756. Streadbeck, Arval L. "Allusions to Christian Redemp-
       tion in German Literature Before 1500." Diss. Stanford
       University, Stanford, Cal., 1953.

1757. Stringer, Gary. "Learning 'Hard and Deepe': Biblical
       Allusion in Donne's 'A Valediction: Of My Name in the
       Window.'" *South Central Bulletin* 33 (1973): 227-231.

1758. Strout, Nathaniel. "A Biblical Framework for Orgog-
       lio's Fall: A Note on *The Faerie Queene* I, viii, 22."
       Notes and Queries 32 (1985): 21-23.

1759. Studer, Basilio. "'Ea specie, videri quam voluntas
       elegerit, non natura formaverit.' Zu einem Ambrosius-
       Zitat in Augustins Schrift *De videndo Deo* (ep. 147)."
       Vetera Christianorum 6 (1969): 91-143, and 7 (1970):
       125-154.

1760. Stueckrath, Joern. "Der literarische Held als Leser:
      Ein historisch-typologischer Prospekt." *Literatur-
      Sprache-Unterricht: Festschrift fuer Jakob Lehmann zum
      65. Geburtstag.* Eds. Michael Krejci and Karl Schuster.
      Bamberg, W. Germany: Bayerische Verlagsanstalt, 1984.
      102-108.

1761. -----. "Zur Poetik der Zitatmontage: Helmut Heissen-
      buettels Text 'Deutschland 1944.'" *Replik* 4-5 (1970):
      16-32.

1762. Stull, William L. "Richard Brautigan's *Trout Fishing
      in America*: Notes of a *Native Son.*" *American Lit-
      erature* 56 (1984): 68-80.

1763. Stump, Debra. "A Matter of Choice: King's *Cujo* and
      Malamud's *The Natural.*" *Discovering Stephen King.* Ed.
      Darrell Schweitzer. Starmont Studies in Literary Crit-
      icism 8. Mercer Island, Wash.: Starmont, 1985. 131-
      140.

1764. Sucre, Guillermo. "La alusión o mención." *Homenaje a
      Angel Rosenblatt. Estudios filológicos y lingüísticos.*
      Caracas, Venezuela: Inst. Pedagógico, 1974. 479-486.

1765. Suerbaum, Ulrich. "Intertextualitaet und Gattungs-
      wechsel: Beispielreihen und Hypothesen." *Intertextua-
      litaet: Formen, Funktionen, anglistische Fallstudien.*
      Eds. U. Broich and M. Pfister. Tuebingen, W. Germany:
      Niemeyer, 1985. 58-77.

1766. Sullivan, J. P. *Ezra Pound and Sextus Propertius: A
      Study in Creative Translation.* London: Faber & Faber,
      1964.

1767. Sullivan, William J. "The Allusion to Jenny Lind in
      Daniel Deronda." *Nineteenth Century Fiction* 29 (1974):
      211-214.

1768. -----. "Music and Musical Allusion in *The Mill on the
      Floss.*" *Criticism* 16 (1974): 232-246.

1769. Summers, Claude J., and Ted-Larry Pebworth. "Herbert,
      Vaughan, and Public Concerns in Private Modes." *George
      Herbert Journal* 3 (1979-80): 1-21.

1770. Sutherland, Jean Murray. "Shakespeare and Seneca: A
      Symbolic Language for Tragedy." Diss. University of
      Colorado, Boulder, Colo., 1985.

1771. Svensson, Arnold. *Anspielung und Stereotyp: Eine
      linguistische Untersuchung des politischen Sprachge-
      brauchs am Beispiel der SPD.* Opladen, W. Germany:
      Westdeutscher Verlag, 1984.

1772. Swafford, James M. "A Rossetti Allusion in Ford's *The
      Good Soldier.*" *Notes and Queries* 31 (1984): 76-77.

1773. Sweeney, Gerard. *Melville's Use of Classical Mythol-*

ogy. Amsterdam, Holland: Rodopi, 1975. [Diss. University of Wisconsin, 1972.]

1774. Sweeney, S. E. "Io's Metamorphosis: A Classical Subtext for *Lolita*." *Nabokovian* 14 (1985): 44-47.

1775. -----. "Io's Metamorphosis: A Classical Subtext for *Lolita*." *Classical and Modern Literature* 6.2 (1986): 79-88.

1776. -----. "Nymphet - Singing in Singleton." *Nabokovian* 15 (1985): 17-18.

1777. Swiggers, Pierre. "Frege on Reference in Quotation." *Linguisticae Investigationes* 6 (1982): 201-204.

1778. Switalski, W. *Die erkenntnistheoretische Bedeutung des Citats: Ein Beitrag zur Theorie des Autoritaetsbeweises.* Verzeichnis der Vorlesungen am Koenigl. Lyceum Hosianum zu Braunsberg, Sommersemester 1905. Braunsberg, Germany, 1905.

1779. Sykes, Stuart. "'Mise en abyme' in the Novels of Claude Simon." *Forum for Modern Language Studies* 9 (1973): 333-345.

1780. -----. "Ternary Form in Three Novels by Claude Simon." *Symposium* 32 (1978): 25-40.

1781. Szoeverffy, Joseph. "Klassische Anspielungen und antike Elemente in mittelalterlichen Hymnen." *Archiv fuer Kulturgeschichte* 44 (1962): 148-192.

1782. -----. "Ein Schmuckmittel der mittellateinischen Strophen: 'Regelmaessige Zeilenentlehnung' in der Hymnendichtung." *Mittellateinisches Jahrbuch* 7 (1972): 7-40.

1783. "Tableau des citations de Lamartine et de Musset dans les *Cahiers de la quinzaine.*" *Revue des Lettres Modernes* 731-734 (1985): 117-121.

1784. Talbert, Ernest William. "Mythological Allusion and Mythological Moral." *Renaissance Papers* (1964): 3-11.

1785. Tamburri, Anthony J. "Palazzeschi's *Il codice di Perelà*: Breaking the Code." *Italica* 63 (1986): 361-380.

1786. Tammi, Pekka. "Some Remarks on Flaubert and *Ada*." *Vladimir Nabokov Research News-Letter* 7 (Fall 1981): 19-21.

1787. Tanner, Jeri. "A Sixteenth-Century Allusion to Chaucer." *American Notes and Queries* 12 (1973): 3-4.

1788. Tarrant, Dorothy. "Plato's Use of Quotations and Other Illustrative Material." *Classical Quarterly* 45 (1951): 59-67.

1789. Taubeneck, Steven. "Kafka and Kant." *Journal of the Kafka Society of America* 8.1-2 (1984): 20-27.

1790. -----. "Zitat als Realitaet, Realitaet als Zitat: Zu Affinitaeten in der neuen deutschen und amerikanischen Prosa." *Arcadia* 19 (1984): 269-277.

1791. Tavormina, Teresa. "A Liturgical Allusion in the *Scottish Legendary*." *Notes & Queries* 33 (1986): 154-157.

1792. Taylor, Gordon D. "Joyce 'after' Joyce: Oates's 'The Dead.'" *Southern Review* 19 (1983): 596-605.

1793. Teipel, Gottfried. "Zitiergesetze in der romanistischen Tradition." Diss. Kiel, W. Germany, 1953.

1794. Tejerina-Canal, Santiago. "*La muerte de Artemio Cruz y Ortego*: Texto e intertexto." *La Chispa '85: Selected Proceedings.* Ed. Gilbert Paolini. New Orleans, La.: Tulane University, 1985. 349-360.

1795. Telle, E. V. "Une allusion (?) de Charles Estienne à Rabelais en 1553." *Etudes Rabelaisiennes* 8 (1969): 71-78.

1796. Tener, R. H. "An Arnold Quotation as a Clue to R. H. Hutton's *Spectator* Articles." *Notes and Queries* 18 (1971): 100-101.

1797. Tenfelde, Nancy. "Longfellow's Chaucer." *Explicator* 22 (1965): Item 55.

1798. Tenney, Merrill Chapin. "The Quotations From Luke in Tertullian as Related to the Texts of the Second and Third Centuries." Diss. Harvard University, Cambridge, Mass., 1944.

1799. Teodorescu, Anda. "Intertextualitatea si alternantele realului." *Studii si Cercetari Lingvistice* 36 (1985): 25-33.

1800. Tetel, Marcel. "Le *Journal de voyage en Italie* et les *Essais*: Etude d'intertextualité." *Textes et intertextes: Etudes sur le XVIe siècle pour Alfred Glauser.* Eds. Floyd Gray and Marcel Tetel. Paris: Nizet, 1979. 173-192.

1801. -----. "Montaigne et le Tasse: Intertexte et voyage." *Montaigne et les Essais, 1580-1980.* Ed. François Moureau. Paris: Champion, 1983. 306-319.

1802. -----. "Rabelais et Lucien: De deux rhétoriques." *Rabelais's Incomparable Book: Essays on His Art.* Ed. Raymond La Charité. Lexington, Ky.: French Forum, 1986. 127-138.

1803. Tetzeli von Rosador, Elisabeth. "Kunst im Werke George Eliots: Anspielungen, Figuren, Thematik." Diss. Muenchen, W. Germany, 1973.

1804. *Textes et intertextes: Etudes sur le XVIe siècle pour Alfred Glauser.* Eds. Floyd Gray and Marcel Tetel. Paris: Nizet, 1979.

1805. Thale, Jerome, and Rose M. Thale. "Greene's 'Literary Pilgrimage': Allusions in *Travels with My Aunt.*" *Papers on Language and Literature* 13 (1977): 207-212.

1806. Theis, Raimund. "A la recherche de l'identité (perdue?): Butor - Gide." *Le plaisir de l'intertexte: Formes et fonctions de l'intertextualité (roman populaire, surréalisme, André Gide, nouveau roman).* Eds. Raimund Theis and Hans T. Siepe. Bern, Switzerland: Lang, 1986. 227-245.

1807. Thielemann, Leland. "The Thousand Lights and Intertextual Rhapsody: Diderot or Mme Dupin." *Romanic Review* 74 (1983): 316-329.

1808. Thiry-Stassin, Martine. "Quelques allusions médiévales au thème de Narcisse." *Marche Romane* 20.4 (1971): 47-58.

1809. Thomas, Grace Agnes. "Five Hundred Years of Allusion to the Vision of Piers the Plowman, 1362-1863." Diss. Cornell University, Ithaca, N. Y., 1927.

1810. Thomas, Lloyd S. "Conrad's 'Jury Rig' Use of the Bible in 'Youth.'" *Studies in Short Fiction* 17 (1980): 79-82.

1811. Thomas, Sue. "Some Religious Icons and Biblical Allusions in William Golding's *The Spire.*" *Journal of the Australasian Universities Language and Literature Association* 64 (1985): 190-197.

1812. Thompson, R. Ann. "'Our Revels Now Are Ended': An Allusion to *The Franklin's Tale.*" *Archiv fuer das Studium der neueren Sprachen und Literaturen* 212 (1975): 317.

1813. Thompson, William R. "Patterns of Biblical Allusions in Hawthorne's 'The Gentle Boy.'" *South Central Bulletin* 22 (1962): 3-9.

1814. Thormaehlen, Marianne. *The Waste Land: A Fragmentary Wholeness.* Lund, Sweden: Gleerup, 1978.

1815. Thorn-Drury, George. *Some Seventeenth Century Allusions to Shakespeare and His Works, Not Hitherto Collected.* London: Dobell, 1920.

1816. Thornton, Weldon. "An Allusion List for James Joyce's *Ulysses.*" *James Joyce Quarterly* 1 (1963): 17-25.

1817. -----. *Allusions in Ulysses: An Annotated List.* Chapel Hill, N. C.: University of North Carolina Press, 1968. [Diss. University of Texas, Austin, Tex., 1961.]

1818. Tidestroem, Gunnar. *Ombord pa aniara. En studie i Harry Martinsons rymdepos.* Stockholm, Sweden: Aldus, 1975.

1819. Tilley, M. P., and James K. Ray. "Proverbs and Proverbial Allusions in Marlowe." *Modern Language Notes* 50 (1935): 347-355.

1820. Tindall, W. "James Joyce and the Hermetic Tradition." *Journal of the History of Ideas* 15 (1954): 23-39.

1821. Tintner, Adeline R. "O. Henry and Henry James: The Author of the Four Million Views / The Author of the Four Hundred." *Markham Review* 13 (1984): 27-31.

1822. Tobol, Carol E. W., and Ida Washington. "Werther's Selective Reading of Homer." *Modern Language Notes* 92 (1977): 596-601.

1823. Todorov, Tvzetan. *Mikhaïl Bakhtine: Le principe dialogique. Suivi d'écrits du cercle de Bakhtine.* Paris: Seuil, 1981. [Engl. trans. by Wlad. Godzich: Mikhail Bakhtin: The Dialogical Principle. Minneapolis, Minn.: University of Minnesota Press, 1984.]

1824. Toernquist, Egil. "Jesus and Judas: On Biblical Allusions in O'Neill's Plays." *Etudes Anglaises: Grande Bretagne, Etats Unis* 24 (1971): 41-49.

1825. Toker, Leona. "Between Allusion and Coincidence: Nabokov, Dickens, and Others." *Hebrew University Studies in Literature* 12 (1984): 175-198.

1826. Toldberg, Helge. "Allusionerne i Sophus Claussens Digtning." *Danske Studier* 40 (1943): 62-80.

1827. Tololyan, Khachig. "The Fishy Poison: Allusion to Statistics in *Gravity's Rainbow.*" *Notes on Modern American Literature* 4 (1980): Item 5.

1828. Toman, Marshall. "Pinsky's An Explanation of America." *Explicator* 42.3 (1984): 62-64.

1829. Topia, André. "Contrepoints joyciens." *Poétique* 27 (1976): 351-371.

1830. Tournon, André. "De la sagesse des autres à la folie de l'autre (Ronsard, Béroalde de Verville)." *Littérature* 55 (1984): 10-23.

1831. Treglown, Jeremy. "The Satirical Inversion of Some English Sources in Rochester's Poetry." *Review of English Studies* 24 (1973): 42-48.

1832. Treu, Kurt. "Menander-Zitate und ihr Kontext." *Philologus: Zeitschrift fuer das klassische Altertum* 119 (1975): 170-178.

1833. Tristram, Hildegard L. C. "Intertextuelle 'Puns' in

Piers   Plowman."   *Neuphilologische   Mitteilungen*   84
(1983): 182-191.

1834. Tritsmans, Bruno. "La descente en enfer dans 'Les
nuits d'Octobre' de Gérard de Nerval: Les avatars d'un
intertexte." *Nineteenth Century French Studies* 11
(1983): 216-230.

1835. Trowbridge, Ronald Lee. "The Echoes of Swift and
Sterne in the Works of Thomas Carlyle." Diss. University of Michigan, Ann Arbor, Mich., 1967.

1836. Truchet, Sybil. "The Art of Antiquity in Works by Lyle
and Shakespeare." *Cahiers Elisabéthains* 24 (1983): 17-
25.

1837. Trunz, Erich. "Ein Goethezitat bei Thomas Mann."
Goethe-Jahrbuch 94 (1977): 109-112.

1838. -----. "Wie findet man ein Goethe-Zitat." *Goethe: Fuer
Leser der Hamburger Goethe-Ausgabe.* Muenchen, W. Germany: Beck, 1982. 4-13.

.1839. Tucker, G. H. "Ulysses and Jason: A Problem of Allusion in Sonnet XXXI of *Les regrets.*" *French Studies* 36
(1982): 385-396.

1840. Turnbull, Alexander. "Glanz und Elend des Zitats."
Deutsche Zeitung und Wirtschafts-Zeitung 5.73 (1950):
11.

1841. Tuttleton, James W. "The Presence of Poe in *This Side
of Paradise.*" *English Language Notes* 3 (1966): 284-
289.

1842. Tye, J. R. "George Eliot's Unascribed Mottoes." *Nineteenth Century Fiction* 22 (1967-68): 235-249.

1843. Tyler, Joseph. "Moebius Strip and Other Designs Within
the Verbal Art of Julio Cortázar." *La Chispa '85: Selected Proceedings.* Ed. Gilbert Paolini. New Orleans,
La.: Tulane University, 1985. 361-368.

1844. Tyler, Stephen A. "Ethnography, Intertextuality, and
the End of Description." *American Journal of Semiotics*
3.4 (1985): 83-98.

1845. Ugarte, Michael. "Juan Goytisolo's Mirrors: Inter-
textuality and Self-Reflection in *Reivindicación del
Conde Don Julián* and *Juan sin tierra.*" *Modern Fiction
Studies* 26 (1980-81): 613-623.

1846. -----. "Writing as Corruption and Contagion: Intertextuality in the Works of Juan Goytisolo." Diss. Cornell University, Ithaca, N. Y., 1978.

1847. Uhlig, Claus. "Literature as Textual Palingenesis: On
Some Principles of Literary History." *New Literary
History* 16 (1985): 481-513.

1848. -----. *Theorie der Literarhistorie: Prinzipien und Paradigmen*. Heidelberg, W. Germany: Winter, 1982.

1849. Uitti, Karl. "A propos de philologie." *Littérature* 41 (1981): 30-46.

1850. -----. "Intertextuality in *Le Chevalier au Lion*." *Dalhousie French Studies* 2 (1980): 3-13.

1851. Ulloa, Justo C. "Severo Sarduy: Pintura y literatura." *Hispamerica* 14 (1985): 85-94.

1852. Ulonska, Herbert. "Die Funktion der alttestamentlichen Zitate und Anspielungen in den paulinischen Briefen." Diss. Muenster, W. Germany, 1963.

1853. Ungeheuer, Gerold. "Kandlers 'Zweitsinn': *l'allusion* bei Dumarsais." *Angewandte Sprachwissenschaft: Grund-fragen-Bereiche-Methoden: Festschrift fuer Guenther Kandler*. Eds. Guenter Penser and Stefan Winter. Bonn: Bouvier, 1981. 167-187.

1854. Unger, Leonard. "Intertextual Eliot." *Southern Review* 21 (1985): 1094-1109.

1855. Ungerer, Gustav. "Edward Phillips's *The Mysteries of Love and Eloquence* (1658) and Its Shakespeare Allusions." *Seventeenth Century News* 43.3 (1985): 38-42.

1856. Upton, Albert W. "Allusions to James I and His Court in Marston's *Fawn* and Beaumont's *Woman Hater*." *Publications of the Modern Language Association* 44 (1929): 1048-1065.

1857. Uriarte, Ivan. "El intertexto como principio constructivo en los cuentos de *Azul... y su proyección en la nueva narrativa latinoamericana." *Revista Iberoamericana* 52 (1986): 937-943.

1858. Urrello, Antonio. "*Ariel*: Referencialidad y estrategia textual." *Revista Canadiense de Estudios Hispánicos* 10 (1986): 463-474.

1859. Vaget, Hans-Rudolf. "Intertextualitaet im Fruehwerk Thomas Manns: *Der Wille zum Glueck* und Heinrich Manns *Das Wunderbare*." *Zeitschrift fuer deutsche Philologie* 101 (1982): 193-216.

1860. Vaillancourt, Pierre-Louis. "Rhétorique et éthique de la citation." *Renaissance et Reformation* 6 (1982): 103-121.

1861. Valenti, Peter. "Gatsby: Franklin and Hoppy." *Notes on Modern American Literature* 3 (1979): Item 23.

1862. Vande Berg, Michael. "'Taking All Hints To Use Them': The Sources of 'Out of the Cradle Endlessly Rocking.'" *Walt Whitman Quarterly Review* 2.4 (1985): 1-20.

1863. Van Maren, J. W. "Zitate deutscher Mystiker bei Marquard von Lindau." *Amsterdamer Beitraege zur aelteren Germanistik* 20 (1983): 74-85.

1864. Van Nuffel, Pierre. "Rôle et fonctionnement du cliché dans le système intertextuel de l'épopée française médiévale." *Cahiers de l'Institut de Linguistique* 3 (1975-76): 4-29.

1865. Van Rossum-Guyon, Françoise. "Aventures de la citation chez Butor." *Butor: Colloque de Cerisy*. Paris: Union Générale d'Editions, 1974. 17-54.

1866. -----. "De Claude Simon à Proust: Un exemple d'intertextualité." *Les Lettres Nouvelles* 4 (1972): 107-137.

1867. Van Slyke, Gretchen. "Dans l'intertexte de Baudelaire et de Proudhon: Pourquoi faut-il assomer les pauvres?" *Romantisme* 45 (1984): 57-77.

1868. Van Strien-Chardonneau, Madeleine. "Pratiques intertextuelles dans *Our ou vingt ans après.*" *Recherches sur l'oeuvre de Claude Ollier*. Ed. Sjef Houppermans. Groningen, Holland, 1985. 93-119.

1869. Van Wert, William F. "Intertextuality and Redundant Coherence in Robbe-Grillet." *Romanic Review* 73 (1982): 249-257.

1870. Vareille, Jean-Claude. "Butor ou l'intertextualité généralisée." *Le plaisir de l'intertexte: Formes et fonctions de l'intertextualité (roman populaire, surréalisme, André Gide, nouveau roman).* Eds. Raimund Theis and Hans T. Siepe. Bern, Switzerland: Lang, 1986. 277-296.

1871. -----. "Chéri-Bibi: Intertextualité, baroque, et degré zéro de l'écriture." *Europe-Revue Littéraire Mensuelle* 59 (1981): 102-107.

1872. Varvaro, Alberto. "Forme di intertestualità: La narrativa spagnola medievale tra Oriente e Occidente." *Annali Istituto Universitario Orientale, Napoli, Sezione Romanza* 27 (1985): 49-65.

1873. Vasiliu, E. "Intertextualitate: Cîteva disocieri necesare." *Studii si Cercetari Lingvistice* 36 (1985): 3-9.

1874. Veit, Walter. "Intellectual Tradition and Pacific Discoveries, or the Function of Quotation in Georg Forster's *Voyage Round the World.*" *Captain James Cook: Image and Impact*. Ed. Walter Veit. Melbourne, Australia: Hawthorn, 1979. 2: 95-117.

1875. Velli, Guiseppe. "Ispirazione e allusivita nell' *Agamennone* dell' Alfieri." *Italica* 41 (1964): 47-62.

1876. Venuti, Lawrence. "The Politics of Allusion: The Gentry and Shirley's *The Triumph of Peace.*" *English*

Literary Renaissance 16 (1986): 182-205.

1877. Verdaasdonk, Hugo. "Het konsept 'intertekstualiteit.'" *Literair Lustrum 2*. Eds. Kees Fens et al. Amsterdam, Holland: Athenaeum-Polak, 1973. 344-365.

1878. Verhuyck, Paul. "Le *Lai de Désiré*: Narrèmes hagiographiques." *Les Lettres Romanes* 40 (1986): 3-17.

1879. Verrier, Jean. "Ségalen lecteur de Ségalen." *Poétique* 27 (1976): 338-350.

1880. Verweyen, Theodor. "'Die Tragoedie des Coriolanus' bei Brecht und Grass oder ueber die Verarbeitung literarischer Modelle." *Poetica* 16 (1984): 246-275.

1881. -----, and Gunther Witting. "Parodie, Palinodie, Kontradiktio, Kontrafaktur: Elementare Adaptionsformen im Rahmen der Intertextualitaetsdiskussion." *Dialogizitaet*. Ed. Renate Lachmann. Muenchen, W. Germany: Fink, 1982. 202-236.

1882. Vessels, Elizabeth Jane. "A Mythic Light on Eve: The Function of Mythological Allusion in Defining Her Character and Role in the Epic Action of *Paradise Lost*." Diss. Fordham University, Bronx, N. Y., 1972.

1883. Vidal, Jean-Pierre. "*Passacaille*: L'essaimage de la lettre envolée." *Etudes Littéraires* 19.3 (1986-87): 99-118.

1884. -----. "La pédale-vapeur et le sexe des mésanges: Cinq approximations figurales du *Surmâle*." *Alfred Jarry*. Ed. Henri Bordillon. Paris: Belfond, 1985. 205-233.

1885. Viglionese, Paschal C. "Internal Allusion and Symmetry at Mid-Point of Dante's *Commedia*." *Italica* 63 (1986): 237-249.

1886. Villegas, Juan. "*La Celestina* de Alfonso Sastre: Niveles de intertextualidad y lector potencial." *Estreno: Cuadernos del Teatro Español Contemporáneo* 12 (1986): 40-41.

1887. Vincent, Michael. "Transtextual Traps: 'Le rat et l'huître.'" *Papers on French Seventeenth Century Literature* 22 (1985): 39-57.

1888. Vinge, L. "Om Allusioner." *Tidskrift foer Litteraturvetenskop* 3 (1972-73): 138-154.

1889. Voelker, Joe. "27 April." *James Joyce Quarterly* 22 (1985): 325.

1890. Vogler, Thomas A. "Intertextual Signifiers and the Blake of That Already." *Romanticism Past and Present* 9 (1985): 1-33.

1891. Voigts, Manfred. "'Die Mater der Gerechtigkeit': Zur

Kritik des Zitat-Begriffes bei Walter Benjamin." *Antike und Moderne: Zu Walter Benjamins Passagen.* Eds. Norbert W. Bolz and Richard Faber. Wuerzburg, W. Germany: Koenigshausen & Neumann, 1986. 97-115.

1892. -----. "Das Zitat vors Gericht!" *Akzente* 28 (1981): 357-366.

1893. Voldeng, Evelyne. "L'intertextualité dans les écrits féminins d'inspiration féministe." *Voix et Images* 7 (1982): 523-530.

1894. Von Koppenfels, Werner. "Intertextualitaet und Sprachwechsel: Die literarische Uebersetzung." *Intertextualitaet: Formen, Funktionen, anglistische Fallstudien.* Eds. U. Broich and M. Pfister. Tuebingen, W. Germany: Niemeyer, 1985. 137-158.

1895. Von Noe, Guenther. "Das musikalische Zitat." *Neue Zeitschrift fuer Musik* 124 (1963): 134-137.

1896. -----. "Das Zitat bei Richard Strauss." *Neue Zeitschrift fuer Musik* 125 (1964): 234-238.

1897. Von See, Klaus. "Polemische Zitate in der Skaldendichtung." *Skandinavistik* 7 (1977): 115-119.

1898. Voss, Lieselotte. *Literarische Praefiguration dargestellter Wirklichkeit bei Fontane: Zur Zitatstruktur seines Romanwerkes.* Muenchen, W. Germany: Fink, 1985.

1899. Vosskamp, Wilhelm. "Emblematisches Zitat und emblematische Struktur in Schillers Gedichten." *Jahrbuch der Deutschen Schiller-Gesellschaft* 18 (1974): 388-406.

1900. Vultur, Smaranda. "A propos des configurations intertextuelles." *Cahiers Roumains d'Etudes Littéraires* 11.4 (1984): 72-78.

1901. -----. "Intertextualitatea ca principiu de functionare a textului literar." *Studii si Cercetari Lingvistice* 36 (1985): 52-63.

1902. -----. "La place de l'intertextualité dans les théories de la réception du texte littéraire." *Cahiers Roumains d'Etudes Littéraires* 13.3 (1986): 103-109.

1903. -----. "Situer l'intertextualité." *Cahiers Roumains d'Etudes Littéraires* 8.3 (1981): 32-36.

1904. -----. "Text si intertext: Posibilitati de abordare si delimitari." *Studii si Cercetari Lingvistice* 29 (1978): 347-357.

1905. -----. "A Type of Intertextuality: The Quotation in the Critical Discourse." *Revue Roumaine de Linguistique* 28.5 (1983): 397-403.

1906. Waggoner, George R. "Allusions to Chaucer in Stow's *Summarye of the Chronicles of England*, 1570." *Notes and Queries* 201 (1956): 462.

1907. Waiblinger, Franz-Peter. "Zitierte Kritik: Zu den Werther-Zitaten in Ulrich Plenzdorfs *Die neuen Leiden des jungen W.*" *Poetica* 8 (1976): 71-88.

1908. Waite, Alan. "Butor's *Degrés*: Making the Reader Work." *Australian Journal of French Studies* 21 (1984): 180-193.

1909. Walker, Robert G. "Irony and Allusion in Hemingway's *After the Storm.*" *Studies in Short Fiction* 13 (1976): 374-376.

1910. Walla, Friedrich. "Der Dichter als Handwerker: Selbstzitate bei Nestroy. Bemerkungen zu Nestroys Arbeitsweise." *Nestroyana* 3 (1981): 3-13.

1911. Wallace, Malcolm T. "The Wodehouse World I: Classical Echoes." *Cithara* 12 (1973): 41-57.

1912. Walsh, Dennis M. "Christian Allusion in the Fiction of Joseph Conrad." Diss. Univ. of Notre Dame, Ind., 1973.

1913. Walters, Jennifer R. "Butor's Use of Literary Texts in *Degrés.*" *Publications of the Modern Language Association* 88 (1973): 311-320.

1914. Walther, Karl-Klaus. "Versuch ueber das Zitat." *Wissenschaftliche Zeitschrift (Halle-Wittenberg)* 29 (1980): 115-116.

1915. Wang, Jing. "The Mythology of Stone: A Study of Intertextuality of Ancient Chinese Stonelore and Three Classic Novels." Diss. University of Massachusetts, 1985.

1916. Warning, Rainer. "Imitatio und Intertextualitaet: Zur Geschichte lyrischer Dekonstruktion der Amortheologie. Dante, Petrarca, Baudelaire." *Kolloquium Kunst und Philosophie.* Ed. Willi Oelmueller. Muenchen, W. Germany: Schoeningh, 1982. 2: 168-207.

1917. -----. "Imitatio und Intertextualitaet: Zur Geschichte lyrischer Dekonstruktion der Amortheologie. Dante, Petrarca, Baudelaire." *Interpretationen: Das Paradigma der europaeischen Renaissance-Literatur: Festschrift fuer Alfred Noyer-Weidner.* Eds. K. W. Hempfer and G. Regn. Wiesbaden, W. Germany: Steiner, 1983. 288-317.

1918. Wassermann, Earl R. "The Limits of Allusion in *The Rape of the Lock.*" *Journal of English and Germanic Philology* 65 (1966): 425-444.

1919. Watkins, Eric Walter. "The Authorial Allusion: A Clue to the Interpretation of Irony." Diss. University of California, San Diego, Cal., 1984.

1920. Watkins, Floyd C. "Fitzgerald's Jay Gatz and Young Ben Franklin." *New England Quarterly* 27 (1954): 249-252.

1921. Webb, Dorothy M. "Fitzgerald on El Greco: A View of *The Great Gatsby*." *Fitzgerald/Hemingway Annual* (1975): 89-91.

1922. Weigand, Hermann John. "Wagners Siegfried im *Florian Geyer*." Hermann John Weigand. *Faehrten und Funde: Aufsaetze zur deutschen Literatur*. Muenchen, W. Germany: Francke, 1967. 227-231.

1923. Weinberg, Kurt. "Ut musica poesis: The Silence of Mallarmé's Sirens." *Intertextuality: New Perspectives in Criticism*. Eds. Jeanine P. Plottel and Hanna Charney. New York Literary Forum 2. New York: Literary Forum, 1978. 219-235.

1924. Weinbrot, Howard D. "The 'Allusion to Horace': Rochester's Imitative Mode." *Studies in Philology* 69 (1972): 348-368.

1925. Weinstock, Horst. *Die Funktion elisabethanischer Sprichwoerter und Pseudosprichwoerter bei Shakespeare*. Heidelberg, W. Germany: Winter, 1966.

1926. Weisenburger, Steven. "Pynchon's Hereros: A Textual and Bibliographical Note." *Pynchon Notes* 16 (1985): 37-45.

1927. Weiser, David K. "Berryman's Sonnets: *In and Out of the Tradition*." *American Literature* 55 (1983): 388-404.

1928. Weisgerber, Jean. "The Use of Quotations in Recent Literature." *Comparative Literature* 22 (1970): 36-45.

1929. Weiss, Timothy. "The 'Black Beast' Headline: The Key to an Allusion in *Ulysses*." *James Joyce Quarterly* 19 (1982): 183-186.

1930. Weiss, Wolfgang. "Satirische Dialogizitaet und satirische Intertextualitaet." *Intertextualitaet: Formen, Funktionen, anglistische Fallstudien*. Eds. U. Broich and M. Pfister. Tuebingen, W. Germany: Niemeyer, 1985. 244-262.

1931. Weissert, Elisabeth. "Ein Stueck Poetologie: Das Zitat in der lyrischen Dichtung." *Erziehungskunst: Zeitschrift zur Paedagogik Rudolf Steiners* 36 (1972): 53-64.

1932. Wejksnora, Louise R. "Classical Gods and Christian God: Religious Allusions and the Moral of Chaucer's *Troilus and Criseyde*." Diss. City University of New York, 1986.

1933. Welch, Dennis M. "Manipulation in Shirley Jackson's 'Seven Types of Ambiguity.'" *Studies in Short Fiction*

18 (1981): 27-31.

1934. Wells, Daniel A. "An Annotated Checklist of Twain Allusions in *Harper's Monthly*, 1850-1900." *American Literary Realism* 17 (1984): 116-123.

1935. -----. "Mark Twain in the *Atlantic Monthly* to 1910: An Annotated List of Allusions." *Mark Twain Journal* 23 (1985): 21-28.

1936. -----. "Melville Allusions in the *Atlantic Monthly*, 1857-1900." *Melville Society Extracts* 55 (1983): 14-15.

1937. Wells, R. Headlam. "Spenser's Christian Knight: Erasmian Theology in *The Faerie Queene*, Book I." *Anglia* 97 (1979): 350-366.

1938. Wendelmoot, Thomas Leroy. "Masonic Allusions and Themes in the Works of Rudyard Kipling." Diss. University of South Florida, Tampa, Fla., 1980.

1939. Wentersdorf, Karl P. "Allusion and Theme in the Third Movement of Milton's 'Lycidas.'" *Modern Philology* 83 (1986): 275-279.

1940. -----. "Imagery, Structure, and Theme in Chaucer's *Merchant's Tale*." *Chaucer and the Craft of Fiction*. Ed. Leigh A. Arrathoon. Rochester, Michigan: Solaris, 1986. 35-62.

1941. West, Grace Starry. "Going by the Book: Classical Allusions in Shakespeare's *Titus Andronicus*." *Studies in Philology* 79 (1982): 62-77.

1942. Wey, James. "Musical Allusion and Song as Part of the Structure of Meaning of Shakespeare's Plays." Diss. Catholic Univ. of America, Washington, D.C., 1958.

1943. Wheeler, Michael. *The Art of Allusion in Victorian Fiction*. London: Macmillan, 1979.

1944. -----. "Biography, Literary Influence and Allusions as Aspects of Source Studies." *British Journal of Aesthetics* 17 (1977): 149-160.

1945. White, Robert B. "Chaucer's Physician: An Uncollected Allusion 1611." *Notes and Queries* 224 (1979): 102-103.

1946. -----. "An Eighteenth Century Allusion to Chaucer's *Cook's Tale*." *English Language Notes* 7 (1970): 190-192.

1947. Whitford, H. C. "An Uncollected Sixteenth-Century Allusion to *The House of Fame*." *Modern Language Notes* 52 (1937): 31-32.

1948. Whiting, B. J. "Emerson, Chaucer, and Thomas Warton." *American Literature* 17 (1945): 75-78.

1949. -----. "Some Chaucer Allusions, 1923-1942." *Notes and Queries* 187 (1944): 288-291.

1950. Widman, Hans. "Zitate und ihre Schicksale: Ein Beitrag zur Geschichte des geistigen Eigentums." *Das Werck der Bucher. Festschrift fuer Horst Kliemann.* Ed. Fritz Hodeige. Freiburg, W. Germany: Rombach, 1956. 73-85.

1951. Wierzbicka, Anna. "Descriptions or Quotations?" *Sign, Language, Culture.* Eds. A. J. Greimas and Roman Jakobson. The Hague, Holland: Mouton, 1970. 627-644.

1952. Wiesemann, Ursula. "How Should Jesus be Quoted?" *Notes on Translation* 101 (1984): 27-39.

1953. Wilbur, Richard. "Poe and the Art of Suggestion." *University of Mississippi Studies in English* 3 (1982): 1-13.

1954. Wilding, Michael. "Allusion and Innuendo in *Mac-Flecknoe.*" *Essays in Criticism* 19 (1969): 355-370.

1955. Williams, Aubrey. "Swift and the Poetry of Allusion: 'The Journal.'" *Literary Theory and Structure: Essays in Honor of William K. Wimsatt.* Ed. Frank Brady. New Haven, Conn.: Yale University Press, 1973. 227-243.

1956. Williams, Franklin B. "Unnoted Chaucer Allusions, 1550-1650." *Philological Quarterly* 16 (1937): 67-71.

1957. Williams, Milton Bryant. "The Quotations of Barhebraeus in His Schola." Diss. University of Chicago, Ill., 1928.

1958. Williams, Paul O. "The Borrowed Axe: A Biblical Echo in *Walden?*" *Thoreau Society Bulletin* 83 (1963): 2.

1959. Williams, Philip. "A 1593 Chaucer Allusion." *Modern Language Notes* 69 (1954): 45.

1960. Willoughby, Edwin. "A Chaucer Allusion of 1608." *Notes and Queries* 159 (1930): 225.

1961. -----. "A Sixteenth-Century Allusion to Chaucer." *Notes and Queries* 159 (1930): 134-135, 367.

1962. Wilson, A. J. N. "Andrew Marvell: 'An Horatian Ode Upon Cromwell's Return From Ireland': The Thread of the Poem and His Use of Classical Allusion." *Critical Quarterly* 11 (1969): 325-341.

1963. Wilson, Christopher P. "Tempests and Teapots: Harriet Beecher Stowe's *The Minister's Wooing.*" *New England Quarterly* 58 (1985): 554-577.

1964. Wilson, Elkin C. "Chaucer Allusions." *Notes and Queries* 173 (1937): 457-458.

1965. Wilson, Raymond J. "Allusion and Implication in John

Fowles's 'The Cloud.'" *Studies in Short Fiction* 20
(1983): 17-22.

1966. Wilss, Wolfram. "Beobachtungen zur Anspielungstechnik
in der deutschen Gegenwartssprache." *Grazer linguistische Studien* 11-12 (1980): 368-390.

1967. Wimsatt, W. K. "One Relation of Rhyme to Reason:
Alexander Pope." *Modern Language Quarterly* ·5 (1944):
323-338.

1968. Winspur, Steven. "Lautréamont and the Question of the
Intertext." *Romanic Review* 76 (1985): 192-201.

1969. Wirtz, Erika A. "Zitat und Leitmotiv bei Thomas Mann."
German Life and Letters 7 (1953-54): 126-136.

1970. Witemeyer, Hugh. "'Of Kings' Treasuries': Pound's
Allusion to Ruskin in *Hugh Selwyn Mauberley.*" *Paideuma*
15 (1986): 23-31.

1971. Wittig, Joseph S. "The Aeneas-Dido Allusion in
Chrétien's *Erec et Enide.*" *Comparative Literature* 22
(1970): 237-253.

1972. Wolf, Bryan J. "A Grammar of the Sublime, or Intertextuality Triumphant in Church, Turner, and Cole."
New Literary History 16 (1985): 321-341.

1973. Wolfzettel, Friedrich. "A propos de quelques aspects
intertextuels des 'Génies du lieu' de Michel Butor."
*Le plaisir de l'intertexte: Formes et fonctions de
l'intertextualité (roman populaire, surréalisme, André
Gide, nouveau roman).* Eds. Raimund Theis and Hans T.
Siepe. Bern, Switzerland: Lang, 1986. 251-276.

1974. Wolpers, Theodor. "Der romantische Leser als Kriegs-
held und Liebhaber: Poetisierung der Realitaet in Walter Scotts *Waverley.*" *Gelebte Literatur in der Literatur: Studien zu Erscheinungsformen und Geschichte
eines literarischen Motivs.* Ed. Theodor Wolpers. Goettingen, W. G.: Vandenhoeck & Ruprecht, 1986. 185-197.

1975. -----. "Schrecken und Vernunft: Die romanlesende Hel-
din in Jane Austens *Northanger Abbey.*" *Gelebte Literatur in der Literatur: Studien zu Erscheinungsformen
und Geschichte eines literarischen Motivs.* Ed. Theodor
Wolpers. Goettingen, W. Germany: Vandenhoeck & Ruprecht, 1986. 168-184.

1976. -----. "Der weibliche Quijote in England: Charlotte
Lennox' *The Female Quixote* und die literarische
Tradition." *Gelebte Literatur in der Literatur: Stu-
dien zu Erscheinungsformen und Geschichte eines lite-
rarischen Motivs.* Ed. Theodor Wolpers. Goettingen, W.
Germany: Vandenhoeck & Ruprecht, 1986. 134-162.

1977. -----. "Zu Begriff und Geschichte des Motivs 'Gelebte
Literatur in der Literatur': Gemeinsames Vorwort der

Beitraeger." *Gelebte Literatur in der Literatur: Studien zu Erscheinungsformen und Geschichte eines literarischen Motivs.* Ed. Theodor Wolpers. Goettingen, W. Germany: Vandenhoeck & Ruprecht, 1986. 7-29.

1978. Wood, Chauncey. "Artistic Intention and Chaucer's Use of Scriptural Allusion." *Revue de l'Université d'Ottawa* 53 (1983): 297-308.

1979. Woods, Barbara Allen. "Unfamiliar Quotations in Brecht's Plays." *Germanic Review* 46 (1971): 26-42.

1980. Woodson, Jon. "Melvin Tolson and the Art of Being Difficult." *Black American Poets Between Worlds. 1940-1960.* Ed. R. Baxter Miller. Knoxville, Tenn.: University of Tennessee Press, 1986. 19-42.

1981. Woolf, Henry Bosley. "An Eighteenth-Century Allusion to Chaucer." *Notes and Queries* 192 (1947): 60.

1982. Wooten, Elizabeth Harper. "Biblical Allusion in the Novels of Richardson." Diss. University of Tennessee, 1973.

1983. Worthen, William B. "Eliot's *Ulysses.*" *Twentieth Century Literature* 27 (1981): 166-177.

1984. Worthington, Mabel P. "Gilbert and Sullivan Songs in the Works of James Joyce." *Hartford Studies in Literature* 1 (1969): 209-218.

1985. -----. "Irish Folk Songs in Joyce's *Ulysses.*" *Publications of the Modern Language Association* 71 (1956): 321-339.

1986. Wright, Nathalia. "Biblical Allusion in Melville's Prose." *American Literature* 12 (1940): 185-199.

1987. Wunberg, Gotthard. "Die Funktion des Zitats in den politischen Gedichten von Hans Magnus Enzensberger." *Neue Sammlung* 4 (1964): 274-282.

1988. Wuthenow, Ralph-Rainer. *Im Buch die Buecher oder: Der Held als Leser.* Frankfurt, W. Germany: Europaeische Verlagsanstalt, 1980.

1989. Wyatt, Bryant N. "*Huckleberry Finn* and the Art of Ernest Hemingway." *Mark Twain Journal* 13 (Summer 1967): 1-8.

1990. Wyatt, Jean. "Art and Allusion in *Between the Acts.*" *Mosaic* 11 (1978): 91-100.

1991. -----. "*Mrs. Dalloway:* Literary Allusion as Structural Metaphor." *Publications of the Modern Language Association* 88 (1973): 440-451.

1992. -----. "The Technique of Literary Allusion in the Novels of Virginia Woolf." Diss. Harvard University,

Cambridge, Mass., 1969.

1993. Yaari, Monique. "Osmose ou parodie: Une lecture intertextuelle de *Paludes.*" *French Forum* 10 (1985): 325-
337.

1994. Yachnin, Paul. "The Significance of Two Allusions in
Middleton's *Phoenix.*" *Notes and Queries* 33 (1986):
375-377.

1995. Yanada, Noriyuki. "Nursery Rhymes Alluded to in D. H.
Lawrence's Novels." *Language and Culture* 11 (1986):
32-63.

1996. Yarrison, Betsy C. "The Symbolism of Literary Allusion
in *Heart of Darkness.*" *Conradiana* 7 (1975): 155-164.

1997. York, R. A. "Bonnefoy and Mallarmé: Aspects of Intertextuality." *Romanic Review* 71 (1980): 307-318.

1998. Yu-Kung, Kao, and Mei Tsu-lin. "Meaning, Metaphor, and
Allusion in T'ang Poetry." *Harvard Journal of Asiatic
Studies* 38 (1978): 281-356.

1999. Zaloscer, Hilde. "Aegypten in Thomas Manns Josephro-
man: Zum Problem des 'Bildzitats.'" *Seminar* 10 (1974):
116-130.

2000. Zamora, Lois. "European Intertextuality in Vargas
Llosa and Cortázar." *Comparative Literature Studies* 19
(1982): 21-38.

2001. Zander, Horst. "Intertextualitaet und Medienwechsel."
*Intertextualitaet: Formen, Funktionen, anglistische
Fallstudien.* Eds. U. Broich and M. Pfister. Tuebingen,
W. Germany: Niemeyer, 1985. 178-196.

2002. Zeitz, Lisa M. "Biblical Allusion and Imagery in
Frederick Douglass' *Narrative.*" *College Language
Association Journal* 25 (1981-82): 56-64.

2003. Zepp, Evelyn H. "The Criticism of Julia Kristeva: A
New Mode of Critical Thought." *Romanic Review* 73
(1982): 80-97.

2004. Zimmermann, Jacquelyn. "L'emploi des citations chez
Montaigne." *Bulletin de la Société des Amis de
Montaigne* 21 (1977): 63-68.

2005. Zimmermann, Manfred. "Ein Zitat aus Oswalds Greifen-
stein-Lied im 16. und 17. Jahrhundert." *Schlern* 55
(1981): 346-348.

2006. Ziolkowski, Theodore. "Figuren auf Pump: Zur Fiktio-
nalitaet des sprachlichen Kunstwerks." *Akten des VI.
internationalen Germanisten-Kongresses Basel 1980 Teil
I.* Eds. Heinz Rupp and Hans-Gert Roloff. Bern, Switzerland: Lang, 1981. 166-176.

2007. Zoberman, Pierre. "Mérimée et la pratique inter-
       textuelle, ou les mésaventures d'une récit." *French
       Forum* 6 (1981): 36-49.

2008. Zook, Alma C. "Star-Gazing at Mansfield Park." *Per-
       suasions* 8 (December 1986): 29-33.

2009. Zulli, Floyd. "Dantean Allusions in *La comédie
       humaine.*" *Italica* 35 (1958): 177-187.

2010. Zumthor, Paul. "Le carrefour des rhétoriqueurs: Inter-
       textualité et rhétorique." *Poétique* 27 (1976): 317-
       337.

2011. -----. "L'intertexte performanciel." *Texte* 2 (1983):
       49-59.

2012. -----. "Intertextualité et mouvance." *Littérature* 41
       (1981): 8-16.

2013. Zurbrugg, Nicholas. "Burroughs, Barthes, and the
       Limits of Intertextuality." *Review of Contemporary
       Fiction* 4 (1984): 86-107.

2014. -----. "The Limits of Intertextuality: Barthes,
       Burroughs, Gysin, Culler." *Southern Review* (Adelaide)
       16 (1983): 250-273.

2015. Zurowski, Maciej. "L'intertextualité, ses antécédents
       et ses perspectives." *Kwartalnik Neofilologiczny* 30
       (1983): 111-125.

ADDENDA

2016. Anderson, Warren D. "Homer and Stephen Crane." *Nine-
       teenth Century Fiction* 19 (1964-65): 77-86.

2017. Apostolescu, Carmen. "*Grup si Psalm*: O posibila
       relatie de intertextualitate." *Studii si Cercetari
       Lingvistice* 36 (1985): 82-91.

2018. Beckman, Gary. "Proverbs and Proverbial Allusions in
       Hittite." *Journal of Near Eastern Studies* 45 (1986):
       19-30.

2019. Box, Mark. "An Allusion in Hume's *An Enquiry Concern-
       ing the Principle of Morals* Identified." *Notes and
       Queries* 33 (1986): 60-61.

2020. D'Ambrosio-Griffith, Gloria R. "Text, Intertext, Vor-
       tex: 'Les chants de Maldoror' and Intertextuality."
       Diss. University of Toronto, Canada, 1986.

2021. Fowler, James. "Catiline Quoted in *The Chances*." *Notes and Queries* 33 (1986): 467-469.

2022. Glowinski, Michal. "O Intertekstualnosci." *Pamietnik Literacki* 77 (1986): 75-100.

2023. Gruber, G. "Das musikalische Zitat als historisches und systematisches Problem." *Musicologica Austriaca* 1 (1977): 121-135.

2024. Hiller, Geoffrey G. "Allusions to Spenser by John Davies and Sir John Davies." *Notes and Queries* 33 (1986): 394-395.

2025. Howard, V. "On Musical Quotation." *Monist* 58 (1974): 307-318.

2026. Johnson, Anthony. "Ben Jonson: An Ungathered Allusion." *Notes and Queries* 33 (1986): 384.

2027. Miola, Robert S. "Another Senecan Echo in Kyd's *The Spanish Tragedy*." *Notes and Queries* 33 (1986): 337.

2028. Prada Oropeza, Renato. "La intertextualidad en *Aura*. Seminario de Semiotica." *Semiosis* 14-15 (1985): 60-85.

2029. Ray, Robert H. "The Herbert Allusion Book: Allusions to George Herbert in the Seventeenth Century." *Studies in Philology* 83.4 (1986) [Special issue].

2030. -----. "Unrecorded Seventeenth-Century Allusions to Donne." *Notes and Queries* 33 (1986): 464-465.

2031. Rudat, Wolfgang E. H. "Milton and the *Miller's Tale*: Chaucerian Allusions in *Paradise Lost*." *Euphorion* 80 (1986): 417-426.

2032. Sarkissian, John. "Allusions to Classical Satire in Ariosto's First and Third *Satire*." *The Early Renaissance: Virgil and the Classical Tradition*. Ed. Anthony L. Pellegrini. Binghamton, N. Y.: Center for Medieval and Early Renaissance Studies, 1984. 107-120.

2033. Wormleighton, Simon. "Some Echoes of Barbusse's *Under Fire* in Wilfred Owen's Poems." *Notes and Queries* 33 (1986): 190-191.

Index to Writers
and Anonymous Texts

792, 847, 1168, 1178,
1249, 1299, 1372, 1386,
1441, 1534, 1585, 1606
Federman, Raymond, 1629
Female Tatler, The, 1558,
1946
Féraud, L'Abbé J. F., 1658
Feydeau, Georges, 1665
Fielding, Henry, 91, 109,
173, 242, 247, 765, 1072,
1631
Fitzgerald, F. Scott, 11,
60, 66, 85, 240, 275, 421,
468, 473, 475, 488, 511,
601, 638, 666, 682, 709,
763, 808, 832, 1062, 1090,
1108, 1298, 1321, 1407,
1416, 1521, 1540, 1541,
1655, 1841, 1861, 1920,
1921
Flaubert, Gustave, 171, 215,
627, 725, 943, 1058, 1136,
1217, 1402, 1421, 1459,
1525, 1537, 1988
Fletcher, John, 187, 2021
Fontane, Theodor, 157, 304,
1185, 1186, 1310, 1378,
1501, 1898
Ford, Ford Madox, 1772
Ford, John, 1306
Forêts, Louis-René des, 919
Forster, Edward Morgan, 643,
1730
Forster, Georg, 1874
Fowles, John, 1965
Freud, Sigmund, 40, 294,
362, 735, 1626
Freytag, Gustav, 623
Frisch, Max, 72, 73, 513,
540, 966
Froeding, Gustaf, 789,
1083
Froissart, Jean, 680, 924,
1285
Frost, Robert, 1593
Fuentes, Carlos, 507, 721,
1794, 2028
Fuller, Thomas, 1438

G

Gaddis, William, 257, 1578
Galindo, Sergio, 1510
Gálvez, Manuel, 303
García Lorca, Federico, 336,
1063
García Márquez, Gabriel, 493
Garret, A., 1239

Gaskell, Elizabeth C., 736,
1297, 1943
Gautier Le Leu, 1082
Gautier, Théophile, 480,
503, 1100
Gay, John, 1133, 1520
Geoffrey of Monmouth, 467
"George Barnwel," 350
Gibbon, Edward, 338
Gide, André, 430, 677, 815,
906, 988, 1262, 1241,
1304, 1806, 1993
Giraudoux, Jean, 1507
Gissing, George Robert, 980
Godwin, William, 1538
Goethe, Johann Wolfgang von,
490, 549, 676, 712, 772,
909, 1043, 1194, 1627,
1822, 1838, 1988
Gogol, Nikolai V., 289
Golding, William, 373, 1811
Góngora y Argote, Luis de,
89, 90, 1423
Gorey, Edward, 314
Goytisolo, Juan, 1318, 1644,
1716, 1845, 1846
Gracq, Julien, 30, 31
Grass, Guenther, 1880
Gray, Simon, 183
Gray, Thomas, 1091
Green, Julien, 111
Greene, Graham, 385, 388,
1805
Greene, Robert, 47
Gries, Johann D., 1140
Grimm, Jacob Ludwig Karl and
Wilhelm Karl, 1513
Guazzo, Stefano, 575
Guillaume de Palerne, 1123
Gullberg, Hjalmar, 789,
1332, 1630
Guy of Warwick, 1287
Gysin, Brion, 2013, 2014

H

Hamann, Johann Georg, 621
Han-Yu, 749
Handke, Peter, 113, 1383
Hao-Ran, 500
Hardy, Frank, 596
Hardy, Thomas, 730, 1721,
1722, 1943
Harper's Monthly, 1934
Harry the Minstrel ("Blind
Harry"; also Hary), 752
Harsnet, Samuel, 311
Hartmann von Aue, 727

Subject Index

other texts, 2006
Chinese literature, 500,
    551, 1026, 1067, 1361,
    1915, 1998
classical allusion, classi-
    cal quotation, classical
    intertextuality, 47, 71,
    79, 99, 185, 193, 209,
    218, 251, 255, 308, 339,
    345, 356, 357, 380, 390,
    406, 430, 450, 463, 476,
    481, 498, 529, 535, 680,
    741, 745, 760, 771, 803,
    820, 824, 857, 884, 911,
    923, 924, 962, 1005, 1032,
    1089, 1099, 1114, 1127,
    1173, 1224, 1238, 1242,
    1253, 1267, 1291, 1334,
    1349, 1396, 1404, 1405,
    1413, 1500, 1501, 1526,
    1529, 1545, 1546, 1548,
    1549, 1550, 1551, 1552,
    1553, 1554, 1556, 1557,
    1600, 1601, 1604, 1627,
    1651, 1653, 1668, 1687,
    1693, 1696, 1703, 1725,
    1736, 1753, 1755, 1770,
    1773, 1774, 1775, 1781,
    1822, 1836, 1839, 1911,
    1924, 1941, 1962, 1971
    (cf., entries on Greek and
    Roman writers)
cliché, 892, 1193, 1771,
    1864
collage, 270, 495, 877,
    1497
concrete poetry, 1013
dancing, 1575
detective fiction, 1244,
    1710
dramatic usage, cf., theater
echo, 353, 546, 736, 812,
    906, 1087, 1153, 1275,
    1320, 1705, 1835, 1911,
    1958
epigraph, 146, 194, 710,
    736, 1019, 1842
ethnography, 1844
exegesis, 437, 469, 793,
    1120, 1456
fairy tale, 341, 475, 1513,
    1514
feminism, 68, 269, 494,
    571, 1893
film, 495, 507, 626, 802,
    1073, 1118, 1161, 1654
fine arts (general), 775,
    950, 986, 987, 1533 (cf.,
    architecture and painting)

folklore, 53, 343, 1225,
    1666, 1747
function (including artistic
    usage), 10, 17, 34, 65,
    74, 75, 99, 120, 125, 136,
    151, 156, 160, 164, 176,
    177, 198, 227, 228, 234,
    250, 257, 261, 267, 286,
    309, 333, 348, 351, 357,
    365, 383, 384, 392, 428,
    465, 497, 509, 527, 533,
    540, 558, 562, 563, 590,
    594, 640, 642, 643, 650,
    674, 710, 719, 720, 726,
    730, 745, 746, 761, 790,
    797, 807, 820, 857, 870,
    878, 888, 890, 904, 908,
    910, 916, 929, 941, 951,
    965, 1000, 1004, 1011,
    1027, 1033, 1037, 1072,
    1078, 1080, 1081, 1093,
    1111, 1142, 1153, 1177,
    1182, 1183, 1185, 1186,
    1190, 1202, 1219, 1226,
    1237, 1277, 1282, 1311,
    1352, 1378, 1397, 1431,
    1497, 1507, 1511, 1516,
    1522, 1535, 1545, 1547,
    1553, 1555, 1562, 1563,
    1588, 1602, 1609, 1615,
    1616, 1618, 1623, 1638,
    1679, 1683, 1684, 1693,
    1705, 1711, 1719, 1721,
    1738, 1745, 1773, 1778,
    1782, 1788, 1803, 1852,
    1864, 1868, 1874, 1882,
    1898, 1899, 1901, 1925,
    1927, 1928, 1939, 1942,
    1943, 1962, 1969, 1978,
    1987, 1991, 1992, 2004
genre, 54, 256, 366, 900,
    1051, 1129, 1272, 1765,
    2001
geographical allusion, 695
Hebrew tradition, 95, 979
historical allusion, 573,
    797, 1023, 1245, 1521,
    1672
humor, 53, 851, 1473 (cf.,
    black humor)
hymns, 1781, 1782
imitation, 90, 248, 366,
    435, 544, 693, 718, 1039,
    1065, 1242, 1364, 1695,
    1916, 1917, 1924
"Interauktorialitaet," 1599
intertextuality (general,
    theory), 24, 27, 39, 41,
    57, 67, 82, 83, 84, 93,

About the Compiler

UDO J. HEBEL (Dr. phil.) teaches American Studies at Johannes Gutenberg-Universität Mainz, West Germany. Dr. Hebel has contributed articles to *Literatur in Wissenschaft und Unterricht* and *Praxis des Neusprachlichen Unterrichts.*